THE SERMONS OF

JOHN DONNE

Selected and Introduced
by THEODORE A. GILL

LIVING AGE BOOKS

published by MERIDIAN BOOKS, INC.   *New York*

Theodore A. Gill

Theodore A. Gill was born in 1920 and educated at Princeton Theological Seminary, Union Theological Seminary, and the University of Zurich, from which he received his doctorate. At present he is managing editor of *The Christian Century*.

FOR KATIE AND TEDDY,
WHO ARE GLAD IT IS
DONE.

A Living Age Books Original
Published May 1958 by Meridian Books, Inc.
First Printing April 1958

CONTENTS

INTRODUCTION by Theodore A. Gill

It is a long time since anyone was caught in a crush trying to get to a sermon by John Donne. But when those sermons were delivered in neighborhood church, court chapel, or cathedral there was no greater attraction in London's public life. On the days when Dr. Donne preached, going to church was *de rigeur*. Packed into a capacity congregation would be members of the royal family, the Archbishop of Canterbury, the first lords and ladies, Francis Bacon, "diverse other great men" . . . and always the people. On at least one occasion noblemen and gentlemen so swarmed to a Lincoln's Inn sermon that "two or three were endangered and taken up dead for the time, with the extreme press and thronging."

Contemporary testimony accounts variously for the preacher's extraordinary appeal. A Dutch diplomat mentions the "wealth of his unequalled wit, and yet more incomparable eloquence in the pulpit." Izaak Walton, earliest of Donne's biographers, described his idol as "preaching the Word so, as shewed his own heart was possest with those very thoughts, and joyes that he labored to distill into others: A Preacher in earnest, weeping sometimes for his Auditory, sometimes with them: always preaching to himself, like an Angel from a cloud, but in none . . ." In the flood of poems about the preacher written by the gifted devotées who flocked to his church while he lived and adorned his tomb and his memory when he died, "Golden Chrysostome" and "Nestor" were the modest names by which his rank and their affection were shown. In English and in Latin his gifts were celebrated by those who under this preaching were regularly "ravished," "thunderstruck," "melted," and driven to "groan and grieve."

Even at three centuries remove the fanatic tinge to this devotion comes through. There was a cult of John Donne in the church of his day. The congregation sat in awe below the tall, pale, distant preacher where he stood dim in his high pulpit. Each hour-long sermon (the hour-glass was with him in the pulpit) poured its learning and its eloquence, its terror and its ecstasy, its passion and its compassion on congregations accustomed to find art in preaching and predisposed to take their truth from John Donne.

1.

It was the style, the matchless, magnificent style of the sermons that accounts for a good part of the preachers extraordinary popularity. And that style was not coincidental. The preaching itself came directly, dramatically, with the whole thrust of the person, pouring the great, rolling, ringing periods from pulpit to pew, precipitously, apparently without premeditation. But there was careful premeditation, and the testimony of the written texts, set down days or years after the sermons were delivered, is that this prose was often more carefully, consciously contrived than much of Donne's poetry—appreciated latterly, at least, for its very roughness. The literary man, come late to the pulpit, brought his writing gifts to the altar and an author's piety required the refinement and enhancement of those gifts. His "refinement" was in the direction of a more traditional poesy, so that those today who are enthusiastic about

Donne's poetry for its impromptu brokenness are less excited about the developments in his more calculated sermonic style (T. S. Eliot, for instance, can be quite short about the sermons, preferring with unaccountable prissiness the distant formalities of Andrewes.)

Yet for the original hearer and for the present reader (who ought, on reading sermons as in reading plays, to run his vision through his throat) there is an exaltation in the steadier beat of the great rhythms, in the longer sweep of the lines, in the projected flight of the prose. And all this had its effect on those palpitant congregations. The effects may not have been calculated by the preacher, but his preaching was—in every carefully selected, pre-tested, well-set word. For the preacher, said Donne, "shall not present the messages of God rudely, barbarously, extemporally; but with such meditation and preparation as appertains to so great an imployment, from such a King as God, to such a State as his Church . . . That Ambassadour should open himself to a shrewd danger and surprisall, that should defer the thinking upon his Oration, till the Prince, to whom he was sent, was reading his letters of Credit: And it is a late time of meditation for a Sermon, when the Psalm is singing."

So the sermons with their "diamond dust of rhetorical brilliancies" (DeQuincy) had their own effect in their original day. It is an effect which the intervening centuries have done nothing to dim. If anything, time has augmented the impression. For the grand English of the early seventeenth century, though spoken at its grandest in St. Paul's, was still the language of the day. Dr. Donne spoke it better than most, but a paler version of the very same language was used everyday for all the prosy business of a very ordinary world. Since then, though, the language of John Donne's sermons, little known from those uncirculated texts, has been kept before the public mainly by the devotional treasury stocked so richly in John Donne's day. Life and language so conspired that a whole literature of devotion was set down at the moment when English was loveliest. The King James Version of the Bible is the main repository. But there were many manuals of devotion besides, and above all the Book of Common Prayer, still in use and source, as well, of numerous other directives for worship, all well used.

So the familiar language that seized those congregations long ago, comes specially freighted to current readers. Marvelling as the first hearers did at its invention and artistry, we hear in it too what Donne and his fellows could not, the sound of sanctity which comes from its principle associations for us. Not for Jacobeans, but for us, Jacobean English is the very dialect of divinity. And it is the dialect of Donne. No wonder the rediscovered sermons seem to have acquired stylistic weight during the interim.

2.

But even before the style, there was the man—the enigmatic, rumor-ringed, mysterious person of John Donne. Not many commoners in the pews could have known all the facts about their preacher's life, for that life had spent most of its maturity battering and being battered at the lower edges of the nobility. And even among the wealthy and the titled, there may have been more fast talk than factual knowledge about the Dean of St. Paul's. Yet what could be more attractive to crowds than just this whispered uncertainty about the occupant of England's mightiest Pulpit? What is more alluring than a legend alive?

The most sophisticated observer must admit that there were good reasons for the audience tremors that were at least a part of John Donne's attraction. It was not just gabby women or nervous saints who wondered about the secrets of their favorite divine. Anybody who had even part of the story was entirely justified in a certain puzzlement and uncertainty. It was hard then as it is now to make convincing order or unqualified sense of that story. And no one knew this better than John Donne, aware as he was of the angularities and discontinuities in his character and career beyond those known or even suspected by others. There is double fascination in a mystery that is mysterious to itself, yet uses a pulpit for its passionate self-examination.

X No family in England had suffered more for Roman Catholic Christianity than John Donne's. His mother's two brothers were among the earliest English Jesuits, and both died in exile. Before he was 21, Donne's only brother (with whom he had been educated by Jesuits before both went on to Oxford, Cambridge, and Lincoln's Inn) died in the prison where he had been thrown for sheltering a Roman priest. Donne's mother, who out-lived her famous son, never gave up her Roman Catholicism, still an aggressive, aged champion of her church while living with Donne in the deanery of St. Paul's.

And the erratic heir to this ancestry is that Church of England luminary, Dr. Donne, dean of the cathedral of London, Britain's National Church—John Donne, sharpest critic of the Jesuits, stubborn foe of X Rome.

But there were other even more remarkable (or at any event, more eagerly remarked!) dislocations in the great preacher's past. There was all that youthful poetry, known well only by those privileged to see much-sought handwritten copies, but known about by many who must have relished the juicy suggestion there of dissolute and profligate years. *Jack* Donne, the Dean was to call the author of all those records of dissipation and debauchery. But he was never to disavow Jack Donne nor challenge his records. How could he? The youths who had shared his immoralities and observed his erotic excess were men when he was a man. While memories last, events long past are not forgotten.

But then this rake, this continental traveller, this veteran of two naval expeditions with Essex, this sensuous adventurer, this cynical jiber at woman's fickleness—29-year-old John Donne marries 17-year-old Ann More and is at once a faithful husband and a frequent father, a sober family man who after lean, discouraging years away from the center of things suddenly emerges as the nation's greatest preacher, distinguished scholar, much given to sober charity, quiet benevolence and moral exhortation.

The marriage marks still another dislocation. From his school days on, Donne had been ambitious, clawingly ambitious for civil preferment. Time and again, when churchmen discovered Donne's scholarship and controversial skills, suggestions came that he seek a career whose success could be guaranteed in the church. But Donne would have none of it. He would have place at court or diplomatic commission. His employment as private secretary to Queen Elizabeth's Lord Keeper was an auspicious beginning, especially since he was much appreciated by the Lord Chancellor both as a person and for his intellectual brilliance.

Then, abruptly, the whole advantage was jettisoned and all the advancement jeopardized. Ambition's cool conniving was thrust aside and the impracticality, the doomed foolishness of an elopment with Lord Keeper Egerton's niece threw Donne into the clearly foreseeable disgrace and disfavor which withered all the skillfully nurtured hope of advantage. Then came the grubby years in the "thin little house" at Mitcham with a frequently ailing wife, the "gamesome children," sickness for all, scattered study, no response to any application for court consideration, dwindling resources. And finally, when he was 42, the about face that turned him from the long, vain look at distant honor to an engagement with the church that shortly brought him to the peace and plenty he wanted, but by a road he had long chosen not to take.

Now what made and what makes the person of John Donne fascinating above anything that he said or any of the ways of his saying is precisely the cumulative character of his being. He was not just a courtier become a cleric, a Roman become a Protestant, a libertine become a moralist. He was, high in his Anglican pulpit, something of everything he had ever been. A man with a past, even an exemplary man with a lurid past, is no rare phenomenon, nor is there peculiar appeal in him. The commanding presence, the personality that seizes is the one in which all appetites, ambitions, energies remain, not just in memory but in strength, only now reordered, redirected. John Donne conventionally deprecated Jack Donne, but Jack did not die until John did, and jammed churches knew that.

Donne's youthful motto was *Antes Muerto que Mudado*. The adoring Izaak Walton, wanting always to see in his pastor the pastor he wanted to see, gave the motto a devotional mistranslation, "How much shall I be changed, before I am changed!" That is what Walton wanted the record to prove: how basically altered was the regenerate Donne. But long before the fact, John Donne had had the truer insight. "Rather dead than changed," is what the prescient motto meant. And it was so. Commenting on the ordination of a friend, Donne spoke of and to himself—as he always did:

> Thou art the same materials as before,
> Onely the stampe is changed; but no more.

So it was not the preacher's style alone, but the preacher himself who attracted the pressing throngs to St. Paul's. In this "middle way" Anglican was all the learning and the probing analysis he had from the Jesuits he detested, and in this Protestant an essentially Catholic vision. In this man of the cloth was still the man of the world, bringing his graces to another court. In this honored and acclaimed favorite, old frustrations and futilities still asked their haunting questions. In this good new man the lusty old surged still, and delights foregone had phantasy-life yet, and little phrases deep inside the long sentences of weighty sermons showed the sinner clamoring just beneath the skin of the saint. The preacher drops a reference to men "sorry when appetite too soon decaies" and the congregation knows that the preacher knows that such sorrow is for all the thousand temporary *decaies*, not just for the terminal one. And the people know that the preacher is one with them as he is one with all the men he has been.

It is not just fascination that brings throngs back to such a man. There is reassurance in encounter with one whose confidence is all in spite of himself. There is satisfaction in the trustworthiness of one who has not deceived himself.

3.

The people came to hear what this man said. The man intrigued them, his style dazzled them, but it was that *what* of his saying as much as the *who* and *how* of it that bade the throngs. This cannot be too much insisted. For not everyone who has since concerned himself to make Donne's written sermons more widely available has found the explanation for the crowds' fascination in the substance of the sermons. Such distribution as the sermons have had since the seventeenth century has not always been for their "message," their theology, their point. In fact, one important aspect or another of Donne's sermonic intention has been avoided as an embarrassment or dismissed for its quaintness by most of his commentators. If there is anything new about the mid-twentieth century reacquaintance with and reevaluation of Donne's sermons, it is precisely the breadth and fullness of theological appreciation which it brings to the texts. It is doubtful whether men living any time since the sermons were delivered could hear them as we do today, with something very like the general understanding or over-all agreement they received on the mornings of their statement.

Special care must be taken with such broad claims. Whatever evidence is now brought to sustain them must not be interpreted to imply prophetic prowess in Donne. Neither is twentieth-century theology to be understood as retrograde. Donne was thoroughly seventeenth century in his matter and manner. The theology today which recognizes kinship in Donne's sermons is entirely of this moment.

But the plain fact is that by some long lineal coincidence, by some fluke of breeding or of physique, by some glandular balance or imbalance, by some quirk or twist in heritage or environment (read: providence), John Donne came to his seventeenth-century thinking with a turn of mind and quality of vision never entirely familiar until the twentieth century. And the other plain fact is that the church, alternating between sullen biblicism and vapid generality, has waited till today for that annealing of evangelical conviction and humility necessary to appreciate Donne where he is most bound *and* where he is most free.

Our conceptual hearing is less stopped and our theological sympathies are less cramped than has been the case for other generations. We do not need to pick and choose quite as recklessly as admirers have done in the past—excising now the earthy wisdom, then the plangent orthodoxy—to make total sense of the sermons. As a matter of fact, it is not any particular element that makes Donne's preaching familiar to us today, but it is precisely the variety, the particular mixture of elements in Donne's preaching that gives us a certain "inside" understanding of it.

It is not just Donne's dialectic that makes us kin across three centuries. Neither is it the characteristic approach which we today call existentialist. No more is it his Christocentrism nor his classic anthropology nor his depth insights. Nor his ethical suggestions, nor his warm ecumenicity. Each of these has been hinted at one time or another, one place or another in the history of Christian thinking. It is just because all come whispering or shouting down the millenia to us that we today do not hesitate to work them all together for ourselves. And it is because all of these scattered elements are gathered in Donne's thinking and preaching too that our apprehension of him can be more direct, less labored, than any in his own day or since.

What straight-line thinkers, for instance, could ever appreciate the paradox and indirection of Donne? Enlightenment Christians, still on the prowl for clear and distinct ideas, will go right by Donne where he struggles in his contradictions and complexities. But such Enlightenment Christians will not therefore move more directly to the truth. For it is altogether likely, say Donne and many Christians today, that statement of truth is more a surrounding than a seizing. The dialectic we share with Donne is the simultaneous affirmation of opposites, with the truth a moving, uneasy vibrancy, always to be relocated and reidentified between the extremes. Not an inert midpoint, but a shifting tension between outside possibilities, this is what you work with in stating the profoundest personal truths.

One of Donne's most familiar images gives the picture:

Cragged, and steep, Truth stands, On a huge hill, and hee that will

Reach her, about must, and about must goe.

(Satyre III)

That is not trick or fad in his day or in ours. That is not carelessness or sleight of hand, but honesty. Such thinking and statement proceeds on a knowledge of the diversity of truth, on a confession of the ranginess of truth, and on a recognition of the limitations of language.

It is precisely because of Donne's recurring yes-and-no, his use of paradox to express the contradictions he locates in reality, that we can give him less reserved confidence than he has often had before. Only so can he or anyone hold in uneasy tension the immanence and the transcendence of God, the presence of God in the church and sacraments and the freedom of God from the church and sacraments. Only so can he or we discuss the knowledge of God that is no-knowledge of a mystery, the having and not-having of faith, the sinfulness of the saved.

The same start of surprise comes with recognition of attitudes in Donne which we now identify (with increasing reluctance and embarrassment) as existentialist. We are used to going back one hundred years to Soren Kierkegaard for the first strong leads; and we note certain antecedents for him. But it is startling indeed to come upon such a cluster of these attitudes a full two centuries before Kierkegaard. There is no such ordering of these existence-oriented insights as the Dane gave them, and there is in Donne no sense of their wider philosophical suggestiveness. There is just that anachronistic turn of mind which repeatedly interpreted experience and belief in the manner we now call existentialist. The focus, over and over again, is on men (not *man*) in their immediacy and in their relationships. Thinking and the action implied is individual, decisive, present in its focus. There is a reluctance to generalize and a resistance to system. There is less contemplation of being and more exhortation to become, less interest in the truth in general and more desperation about the truth for me, less talk about God in himself and more concern about God in his relation to us. Thinking involves all of me, is about the existent, commits my whole existence.

Donne's emphasis was on existence, on deciding and doing: "I would fain do something," he wrote Sir Henry Goodyer, ". . . for to choose is to do." And not to choose and do, he warns in his sermons, "is to be nothing." Significant choice comes in the constant crisis of God's mercy which is also judgment, and which is "alwaies perpendicular, right over every one of us." Decision is exhorted as a conscious, deliberate commitment. Thus, we are not to wait for sickness or a death-bed to say our yes to Christ and our no to ourselves. Weakening or relaxing into consent is not the decision that constitutes us as persons: "in the night, in our last night, those thoughts that fall upon us, they are rather dreams, then true rememberings; we do rather dream that we repent, then repent indeed, upon our death-bed." Even Donne's own death was not allowed simply to happen. While he lived it was in terms of decisive action, deliberately arranging the bizarre circumstances of his demise, and finally choosing death when he was ready, *being* as long as he was *choosing,* and then not being. Life was not allowed, even at the end, to be a flaccid continuum supporting random choices and actions. Choice was the vehicle of existence, and when choice chose its end, existence was over.

But even so sketchy an interpretation of Donne's attitudes and actions might not have been countenanced by him (the terms certainly would not have been recognized by him). He resolutely avoided system-making. This was not what even his most admiring analysts have usually heretofore lamented, a failure in Donne's intellectual equipment. It may very well have been that he was not temperamentally inclined to close structural articulation. But the plain evidence of many of his statements is that it was his persuasion of the relativity and tentativeness of doctrinal formulations and the ineluctability of ultimate mystery that necessarily inhibited system-building. Over and over comes the refrain, after serious doctrinal discussion, "It is a problematicall matter, and we say nothing too peremptorily."

Donne probed all doctrines. He found in them helpful illumination of the truth *for him,* and that was the only truth he bothered with. "We do not call an assent to the Gospell, faith, but faith is the application of the Gospell to our selves; not an assurance that Christ dyed, but an assurance that Christ dyed for all." "This is an impropriation without sacriledge, and an enclosure of a Common without damage, to make God mine owne, to finde that all that God sayes is spoken of me, and all that Christ suffered was suffered for me."

But in all his doctrinal digging, Donne never found that bed-rock upon which a system could be built. Time and again he went back at the Trinity, for instance, but to the end he agreed with an early sermonic observation: "I know the explicite Doctrine of the Trinity was not easy to be apprehended then; as it is not easy to be expressed now. It is a bold thing in servants, to inquire curiously into their Master's pedigree, whether he be well descended, or well allied: It is a bold thing too, to inquire too curiously into the eternall generation of Christ Jesus, or the eternal procession of the Holy Ghost. When *Gregory Nazianzen* was pressed by one, to assign a difference between these words, *Begotten,* and *Proceeding* . . . says he . . . Doe thou tell me, what this *Begetting* is, and then I will tell thee, what this *Proceeding* is; and all the world will find us both mad, for going about to expresse inexpressible things."

Donne did not lack the equipment to systematize so

much as he saw no material and felt no inclination to systematize. It would be a brave or foolish critic who would charge this protean mind with any disability. But it is obvious that Donne felt no need systematically to regard theological realities in themselves. The focus was always on the existent I. "For, beloved, we are to consider God, not as he is in himselfe, but as he works upon us." And again, "we consider not mercy as it is radically in God, and an essentiall attribute of his, but productively in us, as it is an action, a working upon us . . ."

In our day, with its prominent christocentrics, Donne might have noted in his own sermons certain leads like those which have lately been developed into enormous "church dogmatics." Certainly passages stand out repeatedly with a bewildering *déjà vu* effect on twentieth-century readers. It is not just in such sentences as could have been written at any time: "Neither does any man know God, except he know him so, as God hath made himselfe known, that is, In Christ." But there are longer stretches where, except for diction, one could swear that he was hearing again, but from the beginning of the seventeenth century, this very christological pounding and blasting that sounded so new at the beginnig of the twentieth century: *"When you are without Christ, you are without God.* Without this, all morall vertues are but diseases; Liberality is but a popular baite, and not a benefit, not an almes; Chastity is but a castration, and an impotency, not a temperance, not mortification; Active valour is but a fury, whatsoever we do, and passive valour is but a stupidity, whatsoever we suffer. Naturall apprehensions of God, though those naturall apprehensions may have much subtilty, Voluntary elections of a Religion, though those voluntary elections may have much singularity, Morall directions for life, though those morall directions may have much severity, are all frivolous and lost, if all determine not in Christianity, in the Notion of God, so as God hath manifested and conveyed himself to us; in God the Father, God the Son, and God the Holy Ghost . . ."

To those who attend Karl Barth's present efforts to interpret all church doctrine in terms of Christ, insisting the correspondence hardest just where the correspondence is hardest to insist (as in Creation and Election), there is something almost eery in some of John Donne's premonitions of the effort. "We use to ascribe the Creation to the Father, but the Father created by the Word, and his Word, is his Son, Christ; *When he prepared the Heavens, I was there,* (saies Christ, of himselfe in the person of Wisdome) *and when he appointed the foundations of the earth, then was I by him, as one brought up with him;* It is not, as one brought in to him, or brought in by him, but with him; one as old, that is, as eternall, as much God as he. We use to ascribe Santification to the Holy Ghost; But the Holy Ghost sanctifies in the Church, And the Church was purchased by the blood of Christ, and Christ remaines Head of the Church, *usque in consummationem,* till the end of the world."

Or again, there are Donne's remonstrances with preachers who think they can know God's mind and discuss his decrees without reference to Christ: "wee are fallen upon such times too, as that men doe not thinke themselves Christians, except they can tell what God meant to doe with them before he meant they should bee Christians; for we can be intended to be Christians, but from Christ; and wee must needs seek a Predestination, without any relation to Christ; a decree in God for salvation, and damnation, before any decree for the reparation of mankind, by Christ. Every Common-placer will adventure to teach, and every artificer will pretend to understand the purpose, yea, and the order too, and method of Gods eternall and unrevealed decree."

The same theological point is made with fuller

pastoral explication in an earlier sermon. "Christ
Jesus to a Christian, should be the onely foundation;
And therefore to place salvation or damnation in such
an absolute Decree of God, as should have no relation
to the fall of man, or reparation in a Redeemer; this
is to remove this stone out of the foundation, for a
Christian may be well content to beginne at Christ:
If any man therefore have laid any other foundation
to his Faith, or any other foundation to his Actions,
possession of great places, alliance in great Families,
strong practise in Courts, obligation upon dependants,
acclamations of people; if he have laid any other foundations for pleasure, and contentment, care of health,
and complexion, appliablenesse in conversation, de-
lightfulnesse in discourses, cheerefulnesse in disport-
ings, interchanging of secrets, and such other small
wares of Courts and Cities as these are: whosoever
hath laid such foundations as these, must proceed as
that Generall did, who when he received a besieged
Towne to mercy, upon condition that in signe of
subjection they should suffer him to take off one row
of stones from their walls, he tooke away the lowest
row, the foundation, and so ruined and demolished
the whole walls of the Citie: So must he that hath
these false foundations, (that is, these habits) divest
the habite, roote out the lowest stone, that is, the
generall, and radicall inclination to these disorders: For
he shall never be able to watch and resist every particular temptation, if he trust onely to his Morall
Constancy; No, not if he place Christ for the roofe to
cover all his sinnes, when he hath done them; his mercy
worketh by way of pardon after, not by way of . . .
priviledge to doe a sinne before hand; but before
hand we must have the foundation in our eye; when
we undertake any particular Action, in the beginning,
we must looke how that will suite with the foundation,
with Christ; for there is his first place, to be *Lapis
fundamentalis.*"

Pendant to today's christocentrism is a political ethics grounded in what a very popular and exceedingly current slogan calls the Lordship of Christ. The idea was generally reclaimed in the years around the Second World War. Yet no one who uses the phrase now could pen a more precise definition for it than Donne did, long since: ". . . when we say *Iesum Dominum,* so, as that we professe him to be the Lord, Then we confesse a vigilancy, a superintendency, a residence, and a permanency of Christ, in his Dominion, in his Church, to the worlds end. If he be the Lord, in his Church, there is no other that rules with him, there is no other that rules for him. The temporall Magistrate is not so Lord, as that Christ and he are Collegues, or fellow-Consuls, that if he command against Christ, he should be as soone obeyed as Christ; for a Magistrate is a Lord, and Christ is the Lord, a Magistrate is a Lord to us, but Christ is the Lord to him, and to us, and to all. None rules with him, none rules for him . . ."

No emphasis in recent theologies has been more discussed, inside and outside those theologies, than their emphasis on the sin of man. Again, by the remarkable coincidence we have been charting, Donne prefigures our contemporaries on this subject, not only in their mood but even in their terms. There is for instance, a current insistence that the sin about which men must be concerned is not a misdemeanor or a whole list of misdemeanors, but is treason: the gravity of our sin is seen not in our regular breaking of God's laws, but in our challenging the right of God to make any laws for us. The distinction is one Donne had drawn: "A man may make a pety larceny high treason so; If being called in question for that lesser offense, he will deny that there is any such Power, any such Soveraigne, any such King, as can call him in question for it . . . At that last Judgement, we shall be arraigned for not cloathing, not visiting, not har-

bouring the poore . . . But yet, all this is but a pety
larceny, in respect of that high treason, of infidelity,"
of denying or doubting God.

The source of such sedition and the essence of such
sin is, we say, pride. And so said Donne. "Man in re-
volt" we say now; "Mans rebellion to *God*," Donne
said. The distortion of our creation reaches back to
beginnings, "original sin" speaks of origins. "The
Angels," Donne claimed, "fell in love with themselves,
and neglected God, and so fell *in aeternum*, for ever."
The corruption by sin reaches through all thought and
action, even the highest. "There is no worke of ours
so good, as that we can looke for thanks at Gods hand
for that worke; no worke, that hath not so much ill
mingled with it, as that we need not cry Gods mercy
for that worke. There was so much corruption in the
getting, or so much vaine glory in the bestowing, as
that no man builds an Hospitall, but his soule lies,
though not dead, yet lame in that Hospitall; no man
mends a high-way, but he is, though not drowned, yet
mired in that way; no man relieves the poore, but he
needs reliefe for that reliefe." With an air of discovery
we have affirmed that the distortion of sin penetrates
religion, the faith, church itself. And we discover the
same in Donne. "Nay beloved, when a man hath used
those wings, which God hath given him, and raised
himselfe to some heighth in religious knowledge, and
religious practise, as *Eutichus,* out of a desire to hear
Paul preach, was got up into a Chamber, and up into
a window of that Chamber, and yet falling asleep,
fell downe dead; so we may fall into a security of our
present state, into a pride of our knowledge, or of
our purity, and so fall lower, then they, who never
came to our heighth." God's ministers are watchmen,
Donne said soon after ordination, "not only to look
into the chamber, and reprehend the wantonnesses
and licentiousnesse of both sexes there . . . but to
note and reprehend those sins, which are done so

much more immediately towards God, as they are done upon colour and pretence of Religion."

Nowhere, though, is Donne's precocity more striking than in the depth of his insight into the individual workings of this general sin. With an uncanny precision he drops himself into the most troubled deeps of personality and traces there the dark submerged currents and resistances that have been studied latterly only by much more technical analysts. There is no secret about how Donne did his probing: he knew himself, and confessed what he knew. Donne's "acute and pervasive self-awareness" was not just "the secret of his genius and his fascination" (Helen C. White), but it was the door to the whole "complicated web of weakness and distraction and self-bewilderment and self-betrayal" which Donne recognized as common to humanity.

There are some brilliant strokes in Donne's limning of the human unconscious. He describes, in his own pictorial way, various mechanisms which can only be compulsions, repressions, rationalizations. There is a sophisticated contemperaneity even about his little asides: "There is no such unhappiness to a sinner, as to be happy; no such cross as to have no crosses." "Those sins which we apprehend even with horror and amazement, when we hear that others have done them we may come to do them with an earnestness, with a delight, with a defense, with a glory . . ." A prayer begs forgiveness for "sinnes which I have so laboured to hide from the world, as that they are now hid from mine own conscience, and mine own memory." Typically, Donne admits a special affection for Ezekiel because of "his extraordinary depth and mysteriousness." Wheels within wheels were John Donne's special competence. How fascinated he would be today in analyzing, with new tools, his own fascination with the worm!

Everywhere in the sermons are the old suggestions

become modern convictions. No sermon is read through without requiring at least one marveling reminder that this was preached more than three hundred years ago. In that proof-text time of baroque biblicism he could write "It must bee Gods *whole Booke,* and not a few mis-understood *Sentences* out of that Booke that must try thee. Thou must not press heavily to thine own damnation every such *Sentence* . . . That which must try thee is the whole *Booke,* the *tenor* and *purpose,* the *Scope* and *intention* of God in his Scriptures."

At a time when Christian ethics was freezing again into a single pattern demanding unanimity and conformity, Donne could speak of circumstances altering requirements and of capacities changing the ethical significance of objectively similar acts. He saw better than most Christians yet have how solvent of pattern-ethics human relativities are. The Christian life, he knew ahead of us, cannot long continue to be understood as achievement of an objective, observable level of goodness. No two men are the same man, no two have the same resistances, no two start at the same place; so no single action ever has one ethical significance. "It is nothing for a sick man that hath lost his taste, to say . . . Depart voluptuousness; nothing in a consumption to say . . . Depart wantonnesse; nothing for a (pauper) Client, to say, . . . I will not bribe." Over and over again Donne made the point that we still have not adequately weighted: "Chastity is not chastity in an old man, but a disability to be unchast; and therefore thou doest not give God that which thou pretendest to give, for thou hast no chastity to give him." And again: "A poore man may have heaven for a penny, that hath no greater store; and, God lookes, that he to whom he hath given thousands, should lay out thousands upon the purchase of heaven. The market changes, as the plenty of money changes;

Heaven costs a rich man more than a poore, because he hath more to give."

There is in Donne an interpretation of the ministry which we advertise today as kerygmatic: the preacher a herald on a high tower sounding a trumpet and bringing word from the king. There are hints of a distinction which we now describe in terms of "I-Thou" and "I-it" (Buber). There are statements of the response elicited by the unmerited mercy of God which fit easily into current accounts of "costly grace" (Bonhoefer). The phrase, "the ground of all being" is sometimes preferred to the word God for describing the focus of our ultimate religious concern (Tillich).

Above all, there is an ecumenical zeal in Donne's preaching which cannot be matched between the first decades of the Reformation and the last decades of present history. Donne's ecumenicity is part of that earlier remarked humility before mystery and reticence about doctrinal absoluteness. "Take heed how you condemne another man for an Heretique, because he beleeves not just as you beleeve, or for a Reprobate, because he lives not just as you live, for God is no accepter of persons." But there is more to this ecumenicity than temperamental equability or Anglican medianism. That Christocentric element in Donne that flings its bond across three centuries is integral to ecumenics, then as now. A country congregation near London heard this, but it might have come instead from any recent meeting of the Faith and Order Commission of the World Council of Churches: "If we would but make Christ Jesus and his peace, the life and soule of all our actions, and all our purposes; if we would mingle that sweetnesse and supplenesse which he loves, and which he is, in all our undertakings; if in all controversies, booke controversies, and sword controversies, we would fit them to him, and see how neere they would meet in him, that is, how neere we might come to be friends, and yet both sides be good Christians; then wee placed this stone in his second right place, who as hee is a Corner stone reconciling God and man in his owne Person, and a Corner stone in reconciling God and mankinde in his Office, so hee desires to bee a Corner stone in reconciling man and man, and setling peace among our selves, not for worldly ends, but for this respect, that wee might all meet in him to love one another, not because wee made a stronger party by that love, not because wee made a sweeter conversation by that love, but because wee met closer in the bosome of Christ Jesus; where wee must at last either rest altogether eternally, or bee altogether eternally throwne out, or bee eternally separated and divorced from one another."

It would be indefensible sophistication to suggest that John Donne was a twentieth-century Christian out of season. Selection of emphases that startle us by their reminiscence and their contemporaneity has been *selection*. They stand out as they do precisely because the flat stretches of dated interpretation and learned impedimenta between the high points etch the sharp relief. The theology is not all viable, the discussion is not all interesting, the development is not all relevant.

More than that, the arrestingly modern elements in John Donne's thought are not the *ex nihilo* emergences suggested by our discussion. They are not simply premonitions of later conclusions; they are products of long lines of Christian deliberation. None of the coincidences between Donne's statements and ours need any other explication than our common concentration on the biblical revelation, and our common indebtedness to generations of biblical and theological scholarship that went before Donne.

There is no mystery, then, in the fact that Donne and we should see some of the same things when we look through a shared tradition to a single source. But there is still a kind of wonder—and this is all that has been insisted—that that distant man and we should have shared so often a single vision. The delight, beyond even the edification in these sermons, is in observing our own observation so long ago. And that, of course, is the edification too. John Donne did no reach ahead to show theology a way, as he did reach forward to show poetry its way. But looking back, we can see ourselves in what we see in him. Listening again to the long, old periods, we hear ourselves with new and critical objectivity when we note what in Donne speaks to us.

To choose nine sermons from John Donne's one hundred and sixty extant sermons is finally an exercise in the arbitrary. No matter how carefully the choice is weighed, there are always omissions the editor cannot believe or bear.

In the case of this selection, however, choice was helpfully limited by availability of trustworthy versions of the sermons. There is today only one reliable source for Donne's sermons: the ten-volume Simpson-Potter edition now being published by the University of California Press. The superlative scholarship of this edition is such that the sermons as now presented are clearly closer to the author's intention than in any earlier (including the original folio) publication. The Simpson-Potter versions are, in a very real sense, *first* editions of Donne's sermons. The little volume here being introduced will have earned its place on the stands if it helps to direct readers' attention to the Simpson-Potter books.

This definitive edition, however, stands now at six volumes. With one exception, therefore, the sermons here presented are from the available three-fifths of the total collection. Fortunately, the publishing schedule at the University of California has spanned Donne's ministry, so in the six available volumes we have examples of Donne's early, middle and late preaching. Only Donne's last sermon, "Death's Duell" has been added here from Alford's now superseded edition of the sermons.

Usually, the sermons are presented here entire. Marginal notations have been generally omitted, only occasionally being added parenthetically to the text, as when they identify sources not otherwise labeled in a quotation. The italics are all John Donne's. Long italicized passages are generally scriptural quotations which are not identified here (Donne put the references in the margins) but which could usually be located with a concordance of the Authorized Version.

Omissions in the text are few and are marked to indicate the character of the words left out. When a repetition or recapitulation occasionally seemed expendable, three points (. . .) indicate the dropping of Donne's English words. Three asterisks (***) denote the excision of a Latin tag and/or Donne's English paraphrase of such a tag. But omissions are rare. Their only justification is the hastening and sustaining of reading in some of the denser passages. They are never allowed to alter style or statement. And they are never meant to make Donne look better than he is.

SERMON PREACHED AT LINCOLN'S INN

Spring, 1618 (Psalms 32:2)

I

EDITOR'S PREFACE

T. S. Eliot, among others, is not impressed by the erotic evidence of John Donne's profane poetry. For his own reasons, and they are not all apparent, Mr. Eliot doubts the libertine reputation of the older poet: "I do not think that we have sufficient evidence that Donne was so *very* dissipated: we are in danger of making an attractive romance about him." [1] The poetic evidence of an immoral youth is dismissed as inconclusive, the young Donne's cynicism is explained as "a poetic convention of the time," the supposedly knowing complaints about the fickleness of women are minimized as "immature bravado." Nor is Eliot any more convinced of the genuineness of Donne's later remorse or repentance.

Then, because there is no more evidence for his strictures than for the more traditional acceptations, Eliot adds an observation which is as generally true as it may be specifically irrelevant: "It is pleasant in youth to think that one is a gay dog, and it is pleasant in age to think that one *was* a gay dog; because as we grow old we all like to think that we have changed, developed and improved; people shrink from acknowledging that they are exactly the same at fifty as they were at twenty-five . . . If Donne in youth

[1] T. S. Eliot, "Donne in Our Times." *A Garland for Donne*, p. 10.

was a rake, then I suspect he was a conventional rake; if Donne in age was devout, then I suspect he was conventionally devout." [2]

It would be remarkably poetic justice if such a statement, claiming to say something about its subject, actually said more about its speaker. For Donne too repeatedly talked about himself when he claimed to be telling of others. He does it in the sermon which follows. Soon after the beginning he paraphrases Jeremiah 15:10. But the farther he goes, the farther he gets from the Old Testament. And suddenly, still claiming to be parsing the prophet, Donne is blurting out himself, clean beyond any meaning of the text: "I preach but the sense of God's indignation upon mine own soul, in a conscience of mine own sins, I impute nothing to another, that I confesse not of my selfe, I call none of you to confession to me, I doe but confesse my selfe to God, and you, I rack no mans memory, what he did last year, last week, last night, I onely gather into my memory, and powr out in the presence of my God, and his Church, the sinfull history of mine own youth . . ."

That is John Donne on John Donne; Jeremiah is left far behind. And though so personal and pointed an outburst is infrequent in Donne's preaching, private reference is everywhere in the sermons. John Donne preached out of himself and he always preached to himself. Far more than in his poems, the variety and thoroughness of Donne's youthful profligacy comes through in his sermons. A sensitive, imaginative poet might well have written all the poems of passion on the basis of one or two startling and memorable adventures. So the poetry is not "sufficient evidence that Donne was so *very* dissipated." But the sermons *are* sufficient evidence that Donne's popular reputation has firm and extensive basis in fact. The sermons are the utterance of a man who knows the world, at its most problematic, from the inside, and in more devious detail than either poems or sermons state.

As will be seen, the same can be said of the genuineness of the poet's repentance. Its reality may not be compelling when rhyme and rhythm have had their way with its expression. But the power and passion in the preacher's remorse are inescapable and unarguable.

There is, however, another reason for noting the paragraph about "the sinfull history of mine own youth" already remarked in this sermon. Besides saying something about John Donne's past, those phrases are a reminder that Donne was ruefully aware of where he was preaching at that moment. Urged on, almost propelled by the king to ordination (January 23, 1615), the forty-two-year-old Donne began his preaching in country towns around London. According to Izaak Walton, Donne's first sermon was delivered at Paddington. Of that utterance there is no other record. The earliest sermon to be preserved is one preached on April 30, 1615, "at Greenwich." The practice preaching in the suburbs evidently continued, but by April 21, 1616, the king's protégé was preaching at Whitehall before the court. A sermon at the historic preaching post, Paul's Cross, came a year later. Donne preached before the queen at Denmark-House near the end of 1617, and repeatedly at Whitehall for the king, whose chaplain he now was.

But meanwhile, on October 24, 1616, John Donne was chosen Divinity Reader for the Benchers of Lincoln's Inn, a post best understood now as chaplain to the principal law school ("the third university") in the kingdom. Preacher and parish were tailored for each other. Brainy academicians delighted in their brilliant pulpiteer, and he plainly gloried in a congregation that could take the best and sharpest he could give. It was, said old Walton, "a love-strife of desert and liberality . . . he constantly and faithfully preaching, they liberally requiting him."

The only ripple in Donne's satisfaction may have been the embarrassment that shows occasionally in the earliest Lincoln's Inn sermons that we possess. Donne had himself been a student at Lincoln's Inn from 1592 to 1594. Eighteen years later he was back—a divine returned to the scene of youthful indiscretions. Old classmates were back too as faculty members and administrators. They remembered. Legends probably lingered, growing no less lurid with the succession of student generations. And Donne remembered. So there is in a sermon like the one before us (Spring, 1618) an appealing self-consciousness which does not characterize sermons preached later, elsewhere. Donne always involved himself in his preaching, but at Lincoln's Inn there was a rueful, winsome note in his confession that breaks through the more measured statement of later, greater sermons. In sermons to come, Donne would reach down to congregations he wanted to know him. At Lincoln's Inn, Donne reached out to those who knew all about him.

So we begin with Donne at his most personal, introducing his sermon with a lovely description of his scriptural preferences, meditating then with his companions on the vagaries of sin, on the persistence of despair even beyond repentance, and on the perseverance of temptation even after prayer.

PREACHED AT LINCOLNS INNE.

Psal. 38.2. For Thine Arrowes Stick Fast in Me, and Thy Hand Presseth Me Sore.

Almost every man hath his *Appetite,* and his *tast* disposed to some kind of *meates* rather then others; He knows what dish he would choose, for his first, and for his second course. We have often the same disposition in our *spirituall Diet;* a man may have a particular love towards such or such a book of Scripture, and in such an affection, I acknowledge, that my spirituall appetite carries me still, upon the *Psalms of David,* for a first course, for the Scriptures of the Old Testament, and upon the *Epistles of Saint Paul,* for a second course, for the New: and my meditations even for these *pub-like exercises* to Gods Church, returne oftnest to these two. For, as a hearty entertainer offers to others, the meat which he loves best himself, so doe I oftnest present to Gods people, in these Congregations, the meditations which I feed upon at home, in those two Scriptures. If a man be asked a reason why he loves one meat better then another, where all are equally good, (as the books of Scripture are) he will at least, finde a reason in some good example, that he sees some man of good tast, and temperate withall, so do: And for my Diet, I have Saint *Augustines* protestation, that he loved the *Book of Psalms,* and Saint *Chrysostomes,* that he loved Saint *Pauls Epistles,* with a particular devotion. I may have another more particular reason, because they are Scriptures, written in such forms, as I have been most accustomed to; Saint *Pauls* being Letters, and *Davids* being Poems: for, God gives us, not onely that which is meerly necessary, but that which is convenient too; He does not onely feed us, but *feed us with marrow, and with fatnesse;* he gives us our instruction in cheerfull forms, not in a sowre, and sullen, and angry, and unacceptable way, but cheerfully, in *Psalms,* which is also a limited, and a restrained form; Not in an *Oration,* not in *Prose,* but in *Psalms;* which is such a form as is both curious, and requires diligence in the making, and then when it is made, can have nothing, no syllable taken from it, nor added to it: Therefore is Gods will delivered to us in *Psalms,* that we might have it the more cheerfully, and that we might have it the more certainly, because where all the words are numbred, and measured, and weighed, the whole work is the lesse subject to falsification, either by substraction or addition. God speaks to us *in oratione strictâ,* in a limited, in a diligent form; Let us (not) speak to him *in oratione solutâ;* not *pray,* not *preach,* not *hear,* slackly, suddenly, unadvisedly, extemporally, occasionally, indiligently; but let all our speech to him, be weighed, and measured in the weights of the *Sanctuary,* let us be content to preach, and to hear within the compasse of our Articles, and content to pray in those *formes* which the Church hath meditated for us, and recommended to us.

This whole Psalm is a *Prayer,* and recommended by *David* to the Church; And a *Prayer* grounded upon *Reasons.* The *Reasons* are multiplyed, and related from the second to the 20. verse. But as the *Prayer* is made to him that is *Alpha,* and *Omega, first,* and *last;* so the *Prayer* is the *Alpha* and *Omega* of the Psalme; the *Prayer* possesses the first and the last verse thereof; and though the Reasons be not left out . . . yet *David* makes up his Circle, he begins, and ends in prayer. But our text fals within his Reasons; He prays in the first verse that God would forbear him, upon the Reasons that follow; of which some are *extrinsecall,* some arising out of the *power,* some out of the

malice, some out of the *scorn* of other men; And some
are *intrinsecall,* arising out of himself, and of his sense
of Gods Judgements upon him; and our Text begins
the Reasons of that last kind, which because *David*
enters, with that particle, not onely of *Connexion,* but
of *Argumentation* too, *For, (Rebuke me not O Lord,
for* it stands thus and thus with me) we shall make it
a first short part, to consider, how it may become a
godly man, to limit God so far, as to present and oppose *Reasons* against his declared purpose, and proceedings. And then in those calamities which he presents for his Reasons in this Text, *For thine arrows
stick fast in me, and thy hand presseth me sore,* we
shall passe by these steps, first, we shall see in what
respect, in what allusion, in what notification he cals
them *arrows:* And therein first, that they are *alienæ,*
they are shot from *others,* they are not in his own
power; a man shoots not an arrow at himselfe; And
then, that they are *Veloces,* swift in coming, he cannot
give them their time; And again, they are *Vix visibiles,*
though they bee not altogether invisible in their coming, yet there is required a quick eye, and an expresse
diligence, and watchfulnesse to discern and avoid
them . . . And secondly, they are *many arrows;* The
victory lies not in scaping one or two; And thirdly,
they *stick in him;* they finde not *David* so good proof,
as to rebound back again, and imprint no sense; And
they stick fast; Though the blow be felt, and the
wound discerned, yet there is not a present cure, he
cannot shake them off; *Infixæ sunt;* And then, with
all this, they *stick fast in him;* that is, in *all him;* in his
body, and soul; in him, in his thoughts, and actions;
in him, in his sins and in his good works too; *Infixæ
mihi,* there is no part of him, no faculty in him, in
which they stick not: for, (which may well bee another
consideration) *That hand,* which shot them, *presses*
him: follows the blow, and *presses him sore,* that is,
vehemently. But yet, (which will be our conclusion)

Sagittæ tuæ, and *manus tua,* These arrows that are shot, and this hand that presses them so sore, are the *arrows,* and is the *hand* of God; and therefore, first, they must have their *Effect,* they cannot be dis-appointed; But yet they bring their comfort with them, because they are his, because no *arrows* from him, no *pressing* with his hand, comes without that *Balsamum* of mercy, to heal as fast as he wounds. And of so many pieces will this exercise consist, this exercise of your *Devotion,* and perchance *Patience.*

First then, this particle of *connexion* and *argumentation, For,* which begins our text, occasions us, in a first part, to consider, that such an impatience in affliction, as brings us toward a *murmuring* at Gods proceedings, and almost to a calling of God to an account, in inordinate expostulations, is a leaven so kneaded into the nature of man, so innate a tartar, so inherent a sting, so inseparable a venim in man, as that the holyest of men have scarce avoided it in all degrees thereof. *Job* had Gods testimony of being an *upright man;* and yet *Job* bent that way, *O that I might have my request,* says *Job, and that God would grant me the thing that I long for.* Well, if God would, what would *Job* aske? *That God would destroy me, and cut me off.* Had it not been as easie, and as ready, and as usefull a prayer, *That God would deliver him?* . . . *Moses* had Gods testimonies of a remarkable and exemplar man, for *meeknesse.* But did God always finde it so? was it a meek behaviour towards God, to say, *Wherefore hast thou afflicted thy servant? Have I conceived all this people, have I begotten them, that thou shouldest say unto me, Carry them in thy bosome? Elias* had had testimonies of Gods care and providence in his behalf; and God was not weary of preserving him, and he was weary of being preserved; He desired that he might dye, and said, *Sufficit Domine, It is enough O Lord, now take my soul. Jonas,* even then, when God was expressing an act of mercy, takes occasion to be angry, and to bee angry *at God,* and to be angry at *the mercy* of God. We may see his fluctuation and distemper, and irresolution in that case, and his transportation; *He was angry,* says the text; very angry; And yet, the text says, *He prayed,* but he prayed *angerly; O Lord take, I beseech thee, my life from me; for it is better for me to dye, then to live.* Better for *him,* that was all he considered; not what was best for the service and glory of God, but best for him. God asks him, *If he doe well to be angry?* And he will not tell him there; God gives him time to vent his passion, and he askes him again after: *Doest thou well to bee angry?* And he answers more angerly, *I doe well to be angry, even unto death. Ieremy* was under this tentation too. *Jonas* was angry because his Prophesie was not performed; because God would not second his Prophesie in the destruction of Nineveh. *Jeremy* was angry because his Prophesie was like to be performed; he preached heavy Doctrin, and therefore his Auditory hated him; *Woe is me, my Mother,* says he, *that thou hast born me a man of strife, and a man of contention to the whole earth!* I preach but the messages of God; (and *væ mihi si non,* wo be unto me if I preach not them) I preach but the sense of Gods indignation upon mine own soul, in a conscience of mine own sins, I impute nothing to another, that I confesse not of my selfe, I call none of you to confession to me, I doe but confesse my self to God, and you, I rack no mans memory, what he did last year, last week, last night, I onely gather into my memory, and powr out in the presence of my God, and his Church, the sinfull history of mine own *youth,* and yet I am a *contentious man,* says *Jeremy,* a worm, and a burthen to every tender conscience, says he, *and I strive with the whole earth,* I am a bitter, and satyricall preacher; This is that that wearies mee, says hee, *I have neither lent on usury,* nor *men have lent me on usury,* yet, as though I were an oppressing lender, or a fraudulent borrower, *every one of them doth curse me*.

This is a naturall infirmity, which the strongest men, being but men, cannot devest, that if their purposes prosper not, they are weary of their industry, weary of their lifes; But this is *Summa ingratitudo in Deum, malle non esse, quàm miserum esse:* There cannot be a greater unthankfulnesse to God then to desire to be *Nothing* at all, rather then to be that, that God would have thee to be; To desire to be out of the world, rather then to glorifie him, by thy patience in it. But when this infirmity overtakes Gods children . . . Learn patience, not from the stupidity of Philosophers, who are but their own *statues,* men of stone, without sense, without affections, and who placed all their glory, in a *Non facies ut te dicam malum,* that no pain should make them say they were in pain; nor from the pertinacy of Heretiques, how to bear a calamity, who gave their bodies to the fire, for the establishing of their Disciples, but take out a new lesson in the times of *Grace;* Consider the Apostles there, *Gaudentes & Gloriantes,* They departed from the Councell, *rejoycing that they were counted worthy,* to suffer rebuke *for his name.* It was *Joy,* and all *Joy,* says S. *James;* It was *Glory,* and all *Glory,* says S. *Paul, Absit mihi, God forbid that I should glory, save in the Crosse of our Lord Jesus Christ;* And if I can glory in that, (to glory in that, is to have a conscience testifying to me, that God receives glory by my use of his correction) I may come to God, reason with God, plead with God, wrastle with God, and be received and sustained by him. This was *Davids* case in our Text: therefore he doth not stray into the infirmities of these great, and good Men, *Moses, Job, Elias, Jeremy,* and *Jonah;* whose errours, it is labour better bestowed carefully to avoid, then absolutely to excuse, for that cannot be done. But *David* presents onely to God the sense of his corrections, and implies in *that,*

that since the cure is wrought, since Gods purpose, which is, by corrections, to bring a sinner to *himself*, and so to *God*, is effected in him, God would now be pleased to remember all his other gracious promises too; and to admit such a zealous prayer as he doth from *Esay* after, *Be not angry, O Lord, above measure*; (that is, above the measure of thy *promises* to repentant sould, or the measure of the *strength* of our bodies) *Neither remember iniquities for ever; But, loe, wee beseech thee, Behold, we are thy people.* To end this first part, (because the other extends it self in many branches) *Then* when we are come to a *sense* of Gods purpose, by his *corrections,* it is a seasonable time to flie to his *mercy,* and to pray, that he would remove them from us; and to present our *Reasons,* to spare us, *for* thy corrections have wrought upon us; *Give us this day, our daily bread,* for thou hast given us stones, and scorpions, tribulations, and afflictions, and we have *fed* upon them, found nourishment even in those tribulations and afflictions, and said thee grace for them, blessed and glorified thy name, for those tribulations, and afflictions; Give us our *Cordials* now, and our *Restoratives,* for thy physick hath evacuated all the peccant humour, and all our naturall strength; shine out in the light of thy countenance now, for this long cold night hath benum'd us; since the *drosse* is now evaporated, now withdraw thy *fire;* since thy hand hath anew cast us, now imprint in us anew *thine Image;* since we have not disputed against thy corrections, all this while, *O Lord open thou our lips now,* and accept our remembering of thee, that we have not done so; Accept our Petition, and the *Reason* of our Petition, *for thine Arrows stick fast in us, and thy hand presseth us sore.*

David in a rectified conscience findes that he may be admitted to present *reasons* against farther corrections, And that this may be received as a reason, *That Gods Arrows are upon him;* for this is a phrase or a

Metaphore, in which Gods indignation is often expressed in the Scripture. *He sent out his Arrows, and scattered them,* sayes *David;* magnifying Gods goodness in his behalf, against his enemies. And so again, *God will ordaine his Arrowes for them that persecute me. Complebo sagittas,* says God, *I will heap mischiefs upon them, and I will spend mine arrows upon them:* yea, *Inebriabo sanguine, I will make mine Arrows drunk in their bloud.* It is *Idiotismus Spiritus sancti,* a peculiar character of the holy Ghosts expressing Gods anger, in that Metaphore of shooting *Arrows.* In this place, some understand by these Arrows, foul and infectious *diseases,* in his body, derived by his *incontinence.* Others, the sting of *Conscience,* and that fearfull choice, which the Prophet offered him, *war, famine,* and *pestilence.* Others, his passionate *sorrow* in the *death* of *Bethsheba's first childe;* or in the *Incest of Amnon* upon his sister, or in the *murder* upon *Amnon* by *Absolon;* or in the *death* of *Absolon* by *Joab;* or in many other occasions of sorrow, that surrounded *David* and his family, more, perchance, then any such family in the body of story. But these *Psalmes* were made, not onely to vent *Davids* present holy passion, but to serve the Church of God, to the worlds end. And therefore, change the person, and wee shall finde a whole quiver of arrows. Extend this *Man,* to all *Mankind;* carry *Davids* History up to *Adams* History, and consider us in that state, which wee inherit from *him,* and we shall see *arrows* fly about our ears, *A Deo prosequente,* the anger of God hanging over our heads, in a cloud of arrows; and *à conscientia remordente,* our own consciences shooting *poisoned arrows* of desperation into our souls; and *ab Homine Contemnente,* Men multiplying arrows of *Detraction,* and *Calumny,* and *Contumely* upon our good name, and estimation. Briefly, in that wound, as wee were all shot in *Adam,* we bled out *Impassibilitatem,* and we sucked in *Impossibilitatem;* There we lost our *Im-*

mortality, our *Impassibility,* our assurance of Paradise, and then we lost *Possibilitatem boni,* says S. *Augustine:* all possibility of recovering any of this by our selves. So that these arrows which are lamented here, are all those miseries, which sinne hath cast upon us; *Labor,* and the childe of that, *Sicknesse,* and the offspring of that, *Death;* and the *security* of conscience, and the *terrour* of conscience; the *searing* of the conscience, and the *over-tendernesse* of the conscience; Gods quiver, and the Devils quiver, and our own quiver, and our neighbours quiver, afford, and furnish arrows to gall, and wound us. These arrows then in our Text, proceeding from *sin,* and sin proceeding from *tentations,* and inducing *tribulations,* it shall advance your spirituall edification most, to fixe your consideration upon those *fiery darts,* as they are *tentations,* and as they are *tribulations.* *Origen* says, he would wish no more, for the recovery of any soul, but that she were able to see *Cicatrices suas,* those scars which these fiery darts have left in her, the deformity which every sinne imprints upon the soul, and *Contritiones suas,* the attenuating and wearing out, and consumption of the soul, by a continuall succession of more, and more wounds upon the same place. An ugly thing in a Consumption, were a fearfull spectacle, And such *Origen* imagins a soul to be, if she could see *Cicatrices,* and *Contritiones,* her illfavourednesse, and her leannesse in the deformity, and consumption of sin. How provident, how diligent a patience did our blessed Saviour bring to his Passion, who foreseeing that that would be our case, our sickness, to be first wounded with *single tentations,* and then to have even the wounds of our soul wounded again, by a daily reiterating of tentations in the same kinde, would provide us physick agreeable to our Disease, Chyrurgery conformable to our wound, first to be *scourged* so, as that his holy body was torn with *wounds,* and then to have those *wounded again,* and often, with more violatings. So then these arrows, are those *tentations* and those *tribulations,* which are accompanied with these qualities of arrows shot at us, that they are *alienæ,* shot from others, not in our power; And *veloces,* swift and sudden, soon upon us; And *vix visibiles,* not discernible in their coming, but by an exact diligence.

First then, these *tentations* are dangerous arrows, as they are *alienæ,* shot from *others,* and not in our own power. It was the Embleme, and Inscription, which *Darius* took for his coin, *Insculpere sagittarium,* to shew his greatnesse, that he could wound afar off, as an Archer does. And it was the way, by which God declared the deliverance of *Israel* from *Syria; Elisha* bids the King open the window East-ward, and shoot an arrow out. The King does shoot: And the Prophet says, *Sagitta salutis Domini, The arrow of the Lords deliverance:* He would deliver *Israel,* by shooting vengeance into *Syria.* One danger in our *arrows,* as they are *tentations,* is, that they come *unsuspectedly;* they come, we know not, *from whence;* from *others;* that's a danger; But in our tentations, there is a greater danger then that, for a man cannot shoot an arrow at *himself;* but we can direct *tentations* upon our selves; If we were in a wildernesse, we could sin; and where we are, we tempt temptations, and wake the Devil, when for any thing that appears, he would sleep. A certain man drew a bow at a venture, says that story; He had no determinate mark, no expresse aime, upon any one man; He drew his bow at a venture, and he hit, and he slew the King *Ahab.* A woman of tentation, *Tendit arcum in incertum,* as that story speaks; shee paints, she curls, she sings, she gazes, and is gazed upon; There's an arrow shot *at randon;* shee aim'd at no particular mark; And thou puttest thy self within shot, and meetest the arrow; Thou soughtest the tentation, the tentation sought not thee. A man is able to oppresse others;

Et gloriatur in malo quia potens, He boasts himselfe because he is able to doe mischief; and *tendit arcum in incertum,* he shoots his arrow at randon, he lets it be known, that he can prefer *them,* that second his purposes, and thou putt'st thy self within shot, and meet'st the arrow, and mak'st thy self his instrument; Thou sought'st the tentation, the tentation sought not thee; when we expose our selves to tentations, tentations hist us, that were not expresly directed, nor meant to us. And even *then,* when we begin to flie from tentations, the arrow overtakes us. *Jehoram* fled from *Jehu,* and *Jehu* shot after him, and shot him through the heart. But this was after *Jehoram* had talk'd with him. After wee have parled with a tentation, debated whether we should embrace it or no, and entertain'd some discourse with it, though some tendernesse, some remorse, make us turn our back upon it, and depart a little from it, yet the arrow overtakes us; some *reclinations,* some *retrospects* we have, a little of *Lots wife* is in us, a little *sociableness,* and *conversation,* a little point of *honour,* not to be false to former promises, a little *false gratitude,* and thankfulnesse, in respect of former obligations, a little of the *compassion* and *charity* of Hell, that another should not be miserable, for want of *us,* a little of this, which is but the good nature of the *Devill,* arrests us, stops us, fixes us, till the arrow, the tentation shoot us in the back, even when wee had a purpose of departing from that sin, and kil us over again. Thus it is, when we *meet* a tentation, and put our selves in the arrows way; And thus it is when we *fly not fast enough,* not *farre enough* from a tentation. But when we doe all *that,* and provide as safely as we can to get, and doe get quickly out of distance, yet, *The wicked bend their bowes, that they may privily shoot at the upright in heart; In occulto;* It is a work of *Darknesse, Detraction;* and they can shoot *in the dark;* they can wound, and not be known. They can

whisper Thunder, and passe an arrow through another mans eare, into mine heart; Let a man be
zealous, and fervent in reprehension of sin, and there
flies out an arrow, that gives him the wound of a
Puritan. Let a man be zealous of the house of God,
and say any thing by way of moderation, for the *re-
pairing* of *the ruines* of that house, and *making up the
differences* of the Church of God, and there flies out
an arrow, that gives him the wound of a *Papist.* One
shoots *East,* and another *West,* but both these arrows
meet in *him,* that means well, to defame him. And
this is the first misery in these arrows, these tentations,
Quia alienæ, they are shot from others, they are not
in our own quiver, nor in our own government.

Another quality that tentations receive from the
holy Ghosts Metaphore of *arrows* is, *Quia veloces,*
because this captivity to sin, comes so swiftly, so im-
petuously upon us. Consider it first in our *making;*
In the generation of *our parents,* we were *conceiv'd
in sin;* that is, they sinn'd in that action; so we were
conceiv'd in sinne; in *their sin.* And in *our selves,* we
were submitted to sin, in that very act of generation,
because then we became in part the subject of *Originall
sin.* Yet, there was no arrow shot *into* us then; there
was no sinne in that *substance* of which we were
made; for if there had been sin in that *substance,*
that substance might be damn'd, though God should
never infuse a soul into it; and *that* cannot be said
well then: God, whose goodnesse, and wisdome will
have that substance to become a *Man,* he creates a
soul for it, or creates a soul *in it,* (I dispute not *that*)
he sends a light, or hee kindles a light, in that lan-
thorn; and here's no arrow shot neither: here's no
sin in *that* soul, that God creates; for there God
should create something that were evill; and that
cannot be said: Here's no arrow shot from the body,
no sin in the *body alone;* None from the soul, no
sin in the *soul alone;* And yet, the *union* of this soul

and body is so accompanied with Gods *malediction*
for our first transgression, that in the instant of that
union of life, as certainly as that *body must die,* so
certainly *the whole Man* must be guilty of *Originall
sin.* No man can tell me out of what *Quiver,* yet here
is an arrow comes so swiftly, as that in the very first
minute of our life, in our quickning in our mothers
womb, wee become guilty of *Adams* sin done 6000
years before, and subject to all those arrows, *Hunger,
Labour, Grief, Sicknesse,* and *Death,* which have been
shot after it. This is the fearfull swiftnesse of this arrow,
that *God himself* cannot get before it. In the first
minute that my soul is infus'd, the Image of God is
imprinted in my soul; so forward is God in my behalf,
and so early does he visit me. But yet *Originall sin* is
there, as soon as that Image of God is there. My soul
is capable of *God,* as soon as it is capable of sin; and
though sin doe not get the start of God, God does not
get the start of sin neither. Powers, that dwell so far
asunder, as *Heaven,* and *Hell, God* and the *Devill,*
meet in an instant in my soul, in the minute of my
quickning, and the Image of *God,* and the Image of
Adam, Originall sin, enter into me at once, in one,
and the same act. So swift is this arrow, *Originall sin,*
from which, all arrows of subsequent tentations, are
shot, as that God, who comes to my first minute of
life, cannot come before death.

And then, a third, and last danger, which we noted
in our tentations, as they are represented by the holy
Ghost, in this Metaphore of *arrows,* is, that they are
vix visibles, hardly discernible. 'Tis true, that tentations doe not light upon us, as *bullets,* that we cannot
see them, till we feel them. An arrow comes not altogether so: but an arrow comes so, as that it is not
discern'd, except we consider which way it comes, and
watch it all the way. An arrow, that findes a man
asleep, does not *wake* him first, and *wound* him after;
A tentation that findes a man negligent, possesses him,

before he sees it. *In gravissimis criminibus, confinia virtutum læ dunt;* This is it that undoes us, that vertues and vices are contiguous, and borderers upon one another; and very often, we can hardly tell, to which action the name of *vice,* and to which the name of *vertue* appertains. Many times, that which comes within an inch of a noble action, fals under the infamy of an odious treason; At many executions, half the company will call a man an *Heretique,* and half, a *Martyr.* How often, an excesse, makes a naturall affection, an unnaturall disorder? . . . *Hamon* lov'd his sister *Tamar;* but a little too well; *Absolon* hated his brothers incest, but a little too ill. Though *love* be good, and *hate* be good, respectively, yet, says S. *Ambrose,* I would neither that love, nor that hate had gone so far. The contract between *Jonathan* and *David,* was, *If I say, The arrow* (is) *on this side of thee, all is wel; If I say, The arrow is beyond thee, thou art in an ill case.* If the arrow, the tentation, be yet on this side of thee, if it have not lighted upon thee, thou art well; God hath directed thy face to it, and thou may'st, if thou wilt, continue thy diligence, watch it, and avoid it. But if the arrow be beyond thee, and thou have cast it at thy back, in a forgetfulnesse, in a security of thy sin, thy case is dangerous. In all these respects, are these arrows, these infirmities, deriv'd from the sin of *Adam,* dangerous, as they are *alienæ,* in the hand of others, as they are *veloces,* swift in seising us, and as they are *vix visibles,* hardly discern'd to be such; And these considerations fell within this first branch of this second part, *Thine arrows, tentations,* as they are arrows, *stick fast in me.*

These dangers are in them, as they are *sagittæ, arrows;* and would be so, if they were but *single* arrows; any *one* tentation would endanger us, any one tribulation would encumber us; but they are *plurall, arrows,* and *many arrows.* A man is not safe, because one arrow hath mist him; nor though he be free from *one* sin. In the execution of *Achan,* all *Israel* threw stones at him, and stoned him. If *Achan* had had some brother, or cousin amongst them, that would have flung over, or short, or weakly, what good had that done him, when he must stand the mark for all the rest? All *Israel* must stone him. A little disposition towards some one vertue, may keep thee from some one tentation; Thou mayst think it pity to corrupt a chast soul, and forbear soliciting her; pity to oppresse a submitting wretch, and forbear to vex him; and yet practise, and that with hunger and thirst, other sins, or those sins upon other persons. But all *Israel* stones thee; arrows flie from every corner; and thy measure is not, *to thank God, that thou art not as the Publican, as some other man,* but thy measure is, *to be pure and holy, as thy father in heaven is pure, and holy,* and to conform thy self in some measure, to thy pattern, Christ Jesus. Against him it is noted, that the Jews took up stones twice to stone him. Once, when they did it, *He went away and hid himself.* Our way to scape these arrows, these tentations, is to goe out of the way, to abandon all occasions, and conversation, that may lead into tentation. In the other place, Christ stands to it, and disputes it out with them, and puts them from it by the *scriptum est;* and that's our safe shield, since we must necessarily live in the way of tentations, (for *coluber in via,* ther is a snake in every path, tentation in every calling) still to receive all these arrowes, upon the *shield of faith,* still to oppose the *scriptum est,* the faithfull promises of God, that he will give us the issue with the tentation, when we cannot avoid the tentation it self. Otherwise, these arrows are so many, as would tire, and wear out, all the diligence, and all the constancy of the best morall man. Wee finde many mentions in the Scriptures of filling of *quivers,* and emptying of *quivers,* and *arrows,* and *arrows,* still in the *plurall, many arrows.* But in all the Bible, I think, we finde

not this word, (as it signifies *tentation,* or *tribulation*)
in the *singular, one arrow,* any where, but once, where
David cals it, *The arrow that flies by day;* And is seen,
that is, known by every man; for, for that, the Fathers,
and Ancients runne upon that Exposition, that that
one arrow common to all, that day-arrow visible to
all, is the *naturall death;* (so the Chalde paraphrase
calls it there expresly, *Sagitta mortis,* The arrow of
death) which every man knows to belong to every man;
(for, as clearly as he sees the Sunne set, he sees his
death before his eyes.) Therefore it is such an arrow,
as the Prophet does not say, *Thou shalt not feel,* but,
Thou shalt not feare the arrow that flies by day. The
arrow, the *singular* arrow that flies by day, is that
arrow that fals upon every man, *death.* But every
where in the Scriptures, but this one place, they are
plurall, many, so many, as that we know not *whence,*
nor *what* they are. Nor ever does any man receive one
arrow alone, any one tentation, but that he receives
another tentation, to hide that, though with another,
and another sin. And the use of arrows in the war, was
not so much to *kill,* as to *rout,* and *disorder* a battail;
and upon that routing, followed *execution.* Every tentation, every tribulation is not *deadly.* But their multiplicity disorders us, discomposes us, unsettles us, and
so hazards us. Not onely every *periodicall* variation
of our years, *youth* and *age,* but every day hath a
divers arrow, every houre of the day, a divers tentation. An old man wonders then, how an arrow from
an eye could wound him, when he was young, and
how *love* could make him doe those things which hee
did *then;* And an arrow from the tongue of inferiour
people, that which we make shift to call *honour,*
wounds him deeper now; and *ambition* makes him
doe as strange things now, as *love* did then; A fair
day shoots arrows of *visits,* and *comedies,* and *conversation,* and so wee goe abroad: and a foul day shoots
arrows of *gaming,* or *chambering,* and *wantonnesse,*

and so we stay at home. Nay, the same sin shoots arrows of *presumption* in God, before it be committed, and of *distrust* and *diffidence* in God after; we doe not *fear* before, and we cannot *hope* after: And this is that misery from this *plurality,* and *multiplicity* of these arrows, these manifold tentations, which *David* intends here, and as often as he speaks in the same phrase of plurality, *vituli multi,* many buls, *canes multi,* many dogs, and *bellantes multi,* many warlike enemies, and *aquæ multæ,* many deep waters compasse me. For as it is said of the spirit of wisdome, that it is *unicus multiplex, manifoldly one, plurally singular:* so the spirit of tentation in every soul is *unicus multiplex,* singularly plurall, *rooted* in some *one* beloved sin, but derived into infinite branches of tentation.

And then, these arrows *stick in us;* the raine fals, but that cold sweat hangs not upon us; Hail beats us, but it leaves no pock-holes in our skin. These arrows doe not so fall about us, as that they misse us; nor so hit us, as they rebound back without hurting us; But we complain with *Jeremy, The sons of his quiver are entred into our reins.* The Roman Translation reads that *filias, The daughters of his quiver;* If it were but so, *daughters,* we might limit these arrows in the signification of tentations, by the many occasions of tentation, arising from *that sex.* But the Originall hath it *filios,* the sons of his quiver, and therefore we consider these arrows in a stronger signification, *tribulations,* as well as *tentations; They stick in us.* Consider it but in one kinde, *diseases,* sicknesses. They stick to us so, as that we are not sure, that any old diseases mentioned in Physicians books are worn out, but that every year produces *new,* of which they have no mention, we are sure. We can scarce expresse the number, scarce sound the names of the diseases of mans body; 6000 year hath scarce taught us what they are, how they affect us, how they shall be cur'd in us, nothing, on this side the *Resurrection,* can teach us. They stick to us so, as that they passe by *inheritance,* and last more generations in families, then the inheritance it self does; and when no land, no Manor, when no title, no honour descends upon the heir, the stone, or the gout descends upon him. And as though our bodies had not *naturally diseases,* and infirmities enow, we contract more, inflict more, (and that, out of necessity too) in *mortifications,* and *macerations,* and *Disciplines* of this rebellious flesh. I must have this body with me to heaven, or else salvation it self is not perfect; And yet I cannot have this body thither, except as S. *Paul* did his, *I beat down this body,* attenuate this body by mortification . . . I have not body enough for my body, and I have too much body for my soul; not body enough, not bloud enough, not strength enough, to sustain my self in *health,* and yet body enough to destroy my soul, and frustrate the grace of God in that miserable, perplexed, riddling condition of man; sin makes the body of man miserable, and the remedy of sin, *mortification,* makes it miserable too; If we enjoy the good things of this world, . . . wee doe but carry an other wall about our prison, an other story of unwieldly flesh about our souls; and if wee give our selves as much *mortification* as our body needs, we live a life of *Fridays,* and see no *Sabbath,* we make up our years of *Lents,* and see no other *Easters,* and whereas God meant us *Paradise,* we make all the world a *wildernesse.* Sin hath cast a curse upon all the creatures of the world, they are all worse then they were at first, and yet we dare not receive so much blessing, as is left in the creature, we dare not eat or drink, and enjoy them. The *daughters* of Gods quiver, and the *sons* of his quiver, the arrows of *tentation,* and the arrows of *tribulation,* doe so stick in us, that as he lives miserably, that lives in sicknes, and he as miserably, that lives in *physick:* so *plenty* is a misery, and *mortification* is a misery too;

plenty, if we consider it in the *effects,* is a disease too, a continuall hunger, and fasting; and if we consider it at best, and in the effects, mortification is but a *continuall physick,* which is misery enough.

They stick, and they *stick fast; altè infixæ;* every syllable aggravates our misery. Now for the most past, experimentally, we know not whether they stick fast or no, for we never goe about to pull them out: these arrows, these tentations, come, and welcome: we are so far from offering to pull them out, that we fix them faster and faster in us; we assist our tentations: yea, we take preparatives and fomentations, we supple our selves by *provocations,* lest our flesh should be of proof against these arrows, that death may enter the surer, and the deeper into us by them. And he that does in some measure, soberly and religiously, goe about to draw out these arrows, yet never consummates, never perfects his own work; He pulls back the arrow a little way, and he sees *blood,* and he feels *spirit* to goe out with it, and he lets it alone: He forbears his sinfull companions, a little while, and he feels a *melancholy* take hold of him, the spirit and life of his life decays, and he falls to those companions again. Perchance he rushes out the arrow with a sudden, and a resolved vehemence, and he leaves the head in his body: He forces a divorce from that sinne, he removes himself out of distance of that tentation; and yet he surfets upon cold meat, upon the sinfull remembrance of former sins, which is a dangerous rumination, and an unwholesome chawing of the cud; It is not an ill derivation of repentance, that *pœnitere* is *pœnam tenere;* that's true repentance, when we continue in those means, which may advance our repentance. When *Joash* the King of *Israel* came to visit *Elisha* upon his sick bed, and to consult with him about his war, *Elisha* bids the King smite the ground, and he smites it thrice, and ceases: Then the man of God was angry, and said, *Thou shouldst have smitten five or*

*sixe times, and so thou shouldst have smitten thine
enemies, till thou hadst consumed them.* Now, how
much hast thou to doe, that hast not pull'd at this
arrow at all yet? Thou must pull thrice and more,
before thou get it out; Thou must *doe,* and *leave undone* many things, before thou deliver thy selfe of
that arrow, that sinne that transports thee. One of
these arrows was shot into Saint *Paul* himselfe, and it
stuck, and stuck fast; whether an arrow of *tentation,*
or an arrow of *tribulation,* the Fathers cannot tell;
And therefore, wee doe now, (not inconveniently) all
our way, in this exercise, mingle these two considerations, of tentation, and tribulation. Howsoever Saint
Paul pull'd thrice at this arrow, and could not get it
out; *I besought the Lord thrice,* says he, *that it might
depart from mee.* But yet, *Joash* his thrice striking
of the ground, brought him some victory; Saint *Pauls*
thrice praying, brought him in that provision of
Grace, which God cals *sufficient for him.* Once pulling
at these arrows, a slight consideration of thy sins will
doe no good. Doe it *thrice;* testifie some true desire by
such a diligence; Doe it now as thou sitt'st, doe it again
at the *Table,* doe it again in thy *bed;* Doe it *thrice,*
doe it in thy *purpose,* do it in thine *actions,* doe it in
thy *constancy;* Doe it thrice, within the wals of thy
flesh, in thy self, within the wals of thy *house* in thy
family, and in a holy and *exemplar conversation*
abroad, and God will accomplish *thy work,* which is
his work in thee; And though the arrow be not utterly
pull'd out, yet it shall not fester, it shall not *gangrene;*
Thou shalt not be cut off from the body of Christ, in
his Church here, nor in the Triumphant Church hereafter, how fast soever these arrows did stick upon thee
before. God did not refuse *Israel* for her wounds, and
bruises, and putrefying sore, though from the sole
of the foot, to the crown of the head, but because
those wounds were not closed, nor bound up, nor
suppled with ointments, therefore he refused her.

God shall not refuse any soul, because it hath been shot with these arrows . . . But that soul that can pour out flouds of tears, for the losse, or for the absence, or for the unkindnes, or imagination of an unkindness of a friend, mis-beloved, beloved a wrong way, and not afford one drop, one tear, to wash the wounds of these arrows, that soul that can squeaze the wound of Christ Jesus, and spit out his bloud in these blasphemous execrations, and shed no drop of this bloud upon the wounds of these arrows; that soul, and only that soul, that refuses a cure, does God refuse; not because they fell upon it, and stook, and stook fast, and stook long, but because they never, never went about to pull them out; never resisted a tentation, never lamented a transgression, never repented a recidivation.

Now this is more put home to us in the next addition, *Infixæ mihi*, they stick, and stick fast, *in mee*, that is, *in all mee*. That that sins must be sav'd or damn'd; That's not the soul alone, nor body alone, but *all*, the whole man. God is the God of *Abraham*, as he is the God of the living; Therefore *Abraham* is alive; And *Abraham* is not alive, if his body be not alive; Alive *actually* in the person of *Christ;* alive in an *infallible assurance* of a particular resurrection. Whatsoever belongs to *thee*, belongs to thy *body* and *soul;* and these arrows stick fast *in thee;* In *both*. Consider it in both; in things belonging to the body and to the soul; We need clothing; Baptisme is Gods Wardrobe; there *Induimur Christo;* In Baptisme we put on Christ; there we are invested, apparell'd in Christ; And there comes an arrow, that cuts off *half* our garment, (as *Hanon* did *Davids* servants) A tentation that makes us think, it is enough to be *baptized*, to professe the name of Christ; for *Papist*, or *Protestant*, it is but the *train* of the garment, matter of *civility*, and *policy*, and *government*, and may be cut off, and the garment remain still. So we need *meat, suste-*

nance, and then an arrow comes, a tentation meets us, *Edite, & bibite, Eat and drink, to morrow you shall die;* That there is no life, but this life, no blessednesse but in worldly abundances. If we need *physick,* and God offer us his physick, medicinall corrections, there flies an arrow, a tentation, *Medice cura teipsum,* that hee whom wee make our Physician, died himselfe, of an infamous disease, that Christ Jesus from whom we attend our salvation, could not save himself. In our clothing, in our diet, in our physick, things which carry our consideration upon the *body,* these arrowes stick fast in us, in that part of us. So in the more spirituall actions of our souls too. In our *alms* there are *trumpets* blowne, there's an arrow of *vaine-glory;* In our *fastings,* there are *disfigurings,* there's an arrow of *Hypocrisie;* In our *purity,* ther is contempt of others, there's an arrow of *pride;* In our *coming* to Church, there is *custome* and *formality;* In hearing *Sermons,* ther is *affection* to the parts of the Preacher. In our sinfull actions these arrows abound; In our best actions they lie hid; And as thy soul is in every part of thy body; so these arrows are in every part of thee, body, and soul; they stick, and stick fast, in thee, in all thee.

And yet there is another weight upon us, in the Text, there is still a *Hand* that follows the blow, and presses it, *Thy hand presses me sore;* so the Vulgat read it, *Confirmasti super me manum tuam, Thy hand is settled upon mee;* and the Chalde paraphrase carries it farther then, to *Mansit super me vulnus manus tuæ;* Thy hand hath wounded mee, and that hand keeps the wound open. And in this sense the Apostle says, *It is a fearfull thing to fall into the hands of the living God.* But as God leaves not his children without *correction,* so he leaves them not without *comfort,* and therefore it behoves us to consider his hand upon these arrows, more then one way.

First, because his hand is upon the arrow, it shall

certainly hit the mark; Gods purpose cannot be disap-
pointed. If men, and such men, *left-handed men,* and
so many, 700 left-handed men, and so many of *one
Tribe, 700 Benjamites,* could sling stones at a hairs
breadth, and not fail, God is a better *Mark-man* then
the left-handed Benjamites; his arrows alwayes hit
as he intends them. Take them then for tribulation,
his hand is upon them; Though they come from the
malice of *men,* his hand is upon them. S. *Ambrose*
observes, that in afflictions, Gods hand, and the Devils
are but one hand. *Stretch out thy hand,* says Satan to
God, concerning *Job;* And, *all that he hath is in thy
hand,* says God to Satan. *Stretch out thy hand, and
touch his bones,* says Satan again to God; And again,
God to Satan, *He is in thy hand, but touch not his
life.* A difference may be, that when Gods purpose is
but to punish, as he did *Pharaoh,* in those severall
premonitory plagues, there it is *Digitus Dei;* It was
but a *finger,* and Gods finger. When *Balshazzar* was
absolutely to be destroyed, there were *Digiti,* and
Manus hominis, mens fingers, and upon a mans hand.
The arrows of men are ordinarily more venimouse,
and more piercing, then the arrows of God. But as it is
in that story of *Elisha,* and *Joash,* The Prophet bade
the King shoot, but *Elisha* laid his hand upon the
Kings hand; So from what instrument of Satan soever,
thy affliction come, Gods hand is upon *their hand*
that shoot it, and though it may *hit* the mark according to *their* purpose, yet it hath the *effect,* and it
works according to *his.*

Yea, let this arrow be considered as a *tentation,* yet
his hand is upon it; at least God *sees* the shooting of
it, and yet *lets* it flie. Either hee *tries* us by these arrows, what proof we are; Or he *punishes* us by those
arrows of new sins, for our former sins; and so, when
he hath lost one arrow, he shoots another. He shoots
a *sermon,* and that arrow is lost; He shoots a *sicknesse,*
and that arrow is lost; He shoots a *sin;* not that *he* is

authour of any sin, as *sin;* but as *sin is a punishment* of sin, he *concurs* with it. And so he shoots arrow after arrow, permits sin after sin, that at last some sin, that draws affliction with it, might bring us to understanding; for that word, in which the Prophet here expresses this sticking, and this fast sticking of these arrows, which is *Nachath,* is here, (as the Grammarians in that language call it) in *Niphal, figere factæ,* they were made to stick; Gods hand is upon them, the *work* is his, the *arrows* are his, and the *sticking* of them is his, whatsoever, and whosesoever they may be.

His hand shoots the arrow, as it is a *tribulation* he *limits* it, whosoever inflict it. His hand shoots it, as it is a *tentation,* He *permits* it, and he orders it, whosoever offer it. But it is especially from his hand, as it hath a *medicinall nature* in it; for in every *tentation,* and every *tribulation,* there is a *Catechisme,* and *Instruction;* nay, there is a *Canticle,* a *love-song,* an *Epithalamion,* a *mariage song* of God, to our souls, wrapped up, if wee would open it, and read it, and learn that new tune, that musique of God; So when thou hear'st *Nathans* words to *David, The child that is born unto thee, shall surely die,* (let that signifie, the children of thy labour, and industry, thy *fortune,* thy *state* shall perish) so when thou hear'st Gods word to *David, Choose famine, or war, or pestilence, for the people,* (let that signifie, those that depend upon thee, shal perish) so when thou hear'st all the judgements of God, as they lie in the body of the Scriptures, so the applications of those judgements, by Gods Ministers, in these services, upon emergent occasions, all these are arrows shot by the hand of God, and that child of God, that is accustomed to the voice, and to the ear of God, to speak with him in *prayer,* when God speaks to him, in any such voice here, as that to *David,* or *Hezekiah,* though this be a shooting of arrows, *Non fugabit eum vir sagittarius, The arrow,* (as we read it) *The Archer,* (as the Romane Edition

reades it) cannot make that child of God afraid, afraid
with a distrustfull fear, or make him loth to come
hither again to hear more, how close soever Gods
arrow, and Gods archer, that is, his word in his
servants mouth, come to that Conscience now, nor
make him mis-interpret that which he does hear, or call
that *passion* in the Preacher, in which the Preacher
is but *sagittarius Dei,* the deliverer of Gods arrows;
for Gods arrows, are *sagittæ Compunctionis,* arrows
that draw bloud from the eyes; Tears of repentance
from *Mary Magdalen,* and from *Peter;* And when
from thee? There is a *probatum est* in S. *Augustine,*
Sagittaveras cor meum, Thou hast shot at my heart;
and how wrought that? To the withdrawing of his
tongue, *à nundinis loquacitatis,* from that market in
which I sold my self, (for S. *Augustine* at that time
taught *Rhetorique*) to turn the stream of his eloquence, and all his other good parts, upon the service
of God in his Church. You may have read, or heard
that answer of a *Generall,* who was threatened with
that danger, that his enemies arrows were so many,
as that they would cover the Sun from him; *In umbra
pugnabimus;* All the better, says he, for then we shall
fight in the shadow. Consider all the arrows *tribulation,* even of *tentation,* to be directed by the hand of
God, and never doubt to fight it out with God, to lay
violent hands upon heaven, to wrastle with God for
a blessing, to charge and presse God upon his contracts and promises, for *in umbra pugnabis,* though
the clouds of these arrows may hide all suns of worldly
comforts from thee, yet thou art still *under the shadow
of his wings.* Nay, thou are still, for all this shadow,
in the light of his countenance. To which purpose
there is an excellent use of this Metaphor of arrows,
Habakkuk 3. 11. where it is said, that *Gods servants
shall have the light of his arrows, and the shining of
his glittering spear:* that is, the light of his presence,
in all the instruments, and actions of his corrections.

To end all, and to dismisse you with such a re-collection, as you may carry away with you; literally, primarily, this text concerns *David:* He by *tentations* to sin, by *tribulations* for sin, by *comminations,* and *increpations* upon sin, was bodily, and ghostly become a quiver of arrows of all sorts; they *stook,* and stook *fast,* and stook *full* in him, in *all* him. The Psalm hath a *retrospect* too, it looks back to *Adam,* and to every particular man in his loines, and so, *Davids* case is our case, and all these arrowes stick in all us. But the Psalm and the text hath also a *prospect,* and hath a *propheticall* relation from *David* to our Saviour Christ Jesus. And of him, and of the multiplicity of these arrows upon him in the exinanition, and evacuation of himself, in this world for us, have many of the *Ancients* interpreted these words literally, and as in their first and primary signification; Turne we therefore to *him,* before we goe, and he shall return home with us. How our first part of this text is applyable to *him,* that our prayers to God, for ease in afflictions, may be grounded upon reasons, out of the sense of those afflictions, Saint *Basil* tels us, that Christ therefore prays to his Father now in heaven, to spare mankinde, because man had suffered so much, and drunk so deep of the bitter cup of his anger, in his person and passion before: It is an avoidable plea, from Christ in heaven, for us, *Spare them O Lord in themselves, since thou didst not spare them in me.* And how far he was from sparing thee, we see in all those severall weights which have aggravated his hand, and these arrowes upon us: If they be heavy upon us, much more was their weight upon *thee,* every *dram* upon us was a *Talent* upon thee, *Non dolor sicut dolor tuus,* take *Rachel* weeping for her children, *Mary* weeping for her brother *Lazarus, Hezekiah* for his health, *Peter* for his sins, *Non est dolor sicut dolor tuus.* The arrows that were shot at thee, were *Alienæ,* Afflictions that belonged to *others;* and did not onely come from *others*, as ours doe; but they were *alienæ* so, as that they should have fallen upon others; And *all* that should have fallen upon all others, were shot at *thee*, and lighted upon thee. Lord, though we be not capable of sustaining that part, this *passion* for others, give us *that*, which we may receive, *Compassion with* others. They were *veloces*, these arrows met swiftly upon thee; from the sin of *Adam* that induced *death*, to the sin of the last man, that shall not sleep, but be changed, when thy hour came they came all upon thee, in that hour. Lord put this swiftnesse into our sins, that in this one minute, in which our eyes are open towards thee, and thine eares towards us, our sins, all our sins, even from the *impertinent frowardnesse of our childhood*, to the *unsufferable frowardnesse* of our age, may meet in our present *confessions*, and *repentances*, and never appear more. They were (as ours are too) *Invisibles*; Those arrows which fell upon thee, were so *invisible*, so undiscernible, as that to this day, thy Church, thy School cannot see, what kinde of arrow thou tookest into thy soul, what kinde of affliction it was, that made thy *soul heavy unto death*, or dissolved thee into a gelly of blood in thine agony. Be thou O Lord, a Father of Lights unto us, whatsoever is necessary for us to know, and be a light of *understanding* and *grace* before, and a light of *comfort* and *mercy* after any sin hath benighted us. These arrows were, as *ours* are also, *plures*, plurall, many, infinite; they were the sins of some that shall never thank thee, never know that thou borest their sins, never know that they had any such sins to bee born. Lord teach us to number thy corrections upon us, so, as still to see thy torments suffered for us, and our own sins to be infinitely more that occasioned those torments, then those corrections that thou layst upon us. Thine arrows *stook* and *stook fast in thee*; the weight of thy torments, thou wouldest not cast off, nor lessen, when at thy execution they offered thee, that stupefying drink, (which was the civill charity of those times to condemned persons, to give them an easier passage, in the agonies of death) thou wouldest not tast of that cup of ease. Deliver us, O Lord, in all our tribulations, from turning to the miserable comforters of this world, or from wishing or accepting any other deliverance, then may improve and make better our Resurrection. These arrows were in *thee,* in *all thee:* from thy *Head* torn with thorns, to thy *feet* pierced with nayls; and in thy *soul* so as we know not how, so as to extort a *Si possibile, If it be possible let this cup passe,* and an *Vt quid dereliquisti, My God, my God, why hast thou forsaken me?* Lord, whilest we remain entire here, in body and soul, make us, and receive us an entire sacrifice to thee, in directing body and soul to thy glory, and when thou shalt be pleased to take us in pieces by death, receive our souls to thee, and lay up our bodies for thee, in consecrated ground, and in a *Christian buryall.* And lastly, thine arrows were followed, and *pressed with the hand of God; The hand of God pressed upon thee,* in that *eternall decree,* in that *irrevocable contract,* between thy *Father* and *thee,* in that *Oportuit pati, That all that thou must suffer, and so enter into thy glory.* Establish us, O Lord, in all occasions of diffidences here; and when thy hand presses our arrows upon us, enable us to see, that *that* very hand, hath from all eternity written, and written in thine own blood, a *decree* of the *issue,* as well, and as soon, as of the *tentation.* In which confidence of which decree, as men, in the virtue thereof already in possession of heaven, we joyn with that Quire in that service, in that *Anthem, Blessing, and glory, and wisdome, and thanksgiving, and honour, and power, and might, be unto our God for ever, and ever,* Amen.

SERMON PREACHED AT THE CHURCH OF ST. CLEMENT DANES

May 30, 1621 (Hosea 2:19)

II

EDITOR'S PREFACE

Mid-way of Donne's five years as Reader in Divinity at Lincoln's Inn, the king dispatched him to Germany with Lord Doncaster. The mission was intended to mediate the quarrel between the Protestant Bohemians and their recently appointed Roman Catholic ruler. As it turned out, the embassy of 1619 was unsuccessful, but for a few months it relieved Donne of the arduous preaching schedule which had taxed him seriously at Lincoln's Inn. The journey was a break too in the hithertofore impenetrably oppressive sorrow which had been on Donne since the death of his wife in 1617. There was some preaching on the continent, of course, and no land travel was particularly restful in the seventeenth century. But it was a considerably lightened father who returned at last to care for his seven motherless children, and a noticeably refreshed preacher who came again to his eager congregations at Lincoln's Inn and at the royal palace.

John Donne had known Lord Doncaster for a long time. When the statesman was still Lord Hay he was one of the first to hear from Donne his intention to take orders. But the earlier friendship was confirmed on the long trip together. Doncaster continued to interest himself in Donne's welfare when they returned. And when Lord and Lady Doncaster wanted to arrange a proper wedding for their friend Margaret

Washington (a century later in Virginia a George Washington would be born into this family) and Robert Sand, it was John Donne whom they asked to officiate.

Finery is always in order at weddings. In a day when full-length wedding sermons were also in order, few preachers could have prepared finer pieces for the occasion than did John Donne. Of the many marriage sermons he must have preached, three are now extant. Of these three, the one which he wrote for the Doncaster-sponsored wedding of a couple he probably did not know well is on every score the finest.

His text is from Hosea, and the reading he chooses is the Genevan translation, still more familiar to him than the version authorized just ten years before by King James. Besides, the Geneva Bible provides the word he wants: "I will *marry* thee unto me" is better for his purposes than "I will *betroth* . . ."

Like most of Donne's sermons, this one wears its skeleton in plain sight. "Divisio" is a marginal note that customarily appears early in Donne's sermons. He begins by "dividing" the text and outlining his development of it. Then, as the sermon progresses, there are repeated reminders of the outline as new points enter. Subsequent homileticians have trained preachers to hide their outlines in an unseamed fabric of talk. Such counsel is excellent if the sermon is first of all a literary creation; it is sadly misplaced counsel, however, if the sermon is first of all an urgent communication. In the latter case, and it was so that Donne understood his preaching, the preacher's mind must order itself to his argument's shape, and the listener must be shown that shape everywhere in the argument. A sermon is not random thoughts, it is ordered reflection. But what is launched as the most ordered reflection will be received as most random thoughts unless the frame of the whole is as clear to the hearer. That frame need not be stated as explicitly as it usually is by Donne, but it should be as obviously there.

Donne needed that "divisio" as much as his congregations did. In this relatively simple wedding sermon, for instance, there are to be three major "parts." First, straightforward words about this present marriage and its secular obligations; second, an extension to consideration of the spiritual marriage between the couple and Christ; third, a rhapsodic prefigurement of the eternal marriage which will fulfill all. Furthermore, each of these parts will have three "circumstances." First, the persons involved in each part, then the action indicated, and finally the duration of that action. When any sermon has nine elements, be glad the structure is plain.

There is marvelous good sense in the household words of part one—and some wonderously quaint exegesis, as when marriage and rhubarb are likened. There is some real theology set to splendid music in parts two and three. The English language, at least, has rarely been used more artfully or more movingly than in the first long paragraph of part two, and in the last long paragraph of the sermon.

And do not be deceived by Donne's eschatological rhapsodies in that last. In calmer moments he always described heaven sparely, as being in the presence of God. But it was the whole human being in him, and not just the poet, who knew that poetry must be invoked if you are to speak at all of the ultimately unspeakable.

PREACHED AT A MARIAGE (THE MARRIAGE OF MISTRESS MARGARET WASHINGTON AT THE CHURCH OF ST. CLEMENT DANES, MAY 30, 1621).

Hosea 2.19. And I Will Mary Thee Unto Me for Ever.

The word which is the hinge upon which all this Text turns, is *Erash,* and *Erash* signifies not onely a betrothing, as our later Translation hath it, but a mariage; . . . and so our former Translation had it, and so we accept it, and so shall handle it, *I will mary thee unto me for ever.*

The first mariage that was made, God made, and he made it in Paradise . . . The last mariage which shall be made, God shall make too, and in Paradise too; in the Kingdome of heaven: and at that mariage, I hope in him that shall make it, to meet, not some, but all this company. The mariage in this Text hath relation to both those mariages: It is itself the spirituall and mysticall mariage of Christ Jesus to the Church, and to every mariageable soule in the Church: And it hath a retrospect, it looks back to the first mariage; for to that the first word carries us, because from thence God takes his metaphor, and comparison, *sponsabo, I will mary;* And then it hath a prospect to the last mariage, for to that we are carried in the last word, *in æternum, I will mary thee unto me for ever.* Be pleased therefore to give me leave in this exercise, to shift the scene thrice, and to present to your religious considerations three objects, three subjects: first, a secular mariage in Paradise; secondly,

68

a spirituall mariage in the Church; and thirdly, an eternall mariage in heaven. And in each of these three we shall present three circumstances; first the Persons, *Me* and *Tibi, I will mary thee;* And then the Action, *Sponsabo, I will mary thee;* And lastly the Term, *In æternum, I will mary thee to mee for ever.*

In the first acceptation then, in the first, the secular mariage in Paradise, the persons were *Adam* and *Eve:* Ever since they are He and She, man and woman: At first, by reason of necessity, without any such limitation, as now: And now without any other limitations, then such as are expressed in the Law of God: As the Apostles say in the first generall Councell, *We lay nothing upon you but things necessary,* so we call nothing *necessary* but that which is commanded by God. If in heaven I may have the place of a man that hath performed the Commandements of God, I will not change with him that thinks he hath done more then the Commandements of God enjoyned him. The rule of mariage for degrees and distance in blood, is the Law of God; but for conditions of men, there is no Rule at all given. When God had made *Adam* and *Eve* in Paradise, though there were foure rivers in Paradise, God did not place *Adam* in a Monastery on one side, and *Eve* in a Nunnery on the other, and so a River between them. They that build wals and cloysters to frustrate Gods institution of mariage, advance the Doctrine of Devils in forbidding mariage. The Devil hath advantages enow against us, in bringing men and women together: It was a strange and super-devilish invention, to give him a new advantage against us, by keeping men and women asunder, by forbidding mariage. Between the heresie of the Nicolaitians, that induced a community of women, any might take any; and the heresie of the Tatians that forbad all, none might take any, was a fair latitude. Between the opinion of the *Manichæn* hereticks, that thought women to be made by the Devil, and the

Colliridian hereticks that sacrificed to a woman, as to God, there is a fair distance. Between the denying of them souls, which S. *Ambrose* is charged to have done, and giving them such souls, as that they may be Priests, as the *Peputian* hereticks did, is a faire way for a moderate man to walk in. To make them Mistresses is unmanly, and to make them servants is unnoble; To make them as God made them, wives, is godly and manly too . . . When men have made vows to abstain from mariage, I would they would be content to try a little longer then they doe, whether they could keep that vow or no: And when men have consecrated themselves to the service of God in his Church, I would they would be content to try a little farther then they doe, whether they could abstain or no: But to dissolve mariage made after such a Vow, or after Orders, is still to separate those whom God hath not separated. The Persons are He and She, man and woman; they must be so much; he must be a man, she must be a woman; And they must be no more; not a brother and a sister, not an unckle and a neece; *Adduxit ad eum,* was the case between *Adam* and *Eve;* God brought them together; God will not bring me a precontracted person, he will not have me defraud another; nor God will not bring me a misbeleeving, a superstitious person, he will not have me drawn from himself: But let them be persons that God hath made, man and woman, and persons that God hath brought together, that is, not put asunder by any Law of his, and all such persons are capable of this first, this secular mariage . . .

Now this institution of mariage had three objects: first, *In ustionem,* it was given for a remedy against burning; And then, *In prolem,* for propagation, for children; And lastly, *In adjutorium,* for mutuall help. As we consider it the first way, *In ustionem,* every heating is not a burning; every naturall concupiscence does not require a mariage; nay every flaming is not a burning; though a man continue under the flame of carnall tentation, as long as S. *Paul* did, yet it needs not come presently to a *Sponsabo,* I will mary. God gave S. *Paul* other Physick, *Gratia mea sufficit,* grace to stand under that tentation; And S. *Paul* gave himself other Physick, *Contundo corpus,* convenient disciplines to tame his body. These will keep a man from burning; for *** To be overcome by our concupiscences, that is to burn, but to quench that fire by religious ways, that is a noble, that is a perfect work. When God at the first institution of mariage had this first use of mariage in his contemplation, that it should be a remedy against burning, God gave man the remedy, before he had the disease; for mariage was instituted in the state of innocency, when there was no inordinatenesse in the affections of man, and no burning. But as God created Reubarb in the world, whose quality is to purge choler, before there was any choler to purge, so God according to his abundant forwardnesse to doe us good, created a remedy before the disease, which he foresaw comming, was come upon us. Let him then that takes his wife in this first and lowest sense, *In medicinam,* but as his Physick, yet make her his cordiall Physick, take her to his heart, and fill his heart with her, let her dwell there, and dwell there alone, and so they will be mutuall Antidotes and Preservatives to one another, against all forein tentations. And with this blessing, blesse thou, ô Lord, these whom thou hast brought hither for this blessing: make all the days of their life like this day unto them; and as thy mercies are new every morning, make them so to one another; And if they may not die together, sustain thou the survivor of them in that sad hour with this comfort, That he that died for them both, will bring them together again in his everlastingnesse.

The second use of mariage was *In prolificationem,* for children: And therefore as S. *Augustine* puts the case, To contract before, that they will have no children, makes it no mariage but an adultery: To deny themselves to one another, is as much against mariage as to give themselves to another. To hinder it by Physick, or any other practise; nay to hinder it so far, as by a deliberate wish, or prayer against children, consists not well with this second use of mariage. And yet in this second use, we doe not so much consider generation as regeneration; not so much procreation as education, nor propagation as transplantation of children. For this world might be filled full enough of children, though there were no mariage; but heaven could not be filled, nor the places of the fallen Angels supplied, without that care of childrens religious education, which from Parents in lawfull mariage they are likeliest to receive. How infinite, and how miserable a circle of sin doe we make, if as we sinned in our Parents loins before we were born, so we sin in our childrens actions when we are dead, by having given them, either example, or liberty of sinning. We have a fearfull commination from God upon a good man, upon *Eli,* for his not restraining the licentiousnesse of his sons; *I will doe a thing in Israel,* says God there, *at which every mans eares that heares it shall tingle:* And it was executed, *Eli* fell down and broke his neck. We have also a promise of consolation to women for children, *She shall be saved in Child-bearing,* says the Apostle; but as *Chrysostome* and others of the Ancients observe and interpret that place . . . it is, *Si permanserint,* not if she, but if they, if the children continue in faith, in charity, in holiness, and sobriety: The salvation of the Parents hath so much relation to the childrens goodnesse, as that if they be ill by the Parents example, or indulgence, the Parents are as guilty as the children. Art thou afraid thy childe should be stung with a Snake, and wilt thou let him play with the old Serpent, in opening himself to all tentations? Art thou afraid to let him walk in an ill aire, and art thou content to let him stand in that pestilent aire that is made of nothing but oaths, and execrations of blasphemous mouths round about him? It is S. *Chrysostomes* complaint***we pay dear for our childrens damnation, by paying at first for all their childish vanities, and then for their sinfull insolencies at any rate; and we might have them saved, and our selves to the bargain, (which were a frugall way, and a debt well hedg'd in) for much lesse then ours, and their damnation stands us in. If you have a desire, says that blessed Father, to leave them certainly rich, *Deum iis relinque Debitorem,* Doe some such thing for Gods service, as you may leave God in their debt. He cannot break; his estate is inexhaustible; he will not break promise, nor break day; *He will shew mercy unto thousands in them that love him and keep his Commandements.* And here also may another showre of his benedictions fall upon them whom he hath prepared and presented here; *Let the wife be as a fruitful Vine, and their children like Olive plants:* To thy glory, let the Parents expresse the love of Parents, and the children, to thy glory, the obedience of children, till they both loose that secular name of Parents and Children, and meet all alike, in one new name, all Saints in thy Kingdome, and fellow servants there.

The third and last use in this institution of secular mariage, was, *In adjutorium,* for mutuall help. There is no state, no man in any state, that needs not the help of others. Subjects need Kings, and if Kings doe not need their Subjects, they need alliances abroad, and they need Counsell at home. Even in Paradise, where the earth produced all things for life without labour, and the beasts submitted themselfes to man, so that he had no outward enemy; And in the state of innocency in Paradise, where in man, all the affections submitted themselves to reason, so that he had no inward enemy, yet God in this abundant

Paradise, and in this secure innocency of Paradise, even in the survey of his own works, saw, that though all that he had made was good, yet he had not made all good; he found thus much defect in his own work, that man lacked a helper. Every body needs the help of others; and every good body does give some kinde of help to others. Even into the Ark it self, where God blessed them all with a powerfull and an immediate protection, God admitted onely such as were fitted to help one another, couples. In the Ark, which was the Type of our best condition in this life, there was not a single person. Christ saved once one theef at the last gasp, to shew that there may be late repentances; but in the Ark he saved none but maried persons, to shew, that he eases himself in making them helpers to one another. And therefore when we come to the *Posui Deum adjutorium meum,* to rely upon God primarily for our Help, God comes to the *faciam tibi adjutorium,* I will make thee a help like thy self: not always like in complexion, nor like in years, nor like in fortune, nor like in birth, but like in minde, like in disposition, like in the love of God, and of one another, or else there is no helper. It was no kinde of help that *Davids* wife gave him, when she spoke by way of counsell, but in truth, in scorn and derision, to draw him from a religious act, as the dancing before the Ark, at that time was: It is no help for any respect, to slacken the husband in his Religion. It was but a poor help that *Nabals* wife was fain to give him by telling *David, Alas my husband is but a foole, like his name, and what will you look for at a fools hand?* It is the worst help of all to raise a husband by dejecting her self, to help her husband forward in this world, by forfeiting sinfully, and dishonourably, her own interest in the next. The husband is the helper in the nature of a foundation, to sustain and uphold all; The wife in the nature of the roof, to cover imperfections and weaknesses: The husband in the nature of the head from whence all the sinews flow; The wife in the nature of the hands into which those sinews flow, and enable them to doe their offices. The husband helps as legges to her, she moves by his notion; The wife helps as a staffe to him, he moves the better by her assistance. And let this mutuall help be a part of our present benediction too; In all the ways of fortune let his industry help her, and in all the crosses of fortune let her patience help him; and in all emergent occasions and dangers spirituall, or temporall, *O God make speed to save them, O Lord, make haste to help them.*

We have spoken of the persons, man and woman, him and her; And of the action, first as it is Physick, but cordiall Physick; and then for children, but children to be made the children of God; and lastly for help, but true help and mutuall help; There remains yet in this secular mariage, the Term, how long, for ever, *I will mary thee for ever.* Now though there be properly no eternity in this secular mariage, nor in any thing in this world, (for eternity is onely that which never had beginning, nor ever shall have end) yet we may consider a kind of eternity, a kind of circle without beginning, without end, even in this secular mariage: for first, mariage should have no beginning before mariage; no half-mariage, no lending away of the minde, in conditionall precontracts before, no lending away of the body in unchaste wantonnesse before. The body is the temple of the Holy Ghost; and when two bodies, by mariage are to be made one temple, the wife is not as the Chancell, reserv'd and shut up, and the man as the walks below, indifferent and at liberty for every passenger. God in his Temple looks for first fruits from both; that so on both sides, mariage should have such a degree of eternity, as to have had no beginning of mariage before mariage. It should have this degree of eternity too, this quality of a circle to have no interruption, no breaking in the way by unjust suspitions and jealousies. Where there is *Spiritus immunditiei,* as S. *Paul* cals it, a spirit of uncleannesse, there will necessarily be *Spiritus zelotypiæ,* as *Moses* cals it, a spirit of jealousie. But to raise the Devill in the power of the Devill, to call up one spirit by another spirit, by the spirit of jealousie and suspition, to induce the spirit of uncleannesse where it was not, if a man conjure up a Devill so, God knows who shall conjure it down again. As jealousie is a care and not a suspition, God is not ashamed to protest of himself that he is a jealous God. God commands that no idolatry be committed, *Thou shalt not bow down to a graven Image;* and before he accuses any man to have bowed down to a graven Image, before any Idolatry was committed, he tells them that he *is a jealous God;* God is jealous before there be any harm done. And God presents it as a curse, when he says *My jealousie shall depart from thee, and I will be quiet, and no more angry;* that is, I will leave thee to thy self, and take no more care of thee. Jealousie that implies care, and honour, and counsell, and tendernesse, is rooted in God, for God is a jealous God, and his servants are jealous servants, as S. *Paul* professes of himself, *I am jealous over you with a godly jealousie.* But jealousie that implies diffidence and suspition, and accusation, is rooted in the Devil, for he is the *Accuser of the brethren.*

So then, this secular mariage should be *In æternum,* eternall, for ever, as to have no beginning before, and so too, as to have no jealous interruption by the way; for it is so eternall, as that it can have no end in this life: Those whom God hath joyned, no man, no Devill, can separate so, as that it shall not remain a mariage so far, as that if those separated persons will live together again, yet they shall not be new maried; so farre, certainly, the band of mariage continues still. The Devil makes no mariages; He may have a hand in drawing conveyances; in the temporall conditions there may be practice, but the mariage is made by God in heaven. The Devil can break no mariages neither, though he can by sin break of all the good uses, and take away all the comforts of mariage. I pronounce not now whether Adultery dissolves mariage or no; It is *S. Augustines* wisdome to say, Where the Scripture is silent, let me be silent too: And I may goe lower then he, and say, Where the Church is silent, let me be silent too; and our Church is so far silent in this, as that it hath not said, That Adultery dissolves mariage. Perchance then it is not the death of mariage, but surely it is a deadly wound. We have Authors in the Romane Church that think *fornicationem non vagam,* that such an incontinent life as is limited to one certain person, is no deadly sin. But there is none even amongst them that diminish the crime of Adultery . . . Of that salutation of the Angel to the blessed Virgin *Mary, Blessed art thou amongst women,* we may make even this interpretation, not onely that she was blessed amongst women, that is above women, but that she was *Benedicta,* blessed amongst women, that all women blest her, that no woman had occasion to curse her: And this is the eternity of this secular mariage as far as this world admits any eternity; that it should have no beginning before, no interruption of jealousie in the way, no such approach towards dissolution, as that incontinency in all opinions, and in all Churches is agreed to be. And here also without any scruple of fear, or of suspition of the contrary, there is place for this benediction, upon this couple; Build, ô Lord, upon thine own foundations, in these two, and establish thy former graces with future; that no person ever conplain of either of them, nor either of them of one another, and so he and she are maried *in æternum,* for ever.

We are now come in our order proposed at first, to

our second Part; for all is said that I intended of the
secular mariage. And of this second, the spirituall
mariage, much needs not to be said: There is another
Priest that contracts that, another Preacher that cele-
brates that, the Spirit of God to our spirit. And for
the third mariage, the eternall mariage, is a boldnesse
to speak any thing of a thing so inexpressible as the
joyes of heaven; it is a diminution of them to goe
about to heighten them; it is a shadowing of them to
goe about to lay any colours or lights upon them.
But yet your patience may perchance last to a word
of each of these three Circumstances, The Persons,
the Actions, the Term, both in this spirituall, and in
the eternall mariage.

First then, as in the former Part, the secular
mariage, for the persons there, we considered first
Adam and *Eve,* and after every man and woman, and
this couple in particular; so in this spirituall mariage
we consider first Christ and his Church, for the Persons, but more particularly Christ and my soul. And
can these persons meet? in such a distance, and in such
a disparagement can these persons meet? the Son of
God and the son of man? When I consider Christ to
be *Germen Jehovæ,* the bud and blossome, the fruit
and off-spring of Jehovah, Jehovah himself, and my
self before he took me in hand, to be, not a Potters
vessell of earth, but that earth of which the Potter
might make a vessel if he would, and break it if he
would when he had made it: When I consider Christ
to have been from before all beginnings, and to be
still the Image of the Father, the same stamp upon
the same metall, and my selfe a peece of rusty copper,
in which those lines of the Image of God which were
imprinted in me in my Creation are defaced and
worn, and washed and burnt, and ground away, by
my many, and many, and many sins: When I consider
Christ in his Circle, in glory with his Father, before
he came into this world, establishing a glorious

Church when he was in this world, and glorifying that Church with that glory which himself had before, when he went out of this world; and then consider my self in my circle, I came into this world washed in mine own tears, and either out of compunction for my self or compassion for others, I passe through this world as through a valley of tears, where tears settle and swell, and when I passe out of this world I leave their eyes whose hands close mine, full of tears too, can these persons, this Image of God, this God himself, this glorious God, and this vessell of earth, this earth it self, this inglorious worm of the earth, meet without disparagement?

They doe meet and make a mariage; because I am not a body onely, but a body and soul, there is a mariage, and Christ maries me. As by the Law a man might mary a captive woman in the Warres, if he shaved her head, and pared her nails, and changed her clothes; so my Saviour having fought for my soul, fought to blood, to death, to the death of the Crosse for her, having studied my soul so much, as to write all those Epistles which are in the New Testament to my soul, having presented my soule with his own picture, that I can see his face in all his temporall blessings, having shaved her head in abating her pride, and pared her nails in contracting her greedy desires, and changed her clothes not to fashion her self after this world, my soul being thus fitted by himself, Christ Jesus hath maried my soul, maried her to all the three intendments mentioned in the secular mariage; first, *In ustionem,* against burning; That whether I burn my self in the fires of tentation, by exposing my self to occasions of tentation, or be reserved to be burnt by others in the fires of persecution and martyrdome, whether the fires of ambition, or envy, or lust, or the everlasting fires of hell offer at me in an apprehension of the judgements of God, yet as the Spirit of God shall wipe all tears from mine

eyes, so the tears of Christ Jesus shall extinguish all
fires in my heart, and so it is a mariage, *In ustionem,*
a remedy against burning.

It is so too, *In prolificationem,* for children; first,
væ soli, woe unto that single soul that is not maried
to Christ; that is not come into the way of having
issue by him, that is not incorporated in the Christian Church, and in the true Church, but is yet
either in the wildernesse of Idolatry amongst the Gentiles, or in the Labyrinth of superstition amongst the
Papists, *væ soli,* woe unto that single man that is not
maried to Christ in the Sacraments of the Church;
and *væ sterili,* woe unto them that are barren after
this spirituall mariage, for . . . as soon as Christ had
laid that curse upon the Fig-tree, *Let no fruit grow
upon thee for ever,* presently the whole tree withered;
if no fruit, no leaves neither, nor body left. To be
incorporated in the body of Christ Jesus, and bring
forth no fruits worthy of that profession, is a wofull
state too. *Væ soli:* First, woe unto the Gentiles not
married unto Christ; and *væ sterili,* woe unto inconsiderate Christians, that think not upon their calling,
that conceive not by Christ; but there is a *væ præg-
nanti* too, wo unto them that are with child, and are
never delivered; that have sometimes good concep-
tions, religious dispositions, holy desires to the advancement of Gods truth, but for some collaterall
respects dare not utter them, nor bring them to their
birth, to any effect. The purpose of his mariage to us,
is to have children by us: and this is his abundant and
his present fecundity, that working now, by me in
you, in one instant he hath children in me, and
grand children by me. He hath maried me, *in
ustionem,* and in *prolem,* against burning, and for
children; but can he have any use of me, *in adjutorium,* for a helper? Surely, if I be able to feed him,
and clothe him, and harbour him, (and Christ would
not condemne men at the last day for not doing

these, if man could not doe them) I am able to help him too. Great persons can help him over sea, convey the name of Christ where it hath not been preached yet; and they can help him home again; restore his name, and his truth where superstition with violence hath disseised him: And they can help him at home, defend his truth there against all machinations to displant and dispossesse him. Great men can help him thus; and every man can help him to a better place in his own heart, and his own actions, then he hath had there; and to be so helped in me, and helped by me, to have his glory thereby advanced, Christ hath maried my soul: And he hath maried it *in æternum,* for ever; which is the third and last Circumstance in this spirituall, as it was in the secular mariage.

And here the *æternum* is enlarged; in the secular mariage it was an eternity considered onely in this life; but this eternity is not begun in this world, but from all eternity in the Book of life, in Gods eternall Decree for my election, there Christ was maried to my soul. Christ was never in minority, never under years; there was never any time when he was not as ancient as the Ancient of Days, as old as his Father. But when my soul was in a strange minority, infinite millions of millions of generations, before my soul was a soul, did Christ mary my soul in his eternall Decree. So it was eternall, it had no beginning. Neither doth he interrupt this by giving me any occasion of jealousie by the way, but loves my soul as though there were no other soul, and would have done and suffered all that he did for me alone, if there had been no name but mine in the Book of life. And as he hath maried me to him, *in æternum,* for ever, before all beginnings, and *in æternum,* for ever, without any interruptions, so I know, that *whom he loves he loves to the end,* and that he hath given me, not a presumptuous impossibility, but a modest infallibility, that no sin of mine shall divorce or separate me from him; for, that which ends the secular mariage, ends not the spirituall: not death, for my death does not take me from that husband, but that husband being by his Father preferr'd to higher titles, and greater glory in another state, I doe but goe by death where he is become a King, to have my part in that glory, and in those additions which he hath received there. And this hath led us to our third and last mariage, our eternall marriage in the triumphant Church.

And in this third mariage, the persons are, the Lamb and my soul; *The mariage of the Lamb is come, and blessed are they that are called to the mariage Supper of the Lamb,* says S. *John* speaking of our state in the generall Resurrection. That Lamb who was *brought to the slaughter and opened not his mouth,* and I who have opened my mouth and poured out imprecations and curses upon men, and execrations and blasphemies against God upon every occasion; That Lamb who *was slain from the beginning,* and I who was slain by him who *was a murderer from the beginning;* That *Lamb which took away the sins of the world,* and I who brought more sins into the world, then any sacrifice but the blood of this Lamb could take away: This Lamb and I (these are the Persons) shall meet and mary; there is the Action.

This is not a clandestine mariage, not the private seal of Christ in the obsignation of his Spirit; and yet such a clandestine mariage is a good mariage: Nor it is not such a Parish mariage, as when Christ maried me to himself at my Baptisme, in a Church here; and yet that mariage of a Christian soul to Christ in that Sacrament is a blessed mariage: But this is a mariage in that great and glorious Congregation, where all my sins shall be laid open to the eys of all the world, where all the blessed Virgins shall see all my uncleannesse, and all the Martyrs see all my tergiversations, and all the Confessors see all my double dealings in Gods cause; where *Abraham* shall see my faithlesnesse in Gods promises; and *Job* my impatience in Gods corrections; and *Lazarus* my hardness of heart in distributing Gods blessings to the poore; and those Virgins, and Martyrs, and Confessors, and *Abraham,* and *Job,* and *Lazarus,* and all that Congregation, shall look upon the Lamb and upon me, and upon one another, as though they would all forbid those banes, and say to one another, Will this Lamb have any thing to doe with this soule? and yet there and then this Lamb shall mary me, and mary me *In æternum,* for ever, which is our last circumstance.

It is not well done to call it a circumstance, for the eternity is a great part of the essence of that mariage. Consider then how poore and needy a thing, all the riches of this world, how flat and tastlesse a thing, all the pleasures of this world, how pallid, and faint and dilute a thing, all the honours of this world are, when the very Treasure, and Joy, and glory of heaven it self were unperfect, if it were not eternall, and my mariage shall be soe, *In æternum,* for ever.

The Angels were not maried so; they incurr'd an irreparable Divorce from God, and are separated for ever, and I shall be maried to him, *in æternum,* for ever. The Angels fell in love, when there was no object presented, before any thing was created; when there was nothing but God and themselves, they fell in love with themselves, and neglected God, and so fell *in æternum,* for ever. I shall see all the beauty, and all the glory of all the Saints of God, and love them all, and know that the Lamb loves them too, without jealousie, on his part, or theirs, or mine, and so be maried *in æternum,* for ever, without interruption, or diminution, or change of affections. I shall see the Sunne black as sackcloth of hair, and the Moon become as blood, and the Starres fall as a Figge-tree casts her untimely Figges, and the heavens roll'd up together as a Scroll. I shall see a divorce between Princes and their Prerogatives, between nature and all her elements, between the spheres, and all their intelligences, between matter it self, and all her forms, and my mariage shall be, *in æternum,* for ever. I shall see an end of faith, nothing to be beleeved that I doe not know; and an end of hope, nothing to be wisht that I doe not enjoy, but no end of that love in which I am maried to the Lamb for ever. Yea, I shall see an end of some of the offices of the Lamb himself; Christ himself shall be no longer a Mediator, an Intercessor, an Advocate, and yet shall continue a Husbànd to my soul for ever. Where I shall be rich enough without Joynture, for my Husband cannot die; and wise enough without experience, for no new thing can happen there; and healthy enough without Physick, for no sicknesse can enter; and (which is by much the highest of all) safe enough without grace, for no tentation that needs particular grace, can attempt me. There, where the Angels, which cannot die, could not live, this very body which cannot choose but die, shall live, and live as long as that God of life that made it. Lighten our darkness, we beseech thee, ô Lord, that in thy light we may see light: Illustrate our understandings, kindle our affections, pour oyle to our zeale, that we may come to the mariage of this Lamb, and that this Lamb may come quickly to this mariage: And in the mean time bless these thy servants, with making this secular mariage a type of the spirituall, and the spirituall an earnest of that eternall, which they and we, by thy mercy, shall have in the Kingdome which thy Son our Saviour hath purchased with the inestimable price of his incorruptible blood. To whom, etc.

SERMON PREACHED AT ST. PAUL'S CATHEDRAL

London, 1624 (Isaiah 7:14)

III

EDITOR'S PREFACE

Ambition had much to do with John Donne's long
hesitation about entering the ministry. But ambition
had something to do, too, with his decision to be
ordained when that finally came. At first he had
hoped for secular preferment, and so had kept himself ready until there could no longer be any reasonable hope that such advantage was coming. Even
then he hesitated about taking orders until the king
himself made it plain that only in the clergy could
Donne hope for the benefits of royal favor. According
to Walton, it was the Earl of Somerset who finally located the intention of James I when Somerset im-
portuned him to appoint the middle-aged and still
waiting Donne to a vacant court clerkship. The king
refused with an explanation swiftly relayed to Donne:
"I know Mr. Donne is a learned man, has the abilities
of a learned Divine, and will prove a powerful
preacher; and my desire is to prefer him that way,
and in that way I will deny you nothing for him."

So it was on the promise of ecclesiastical favor that
Donne reluctantly gave up his governmental ambitions and moved slowly toward his ordination. King
James was as good as his word. Donne became a court
chaplain almost at once, was soon appointed to the
highly congenial ministry at Lincoln's Inn, and
through royal solicitude was sent on a diplomatic

mission just when such diversion was needed for his health's sake. He returned happily to his congregations.

But then the royal favor faltered—or so it seemed to Donne, who would soon have his fiftieth birthday. Considering his late start, and remembering the early end likely for anybody in the seventeenth century, it is perhaps understandable that even a delay in advancement could look like the end of the road to him. Important pulpits fell empty, but still the king hesitated, others were appointed to the vacancies, and Donne despaired again. There is no indication of any unhappiness with Lincoln's Inn, but he knew that if he were going anywhere he had soon to be on his way.

Then late in 1621 Valentine Cary, Dean of St. Paul's, was appointed to the bishopric of Exeter. He could not be consecrated at once, however, because the Archbishop of Canterbury was under judgment of involuntary manslaughter for accidently shooting a game warden in Lord Zouch's park. When that was straightened out, "the king sent to Dr. Donne, and appointed him to attend him at dinner the next day. When his Majesty was sate down, before he had eat any meat, he said after his pleasantest manner, *Dr. Donne, I have invited you to Dinner; and, though you sit not down with me, yet will I carve to you a dish that I know you love well; for knowing you love London, I do therefore make you Dean of Paul's;* and when I have dined, then do you take your beloved dish home to your study; say grace there to your self, and much good may it do you" (Walton).

So on Christmas Day, 1621, John Donne preached his first sermon as Dean of St. Paul's. St. Paul's: Cathedral of London since 604, Britain's National Church, center of English ecclesiastical history, *the* British pulpit any time in the thirteen and one half centuries of its existence. Six years after his ordination, John Donne was Dean of St. Paul's.

The Dean, by terms of his appointment, was to preach on Christmas Day, Easter Sunday, Whitsunday and on any other occasion of his choice. We do not have all of Donne's cathedral sermons, but we do have a complete file of the Christmas and Easter sermons preached at St. Paul's. The Christmas Day sermon which follows would probably not be chosen as one of Donne's greatest, all around. It has more than its share of the hair-splitting and authority name-dropping in which Donne too often out-did even the artificial high-style of his day. The tedious and by now utterly irrelevant argument about Mary's physique drones on out of all conscience at the end. And the beginning is a crusty, dry outline of the whole.

But break through those first brittle paragraphs and what a molten, glowing word on the mercies and grace of God there is beneath. Donne's preoccupation with sin and death is often noted. Here is that glad crying of the goodness of God which must be remembered as the context for his darkest speech. It is for these glorious pages that the sermon is to be read. Here is the gospel, the good news of the limitless and ever-present love of God, sung as few men have ever been graced to sing it. Read the long passage from "We begin with that which is elder than our beginning" to "and all times are his seasons." Read with a grateful eye for the message; the ear will be grateful for the music. George Saintsbury called this "a passage than which I hardly know anything more exquisitely rhythmed in the whole range of English from Aelfric to Pater."

PREACHED AT PAULS,
UPON CHRISTMAS DAY,
IN THE EVENING, 1624.

*Esaiah 7.14. Part of the First Lesson, That Evening.
Therefore the Lord Shall Give You A Signe; Behold,
A Virgin Shall Conceive, and Beare A Son, and Shall
Call His Name Immanuel.*

Saint *Bernard* spent his consideration upon three remarkable conjunctions, this Day. First, a Conjunction
of God, and Man in one person, Christ Jesus; Then a
conjunction of the incompatible Titles, Maid and
Mother, in one blessed woman, the blessed Virgin
Mary: And thirdly a conjunction of Faith, and the
Reason of man, that so beleeves, and comprehends
those two conjunctions. Let us accompany these three
with another strange conjunction, in the first word
of this Text, *Propterea, Therefore;* for that joynes the
anger of God, and his mercy together. God chides and
rebukes the King *Achaz* by the Prophet, he is angry
with him, and *Therefore,* sayes the Text, because he
is angry he will give him a signe, a seale of mercy,
*Therefore the Lord shall give you a signe, Behold, a
Virgin, &c.* This *Therefore,* shall therefore be a first
part of this Exercise, That God takes any occasion to
shew mercy; And a second shall be, The particular
way of this mercy, declared here, *The Lord shall give
you* a signe; And then a third and last, what this
signe was, *Behold, a Virgin, &c.*

In these three parts, we shall walk by these steps;
Having made our entrance into the first, with that
generall consideration, that Gods mercy is alwaies in

season, upon that station, upon that height we shall
look into the particular occasions of Gods mercy here,
what this King *Achaz* had done to alien God, and to
avert his mercy, and in those two branches we shall
determine that part. In the second, we shall also first
make this generall entrance, That God persists in his
own waies, goes forward with his own purposes, And
then what his way, and his purpose here was, he would
give them a signe: and farther we shall not extend
that second part. In the third we have more steps to
make; First, what this sign is in generall, it is, that
there is a Redeemer given. And then how, thus; First,
Virgo concipiet, a Virgin shall conceive, she shall be
a Virgin then; And *Virgo pariet, a Virgin shall bring
forth,* she shall be a Virgin then; And *Pariet filium,
she shall beare a Son,* and therefore he is of her substance, not only man, but man of her; And this Virgin
shall call this Son *Immanuel, God with us,* that is,
God and Man in one person. Though the Angel at
the Conception tell *Ioseph,* That he shall call his
name Jesus, and tell *Mary* her selfe, that she shall
call his name Jesus, yet the blessed Virgin her selfe shall
have a further reach, a clearer illustration, She shall
call his name *Immanuel, God with us:* Others were
called *Iesus, Iosuah* was so, divers others were so; but,
in the Scriptures there was never any but Christ called
Immanuel. . . . And then that all this should be
established, and declared by an infallible signe, with
this *Ecce, Behold;* That whosoever can call upon God
by that name *Immanuel,* that is confesse Christ to
bee come in the flesh, that Man shall have an *Ecce,*
a light, a sign, a token, an assurance that this *Immanuel,* this Jesus, this Saviour belongs unto him, and
he shall be able to say, *Ecce, Behold, mine eyes have
seen thy salvation.*

We begin with that which is elder then our beginning, and shall over-live our end, The mercy of God.
I will sing of thy mercy and judgement, sayes *David;*

when we fixe our selves upon the meditation and
modulation of the mercy of God, even his judgements
cannot put us out of tune, but we shall sing, and be
chearefull, even in them. As God made grasse for
beasts, before he made beasts, and beasts for man,
before he made man: As in that first generation, the
Creation, so in the regeneration, our re-creating, he
begins with that which was necessary for that which
followes, Mercy before Judgement. Nay, to say that
mercy was first, is but to post-date mercy; to preferre
mercy but so, is to diminish mercy; The names of first
or last derogate from it, for first and last are but ragges
of time, and his mercy hath no relation to time, no
limitation in time, it is not first, nor last, but eternall,
everlasting; Let the Devill make me so far desperate
as to conceive a time when there was no mercy, and
he hath made me so far an Atheist, as to conceive a
time when there was no God; if I despoile him of his
mercy, any one minute, and say, now God hath no
mercy, for that minute I discontinue his very God-
head, and his beeing. *** But the true roote of the
word mercy, through all the Prophets, is *Racham,* and
Racham is *diligere,* to love; as long as there hath been
love (and *God is love*) there hath been mercy: And
mercy considered externally, and in the practise and
in the effect, began not at the helping of man, when
man was fallen and become miserable, but at the making of man, when man was nothing. So then, here we
consider not mercy as it is radically in God, and an
essentiall attribute of his, but productively in us, as
it is an action, a working upon us, and that more
especially, as God takes all occasions to exercise that
action, and to shed that mercy upon us: for particular
mercies are feathers of his wings, and that prayer,
*Lord let thy mercy lighten upon us, as our trust is in
thee,* is our birdlime; particular mercies are that cloud
of Quailes which hovered over the host of Israel, and
that prayer, *Lord let thy mercy lighten upon us,* is

our net to catch, our Gomer to fill of those Quailes.
The aire is not so full of Moats, of Atomes, as the
Church is of Mercies; and as we can suck in no part
of aire, but we take in those Moats, those Atomes;
so here in the Congregation we cannot suck in a word
from the preacher, we cannot speak, we cannot sigh
a prayer to God, but that that whole breath and aire
is made of mercy. But we call not upon you from this
Text, to consider Gods ordinary mercy, that which he
exhibites to all in the ministery of his Church; nor
his miraculous mercy, his extraordinary deliverances
of States and Churches; but we call upon particular
Consciences, by occasion of this Text, to call to minde
Gods occasionall mercies to them; such mercies as a
regenerate man will call mercies, though a naturall
man would call them accidents, or occurrences, or con-
tingencies; A man wakes at midnight full of unclean
thoughts, and he heares a passing Bell; this is an
occasionall mercy, if he call that his own knell, and
consider how unfit he was to be called out of the
world then, how unready to receive that voice, *Foole,
this night they shall fetch away thy soule.* The adul-
terer, whose eye waites for the twy-light, goes forth,
and casts his eyes upon forbidden houses, and would
enter, and sees a *Lord have mercy upon us* upon the
doore; this is an occasionall mercy, if this bring him to
know that they who lie sick of the plague within, passe
through a furnace, but by Gods grace, to heaven; and
hee without, carries his own furnace to hell, his lust-
full loines to everlasting perdition. What an occasionall mercy had Balaam, when his Asse Catechized
him? What an occasionall mercy had one Theefe,
when the other catechized him so, *Art thou not
afraid being under the same condemnation?* . . . If
I should declare what God hath done (done occasionally) for my soule, where he instructed me for feare
of falling, where he raised me when I was fallen,
perchance you would rather fixe your thoughts upon

my illnesse, and wonder at that, then at Gods goodnesse, and glorifie him in that; rather wonder at my
sins, then at his mercies, rather consider how ill a man
I was, then how good a God he is. If I should inquire
upon what occasion God elected me, and writ my
name in the book of Life, I should sooner be afraid
that it were not so, then finde a reason why it should
be so. God made Sun and Moon to distinguish seasons,
and day, and night, and we cannot have the fruits of
the earth but in their seasons: But God hath made no
decree to distinguish the seasons of his mercies; In
paradise, the fruits were ripe, the first minute, and in
heaven it is alwaies Autumne, his mercies are ever in
their maturity. We ask *panem quotidianum,* our daily
bread, and God never sayes you should have come
yesterday, he never sayes you must againe to morrow,
but *to day if you will heare his voice,* to day he will
heare you. If some King of the earth have so large an
extent of Dominion, in North, and South, as that he
hath Winter and Summer together in his Dominions,
so large an extent East and West, as that he hath day
and night together in his Dominions, much more hath
God mercy and judgement together: He brought light
out of darknesse, not out of a lesser light; he can
bring thy Summer out of Winter, though thou have
no Spring; though in the wayes of fortune, or understanding, or conscience, thou have been benighted till
now, wintred and frozen, clouded and eclypsed,
damped and benummed, smothered and stupified till
now, now God comes to thee, not as in the dawning
of the day, not as in the bud of the spring, but as
the Sun at noon to illustrate all shadowes, as the
sheaves in harvest, to fill all penuries, all occasions invite his mercies, and all times are his seasons.

If it were not thus in generall, it would never have
been so in this particular, in our case, in the Text,
in King *Achaz;* If God did not seeke occasion to doe
good to all, he would never have found occasion to

doe good to King *Achaz.* Subjects are to look upon the faults of Princes, with the spectacles of obedience, and reverence, to their place, and persons; little and dark spectacles, and so their faults, and errors are to appeare little, and excusable to them; Gods perspective glasse, his spectacle is the whole world; he looks not upon the Sun, in his spheare onely, but as he works upon the whole earth: And he looks upon Kings, not onely what harme they doe at home, but what harme they occasion abroad; and through that spectacle, the faults of Princes, in Gods eye, are multiplyed, farre above those of private men. *Achaz* had such faults, and yet God sought occasion of Mercy. *Iotham,* his Father, is called *a good King,* and yet all Idolatry was not removed in his time, and he was a good King, for all that. *Achaz* is called *ill,* both because himselfe sacrificed Idolatrously, (And the King was a commanding person) And because he made the Priest *Vriah* to doe so, (And the Priest was an exemplar person) And because he made his Son commit the abominations of the heathen; (And the actions of the Kings Son pierce far in leading others.) *Achaz* had these faults, and yet God sought occasion of mercy. *If the evening skie be red, you promise your selves a faire day,* sayes Christ; you would not doe so if the evening were black and cloudy: when you *see the fields white with corne, you say harvest is ready;* you would not doe so if they were white with frost. *If ye consent, and obey, you shall eat the good things of the Land,* sayes God in the Prophet; shall ye doe so if you refuse, and rebell? *Achaz* did, and yet God sought occasion of mercy. There arise diseases for which there is no *probatum est,* in all the bookes of Physitians; There is scarce any sin of which we have not had experiments of Gods mercies; He concludes with no sin, excludes no occasion, precludes no person: And so we have done with our first part, Gods generall disposition, for the Rule, declared in *Achaz* case for the example.

Our second part consists of a Rule, and an Example too: The Rule, That God goes forward in his own wayes, proceeds, as he begun, in mercy; The Example, what his proceeding, what his subsequent mercy to *Achaz* was. One of the most convenient Hieroglyphicks of God, is a Circle; and a Circle is endlesse; whom God loves, hee loves to the end: and not onely to their own end, to their death, but to his end, and his end is, that he might love them still. His hailestones, and his thunder-bolts, and his showres of bloud (emblemes and instruments of his Judgements) fall downe in a direct line, and affect and strike some one person, or place: His Sun, and Moone, and Starres, (Emblemes and Instruments of his Blessings) move circularly, and communicate themselves to all. His Church is his chariot; in that, he moves more gloriously, then in the Sun; as much more, as his begotten Son exceeds his created Sun, and his Son of glory, and of his right hand, the Sun of the firmament; and this Church, his chariot, moves in that communicable motion, circularly; It began in the East, it came to us, and is passing now, shining out now, in the farthest West. As the Sun does not set to any Nation, but withdraw it selfe, and returne againe; God, in the exercise of his mercy, does not set to thy soule, though he benight it with an affliction. Remember that our Saviour Christ himselfe, in many actions and passions of our humane nature, and infirmities, smothered that Divinity, and suffered it not to worke, but yet it was alwayes in him, and wrought most powerfully in the deepest danger; when he was absolutely dead, it raised him again: If Christ slumbred the God-head in himselfe, The mercy of God may be slumbred, it may be hidden from his servants, but it cannot be taken away, and in the greatest necessities, it shall break out. The Blessed Virgin was overshadowed, but it was with the Holy Ghost that overshadowed her: Thine understanding, thy conscience may be so too, and yet it may be the work of the Holy Ghost, who moves in thy darknesse, and will bring light even out of that, knowledge out of thine ignorance, clearnesse out of thy scruples, and consolation out of thy Dejection of Spirit. *God is thy portion,* says *David; David* does not speak so narrowly, so penuriously, as to say, God hath given thee thy portion, and thou must look for no more; but *God is thy portion,* and as long as he is God, he hath more to give, and as long as thou art his, thou hast more to receive. Thou canst not have so good a Title, to a subsequent blessing, as a former blessing; where thou art an ancient tenant, thou wilt look to be preferred before a stranger; and that is thy title to Gods future mercies, if thou have been formerly accustomed to them. The Sun is not weary with sixe thousand yeares shining; God cannot be weary of doing good; And therefore never say, God hath given me these and these temporall things, and I have scattered them wastfully, surely he will give me no more; These and these spirituall graces, and I have neglected them, abused them, surely he will give me no more; For, for things created, we have instruments to measure them; we know the compasse of a Meridian, and the depth of a Diameter of the Earth, and we know this, even of the uppermost spheare in the heavens: But when we come to the Throne of God himselfe, the Orbe of the Saints, and Angels that see his face, and the vertues, and powers that flow from thence, we have no balance to weigh them, no instruments to measure them, no hearts to conceive them: So, for temporall things, we know the most that man can have; for we know all the world; but for Gods mercy, and his spirituall graces, as that language in which God spake, the Hebrew, hath no superlative, so, that which he promises, in all that he hath spoken, his mercy hath no superlative; he shewes no mercy, which you can call his Greatest Mercy, his Mercy is never at the highest; whatsoever he hath done for thy soule, or for any other, in applying himselfe to it, he can exceed that. Onely he can raise a Tower, whose top shall reach to heaven: The Basis of the highest building is but the Earth; But though thou be but a Tabernacle of Earth, God shall raise thee peece by peece, into a spirituall building; And after one Story of Creation, and another of Vocation, and another of Sanctification, he shall bring thee up, to meet thy selfe, in the bosome of thy God, where thou wast at first, in an eternall election: God is a circle himselfe, and he will make thee one; Goe not thou about to square eyther circle, to bring that which is equall in it selfe, to Angles, and Corners, into dark and sad suspicions of God, or of thy selfe, that God can give, or that thou canst receive no more Mercy, then thou hast had already.

This then is the course of Gods mercy, He proceeds as he begun, which was the first branch of this second part; It is always in motion, and alwayes moving towards *All*, alwaies perpendicular, right over every one of us, and always circular, always communicable to all; And then the particular beame of this Mercy, shed upon *Achaz* here in our Text, is, *Dabit signum, The Lord shall give you a signe*. It is a great Degree of Mercy, that he affords us signes. A naturall man is not made of Reason alone, but of Reason, and Sense: A Regenerate man is not made of Faith alone, but of Faith and Reason; and Signes, externall things, assist us all.

In the Creation, it was part of the office of the Sunne and Moone, to be significative; he created them for signes, as well as for seasons; hee directed the Jews to Christ, by signes, by sacrifices, and Sacraments, and ceremonies; and he entertaines us with Christ, by the same meanes to; we know where to finde Christ; In his House, in his Church; And we know at what signe he dwels; where the Word is rightly Preached, and the Sacraments duly administred. It is truly, and wisely

said, *** We must so farre satisfie our selves, with the
word of God, as that we despise not those other sub-
sidiary helps, which God in his Church hath afforded
us (Calvin): which is true (as of Sacraments especially)
so of other Sacramentall, and Rituall, and Ceremoniall
things, which assist the working of the Sacraments.
For, therefore does the Prophet say, when *Achaz* refused a signe, *Is it a small thing to weary* (or disobey)
men, but that you will weary (disobey) *God himselfe?*
He disobeys God, in the way of contumacy, who refuses his signes, his outward assistances, his ceremonies
which are induced by his authority, derived from him,
upon men, in his Church, and so made a part, or a
help, of his ordinary service, as Sacraments and Sacramentall things are.

There are signes of another sort, not fixed by Gods
Ordinance, but signes which particular men, have
sometimes desired at Gods hand, for a farther manifestation of Gods will, in which, it is not, otherwise,
already fully manifested, and revealed. For, to seeke
such signes, in things which are sufficiently declared by
God, or to seeke them, with a resolution, That I will
leave a duty undone, except I receive a signe, this is
to tempt God, and to seeke a way to excuse my selfe,
for not doing that, which I was bound to doe, by the
strength of an old commandement, and ought not to
look for a new signe. But the greatest fault in this
kinde, is, that if God, of his abundant goodnesse, doe
give me a signe, for my clearer directions, and I resist
that signe, I dispute against that signe, I turne it another way, upon nature, upon fortune, upon mistak-
ing, that so I may goe mine owne way, and not be
bound, by beleeving that signe to be from God, to
goe that way, to which God by that signe calls me. And
this was *Achaz* case; God spoke unto him, and said,
Aske a signe (that he would deliver him, from the enemy, that besieged Jerusalem) *and he said, I will not
aske a signe, nor tempt God;* For, though St. *Augus-*

tine, and some with him, ascribe this refusall of *Achaz,* to a religious modesty, yet St. *Hierome,* and with him, the greatest party, justly impute this, for a fault to *Achaz:* both because the signe was offered him from God, and not sought by himselfe, (which is the case that is most subject to errour) And because the Prophet, who understood Gods minde, and the Kings minde to, takes knowledge of it, as of a great fault, *In this, thou hast contemned, and wearyed, not Man but God.* . . . God does give signes, and when he does so, he gives also irradiations, illustrations of the under-standing, that they may be discerned to be his signes; and when they are so, it is but a pretended modesty, to say, we will not tempt God to ask a sign, we will not trouble God to tell us whether this be a sign or no, but against all significations from God, goe on, as though all were but naturall accidents.

God gives signes *recte petentibus,* to them that aske them upon due grounds, . . . He gives signes also *Non petentibus,* without being asked, to illustrate the case, and to confirme the person, . . . But the highest of all, is, to persever in his mercy so far, as to give a signe, though upon the offer thereof, it be refused; And that is *Achaz* case: *Aske ye,* says God, And, *I will not,* says *Achaz,* and then, It is not *Quamvis,* for all that, though thou refuse, but it is *Propterea, There-fore,* because thou refusest, *The Lord himselfe shall give thee a signe.* His fault is carried thus high: Be-cause he had treasure to pay an army, because he had contracted with the Assyrians to assist him with men, therefore he refuses the assistance offered by the Prophet from God, and would faine goe his owne wayes, and yet would have a religious pretext, *He will not tempt God.* Nay his fault is carried thus much higher, That which we read, *Non tentabo, I will not tempt,* is in the Originall, *Nasas;* and *Nasas* is *non Extollam, non glorificabo,* I will not glorifie God so much, that is, I will not be beholden to God for this victory, I will not take him into the league for this action, I will do it of my selfe: And yet, (and then, who shall doubt of the largenesse of Gods mercy?) God proceeds in his purpose: *Aske a signe,* will ye not? *Therefore the Lord shall give you a signe:* Because you will doe nothing for your selfe, the Lord shall doe all; which is so transcendent a mercy, as that, howsoever God afforded it to *Achaz* here, we can promise it to no man hereafter.

We are come to our third part, which is more peculiar to this Day: It is, first, what the signe is in generall, And then, some more particular circumstances, *Behold a Virgin shall conceive, &c.* In generall then, the signe that God gives *Achaz* and his company, is, That there shall bee a Messias, a Redeemer given. Now, how is this future thing, (There shall be a Messias) a signe of their present deliverance from that siege? First, In the notion of the Prophet, it was not a future thing; for, as in Gods owne sight, so in their sight, to whom he opens himselfe, future things are present. So this Prophet says, *Puer datus, filius natus, unto us a child is borne, unto us a Son is given:* He was not given, he was not borne in six hundred yeares after that; but such is the clearenesse of a Prophets sight, such is the infallibility of Gods declared purpose. So then, if the Prophet could have made the King beleeve, with such an assurednesse, as if he had seene it done, that God would give a deliverance, to all mankinde, by a Messias, that had been signe enough, evidence enough to have argued thereupon, That God who had done so much a greater worke, would also give him a deliverance from that enemy, that pressed him then: If I can fixe my selfe, with the strength of faith, upon that which God hath done for man, I cannot doubt of his mercy, in any distresse: If I lacke a signe, I seeke no other but this, That God was made man for me; which the Church and Church-writers, have well expressed by the word Incarnation, for that acknowledges, and

denotes, that God was made my flesh: It were not so
strange, that he who is spirit, should be made my
spirit, my soule, but he was made my flesh: Therefore
have the Fathers delighted themselves, in the variation
of that word; so far, as that *Hilarie* cals it *Corpora-
tionem,* That God assumed my Body; And *Damascen*
cals it *Inhumanationem,* That God became this man,
soule and body; And *Irenaeus* cals it *Adunationem,*
and *Nysen Contemperationem,* A mingling, says one,
an uniting, saies the other, of two, of God and man,
in one person. Shall I aske, what needs all this? what
needed God to have put himselfe to this? I may say
with S. *Augustine,* *** What other way soever God
had taken for our salvation, our curiosity would no
more have beene satisfied in that way, than in this:
But God having chosen the way of Redemption, which
was the way of Justice, God could do no otherwise:
*** saies Irenaeus; As, if a man should get a battaile
by the power of the Devill, without fighting, this were
not a just victory; so, if God, in mans behalfe, had
conquered the devill, without man, without dying, it
had not beene a just conquest. I must not aske why
God tooke this way, to Incarnate his Son; And shall
I aske how this was done? I doe not aske how *Rheu-
barb,* or how *Aloes* came by this, or this vertue, to
purge this, or this humour in my body: *** Even in
naturall things, all the reason of all that is done, is
the power, and the will of him, who infused that vertue into that creature (Augustine). And therefore
much more, when we come to these supernaturall
points, such as this birth of Christ, we embrace S.
Basils modesty, and abstinence, *Nativitas ista silentio
honoretur,* This mysterie is not so well celebrated,
with our words, and discourse, as with a holy silence,
and meditation: *** Nay, (saies that Father) there
may be danger in giving our selves leave, to thinke or
study too much of it. *** Aske not thy selfe over-
curiously, when this mystery was accomplished; be not

over-vehement, over-peremptory, (so far, as to the per-
plexing of thine owne reason and understanding, or so
far, as to the despising of the reasons of other men) in
calculating the time, the day or houre of this nativity:
*** pass over this question, in good time, and with
convenient satisfaction, *Quando,* when Christ was
borne; But *noli inquirere Quomodo,* (saies S. *Basil*
still) never come to that question, how it was done,
*** for God hath given us no faculties to comprehend
it, no way to answer it. That's enough, which we have
in S. *Iohn, Every spirit, that confesses, that Iesus is
come in the flesh, is of God:* for, since it was a coming of Iesus, Iesus was before; so he was God; and
since he came in the flesh, hee is now made man; And,
that God and Man, are so met, is a signe to mee, that
God, and I, shall never bee parted.

This is the signe in generall; That God hath had
such a care of all men, is a signe to me, That he hath
a care of me: But then there are signes of this signe;
Divers: All these; *A Virgin shall conceive,* A Virgin
shall *bring forth,* Bring forth *a Son, And* (whatsoever
have been prophesied before) *she shall call his name
Immanuel.*

First, a Virgin shall be a mother, which is a very
particular signe, and was seene but once. That which
Gellius, and *Plinie* say, that a Virgin had a child, almost 200. yeares before Christ, that which *Genebrard*
saies, that the like fell out in France, in his time, are
not within our faith, and they are without our reason;
our faith stoopes not downe to them, and our Reason
reaches not up to them; of this Virgin in our text, If
that be true, which *Aquinas* cites out of the Roman
story, that in the times of *Constantine* and *Irene,* upon
a dead body found in a sepulchre, there was found this
inscription, in a plate of gold, *Christus nascetur ex
Virgine, & ego credo in eum,* Christ shall be borne of
a Virgin, and I beleeve in that Christ; *** If this be
true, yet our ground is not upon such testimonie; If

God had not said it, I would never have beleeved
it. . . . That this Mother, in our text, was a Virgin,
is a peculiar, a singular signe, given, as such, by God;
never done but then; and it is a singular testimony,
how acceptable to God, that state of virginity is; Hee
does not dishonour physick, that magnifies health;
nor does hee dishonour marriage, that praises Virginity; let them embrace that state, that can; and certainly, many more might doe it, then do, if they
would try whether they could, or no; and if they
would follow S. Cyprians way, *** It is not enough
for a virgin to bee a virgin in her owne knowledge,
but she must governe her selfe so, as that others may
see, that she is one, and see, that shee hath a desire,
and a disposition, to continue so still; *** saies that
Father, She must appeare in such garments, in such
language, and in such motions, (for, as a wife may
weare other clothes, so she may speake other words,
then a virgin may do) as they that see her, may not
question, nor dispute, whether she be a maid or
no. . . . And *Tertullian,* who makes the note, notes
withall, that *** Curious dressings are for publique
eyes; and the Virgin that desires to publish her selfe,
is weary of that state: It is usefully added by him, ***
the eyes of others, that strike upon her, (if she be willing to stand out that battery) dry up that blood, that
should blush, and weare out that chastity, which
should be preserved. So precious is virginity in Gods
eye, as that hee lookes upon that, with a more jealous
eye, than upon other states.

This blessed Mother of God, in our text, was a Virgin: when? *Virgo concipiet,* saies our Text, *A Virgin
shall conceive,* when she conceived, she was a Virgin.
There are three Heresies, all noted by S. *Augustine,*
that impeach the virginity of this most blessed
Woman: The Cerinthians said she conceived by ordinary generation; *Iovinian* said, she was delivered by
ordinary meanes; And *Helvidius* said, she had chil-

dren after: All against all the world besides themselves, and against one another. For the first, that is
enough which S. *Basil* sayes, that if the word Virgin
in our text signified no more but *adolescentulam,* a
yong woman (as they pretend) it had been an impertinent, an absurd thing for the Prophet to have made
that a sign, and a wonder, that a yong woman should
have a childe. This is enough, but that is abundantly
enough, that S. *Matthew,* who spoke with the same
spirit that *Esay* did, sayes in a word, which can admit
no mis-interpretation, That that was fulfilled which
Esay had said, *A Virgin shall conceive;* S. *Matthews*
word without question, is a Virgin, and not a yong
woman, and S. *Matthew* took *Esaies* word to be so too;
and S. *Matthew* (at least he that spake in S. *Matthew*)
did not, could not mistake, and mistake himself, for
it was one and the same Holy Ghost that spake
both. . . . *Virgo concepit,* she was a Virgin then, then
when she had conceived.

She was so to, *In Partu,* then when she was delivered; *Iovinian* denied that: A better then he (*Tertul-*
lian) denied it: *** says he, she was such a Virgin as
knew no man, not such a Virgin as needed no midwife: *** a Virgin in her conception, but a wife in
the deliverance of her Son. Let that be wrapped up
amongst *Tertullians* errors, he had many; The text
cleares it, *A virgin shall conceive, a virgin shall beare*
a Son: The Apostles Creed cleares it, sayes S. *Augus-*
tine, when it sayes, *Born of the Virgin Mary;* and S.
Ambrose cleares it, when hee says, with such indignation, *** It is said, that there are some men so impious, as to deny that she remained a Virgin at the birth
of her Son: S. Ambrose wondred there should be,
scarce beleeved it to be any other then a rumour, or a
slander, that there could be any so impious, as to deny
that: And yet there have beene some so impious, as to
charge *Calvin,* with that impiety, with denying her
to be a Virgin then; It is true, he makes it not a matter

of faith, to defend her perpetuall virginity; but that's not this case, of her Virginity in her Deliverance: And even of that, (of her perpetuall virginity) he saies thus, *** He is over-curious, that will make any doubt of it; but no man will persist in the denyall of it, but a contentious wrangler; And in that very point, S. *Basil* saies fully as much, as *Calvin*. But, at his birth, and after his birth, there is evidence enough in this text, *A Virgin shall conceive, A Virgin shall bring forth, A Virgin shall call him Immanuel*, In all those future, and subsequent Acts, still it is the same person, and in the same condition.

Pariet, & pariet filium, She shall bring forth a Son; If a Son, then of the substance of his Mother; that the Anabaptists deny; But had it not beene so, Christ had not beene true Man, and then, man were yet unredeemed. He is her Son, but not her ward; his Father cannot dye: Her Son, but yet he asked her no leave, to stay at Jerusalem, nor to dispute with the Doctors, nor to goe about his Fathers worke: His setling of Religion, his governing the Church, his dispensing of his graces, is not by warrant from her: They that call upon the Bishop of Rome, in that voyce, *Impera Regibus,* command Kings and Emperors, admit of that voyce, *Impera filio,* to her, that she should command her Sonne. The naturall obedience of children to Parents, holds not in such civill things, as are publique; A woman may be a Queen-Dowager, and yet a subject; The blessed Virgin *Mary* may be in a high ranke, and yet no Soveraigne; *Blessed art thou amongst women,* saies the Angell to her; Amongst women, above women; but not above any person of the Trinity, that she should command her Son. *Luther* was awake, and risen, but he was not readie; Hee had seene light, and looked toward it, but yet saw not so clearely by it, then, when he said, That the blessed Virgin was of a middle condition, betweene Christ, and man; that man hath his conception, and his quickning (by the

infusion of the soule) in originall sin; that Christ had
it in neither, no sin in his conception, none in his inanimation, in the infusion of his soule; But, saies
Luther, howsoever it were at the conception, certainly
at the inanimation, at the quickning, she was preserved from originall sin. Now, what needs this? may
I not say, that I had rather be redeemed by Christ
Jesus then bee innocent? rather be beholden to Christs
death, for my salvation, then to *Adams* standing in his
innocencie? *Epiphanius* said enough, *Par detrimentum
afferunt religioni,* they hurt Religion as much, that
ascribe too little, to the Blessed Virgin, as they who
ascribe too much; much is due to her, and this
amongst the rest, That she had so cleare notions,
above all others, what kind of person, her Son was,
that as *Adam* gave names, according to natures, so the
Prophet here leaves it to her, to name her Son, according to his office, *She shall call his name Immanuel.*

Wee told you at first, that both *Ioseph* and *Mary,*
were told by the Angel, that his name was to be Jesus,
and we told you also, that others, besides him, had
beene called by that name of Jesus: but, as, though
others were called Jesus, . . . yet there is observed
a difference in the pointing, and sounding of those
names, from this our Jesus: so though other women
were called *Mary,* as well as the blessed Virgin, yet the
Euangelists, evermore make a difference, betweene her
name, and the other *Maries;* for Her they call *Mariam,*
and the rest *Maria.* Now this Jesus, in this person, is a
reall, an actuall Saviour, he that hath already really,
and actually accomplished our salvation; But the
blessed Virgin had a clearer illustration, then all that;
for she onely knew, or she knew best, the capacity, in
which he could be a Saviour, that is, as he is *Immanuel, God with us;* for she, and she onely knew, that he
was the Sonne of God, and not of naturall generation
by man. How much is enwrapped in this name *Immanuel,* and how little time to unfold it? I am afraid

none at all; A minute will serve to repeate that which
S. *Bernard* saies, and a day, a life will not serve to
comprehend it; (for to comprehend is not to know a
thing, as far as I can know it, but to know it as far,
as that thing can be knowne; and so onely God, can
comprehend God.) *Immanuel est verbum infans,* saies
the Father; He is the ancient of daies, and yet in minority; he is the Word it selfe, and yet speechlesse; he
that is All, that all the Prophets spoke of, cannot
speake: He addes more, He is *Puer sapiens,* but a
child, and yet wiser then the elders, wiser in the
Cradle, then they in the Chaire: Hee is more, *Deus
lactens,* God, at whose breasts all crestures suck, suck-
ing at his Mothers breast, and deliver us, in all en-
cumbrances; so he is with us; And with us, *usque ad
consummationem,* till the end of the world, in his
Word, and in the Sacraments: for, though I may not
say, as some have said, That by the word of Consecration, in the administration of the Sacrament, Christ
is so infallibly produced, as that, if Christ had never
been incarnate before, yet, at the pronouncing of
those words of consecration, he must necessarily be
incarnate then, yet I may say, that God is as effectually
present, with every worthy receiver, as that hee is not
more effectually present with the Saints in Heaven.

And this is that, which is intimated in that word,
which we seposed at first, for the last of all, *Ecce, Behold; Behold, a* Virgin shall conceive, &c. God does
not furnish a roome, and leave it darke; he sets up
lights in it; his first care was, that his benefits should
be seene; he made light first, and then creatures, to
be seene by that light: He sheds himselfe from my
mouth, upon the whole auditory here; he powres himselfe from my hand, to all the Communicants at the
table; I can say to you all here, *The grace of our Lord
Iesus Christ be with you, and remaine with you all;*
I can say to them all there, *The Body of our Lord
Iesus Christ which was given for you, preserve you to*

everlasting life: I can bring it so neare; but onely the worthy hearer, and the worthy receiver, can call this Lord, this Jesus, this Christ, *Immanuel, God with us;* onely that Virgin soule, devirginated in the blood of *Adam,* but restored in the blood of the Lambe, hath this *Ecce,* this testimony, this assurance, that God is with him; they that have this *Ecce,* this testimony, in a rectified conscience, are Godfathers to this child Jesus, and may call him *Immanuel, God with us;* for, as no man can deceive God, so God can deceive no man; God cannot live in the darke himselfe, neither can he leave those, who are his, in the darke: If he be with thee, he will make thee see, that he is with thee; and never goe out of thy sight, till he have brought thee, where thou canst never goe out of his.

SERMON PREACHED AT ST. PAUL'S CATHEDRAL

London, January 29, 1625
(Psalms 63:7)

IV

SERMONS OF JOHN DONNE

EDITOR'S PREFACE

As Dean of St. Paul's, John Donne was one of the thirty clerical members of the cathedral Chapter. The cathedral properties were divided into thirty benefices, or prebends, and each chapter member was assigned a prebend as his living. Donne came into the Chapter as prebendary of Chiswick.

At St. Paul's, the Psalms were traditionally the book of the cathedral staff. They were divided among the thirty prebendaries, each reciting his five psalms daily, and giving regular occasion to meditation and reflection upon them. Dean Donne drew Psalms 62 to 66. Nothing pleased him more than to give them the special attention to which he was pledged.

The first sentences in the first sermon printed in this volume are witness to Donne's general predisposition toward all the Psalms. "Almost every man hath his *Appetite,* and his *tast* disposed to some kind of meates rather than others . . . We have often the same disposition in our *spirituall Diet;* a man may have a particular love toward such and such a book of Scripture, and in such an affection, I acknowledge, that my spirituall appetite carries me still, upon the *Psalms of David,* for a first course. . ." So to his Lincoln's Inn congregation. In May, 1625, he preached at St. Paul's on Psalm 62:9, explaining to his hearers that out of all the psalms he loved, he was with this sermon beginning to pay special attention to the five "appointed for his Prebend. And of those five Psalmes which belong to mee, this, out of which I read you this Text, is the first. And, by God's grace, (upon like occasione) I shall here handle some part of every one of the other foure Psalms, for some testimony, that those my five Psalmes returne often into my meditation, which I also assure my selfe of the rest of my brethren, who are under the same obligation in this Church."

The greatest of these promised sermons, and one of the most splendid of all his utterances, is the one printed hereafter, "the second of my Prebend Sermons upon my five Psalmes." It is one long hymn of joy, so powerful, so insistent in its relief and gladness that even the most insensitive must suspect unusual circumstances around its conception. Back of the theological and homiletical ebulliance of this sermon is the lifting of the dreadful plague epidemic which had terrorized and decimated London in the summer and fall of 1625.

In July alone there were 5,000 plague deaths in London; in August, 19,000. There was a great scattering as people, unaware of the role of rat fleas in the transmission of bubonic plague, fled from the city and from each other. The King, the Court, and Parliament led the way, leaving London early in July—after a day of fasting during which King and Lords heard two sermons and the House of Commons heard three: the first, three hours long, each of the other two, two hours long. Surely heroic, kill-or-cure measures.

John Donne shipped off his children to outlying towns and adjourned himself to the Chelsea home of Sir John and Lady Danvers (Magdalen Herbert in her first marriage, mother of poet George Herbert, and longtime friend of Donne). Since contagion was the dread, no one visited anyone. In December Donne wrote Sir Henry Goodyer commenting on a report of his own death. "The report of my death hath thus much of truth in it, that though I be not dead, yet am I buried; within a few hours after I immured my self in this house, the infection strook into the town, into so many houses, as that it became ill manners to make any visits." In an earlier letter to Sir Thomas Roe he adds ". . . so I have been in a secular Monastery."

Meanwhile, according to contemporary accounts, a stricken, emptied London echoed to "the howling of dogs, the raving of the sick, and the mourning of the bereaved." What roistering there was went on among those dregs of humanity who looted the empty houses. Later, in his "First Sermon after our Dispersion by the Sickness," Donne has hard words for these "Egyptians" who cried *"Let us eat and drink, and take our pleasure . . . for tomorrow we shall die,* and so were cut off by the hand of God, some even in their robberies, in half-empty houses; and in their drunkenness in voluptuous and riotous houses; and in their lusts and wantonness in licentious houses; and so took in infection and death, like *Judas'* sop, death dipt and soaked in sin. Men whose lust carried them into the jaws of infection in lewd houses, and seeking one sore perished with another; men whose rapine and covetousness broke into houses, and seeking the Wardrobes of others, found their own winding-sheet, in the infection of that house where they stole their own death . . ."

Other passages in the same sermon indicate how powerfully the whole melancholy event worked on Donne's frequently mordant imagination: ". . . consider upon what ground you tread; upon ground so holy, as that all the ground is made of the bodies of Christians, and therein hath received a second consecration. Every puff of wind within these walls, may blow the father into the sons eyes, or the wife into her husbands, or his into hers, or both into their childrens, or their childrens into both. Every grain of dust that flies here, is a piece of a Christian . . ."

But at last the epidemic abated, the citizens returned to London, and the Dean of St. Paul's resumed his preaching. During his prolonged seclusion, Donne had been working on old sermons, writing them out, polishing them off for whatever use his promising elder son John would make of them. Now, having learned from such retrospection, Donne turned with new force and focus to the richest years, both for quantity and quality of his sermons, in his whole ministry. Everything which the earlier years of experience and practise had taught him was in easy command. The failing physical forces of his last years had not begun their serious drain. And the situation in these climactic years, demanding reassurance and stimulation for frightened and depressed peoples, stirred Donne to his superb best.

The second "Prebend Sermon" sets the standard which, if rarely equalled, was often thereafter approached. It is, in thought and expression, what Edmund Gosse called it: "a long poem of victory over death . . . one of the most magnificent pieces of religious writing in English literature," closing with "a majestic sentence of incomparable pomp and melody, which might be selected as typical of Jacobean, or rather, early Stuart prose in its most gorgeous and imperial order."

THE SECOND OF MY PREBEND SERMONS UPON MY FIVE PSALMES. PREACHED AT S. PAULS, JANUARY 29, 1625 (1625/6).

Psal. 63.7. Because Thou Hast Been My Helpe, Therefore in the Shadow Of Thy Wings Will I Rejoyce.

The Psalmes are the Manna of the Church. As Manna tasted to every man like that that he liked best, so doe the Psalmes minister Instruction, and satisfaction, to every man, in every emergency and occasion. *David* was not onely a cleare Prophet of Christ himselfe, but a Prophet of every particular Christian; He foretels what I, what any shall doe, and suffer, and say. And as the whole booke of Psalmes is *** an Oyntment powred out upon all sorts of sores, A Searcloth that souples all bruises, A Balme that searches all wounds; so are there some certaine Psalmes, that are Imperiall Psalmes, that command over all affections, and spread themselves over all occasions, Catholique, universall Psalmes, that apply themselves to all necessities. This is one of those; for, of those Constitutions which are called Apostolicall, one is, That the Church should meet every day, to sing this Psalme. And accordingly, S. *Chrysostome* testifies, That it was decreed, and ordained by the Primitive Fathers, that no day should passe without the publique singing of this Psalme. Under both these obligations, (those ancient constitutions, called the Apostles, and those ancient Decrees made by the primitive Fathers) belongs to me, who have my part in the service of Gods Church, the especiall meditation, and recommendation of this

Psalme. And under a third obligation too, That it is
one of those five psalmes, the daily rehearsing whereof,
is injoyned to me, by the Constitutions of this Church,
as five other are to every other person of our body. As
the whole booke is Manna, so these five Psalmes are
my Gomer, which I am to fill and empty every day of
this Manna.

Now as the spirit and soule of the whole booke of
Psalmes is contracted into this psalme, so is the spirit
and soule of this whole psalme contracted into this
verse. The key of the psalme, (as S. *Hierome* calls the
Titles of the psalmes) tells us, that *David* uttered this
psalme, *when he was in the wildernesse of Iudah;*
There we see the present occasion that moved him;
And we see what was passed between God and him before, in the first clause of our Text; (*Because thou hast
been my helpe*) And then we see what was to come,
by the rest, (*Therefore in the shadow of thy wings will
I rejoyce.*) So that we have here the whole compasse
of Time, Past, Present, and Future; and these three
parts of Time, shall be at this time, the three parts of
this Exercise; first, what *Davids* distresse put him upon
for the present; and that lyes in the Context; secondly,
how *David* built his assurance upon that which was
past; (*Because thou hast been my help*) And thirdly,
what he established to himselfe for the future, (*Therefore in the shadow of thy wings will I rejoyce.*) First,
His distresse in the Wildernesse, his present estate
carried him upon the memory of that which God had
done for him before, And the Remembrance of that
carried him upon that, of which he assured himselfe
after. Fixe upon God any where, and you shall finde
him a Circle; He is with you now, when you fix upon
him; He was with you before, for he brought you to
this fixation; and he will be with you hereafter, for
He is yesterday, and to day, and the same for ever.

For *Davids* present condition, who was now in a
banishment, in a persecution in the Wildernesse of

Judah, (which is our first part) we shall onely insist upon that, (which is indeed spread over all the psalme to the Text, and ratified in the Text) That in all those temporall calamities *David* was onely sensible of his spirituall losse; It grieved him not that he was kept from *Sauls* Court, but that he was kept from Gods Church . . . That spirituall losses are incomparably heavier then temporall, and that therefore, The Restitution to our spirituall happinesse, or the continuation of it, is rather to be made the subject of our prayers to God, in all pressures and distresses, then of temporall, we shall determine that first part. And for the particular branches of both the other parts, (The Remembring of Gods benefits past, And the building of an assurance for the future, upon that Remembrance) it may be fitter to open them to you, anon when we come to handle them, then now. Proceed we now to our first part, The comparing of temporall and spirituall afflictions.

In the way of this Comparison, falls first the Consideration of the universality of afflictions in generall, and the inevitablenesse thereof. It is a blessed Metaphore, that the Holy Ghost hath put into the mouth of the Apostle, *Podus Gloriæ,* That our *afflictions* are but *light,* because there is an *exceeding,* and an *eternall waight of glory* attending them. If it were not for that exceeding waight of glory, no other waight in this world could turne the scale, or waigh downe those infinite waights of afflictions that oppresse us here. There is not onely *Pestis valde gravis (the pestilence grows heavy upon the Land)* but there is *Musca valde gravis,* God calls in but the fly, to vexe Egypt, and even the fly is a heavy burden unto them. It is not onely *Iob* that complains, *That he was a burden to himselfe,* but even *Absaloms* haire was a burden to him, till it was polled . . . *Sand is heavy,* sayes *Solomon;* And how many suffer so? under a sand-hill of crosses, daily, hourely afflictions, that are heavy by their number, if not by their single waight? And *a stone is heavy;* (sayes he in the same place) And how many suffer so? How many, without any former preparatory crosse, or comminatory, or commonitory crosse, even in the midst of prosperity, and security, fall under some one stone, some grindstone, some milstone, some one insupportable crosse that ruines them? But then, (sayes *Solomon* there) *A fooles anger is heavier then both;* And how many children, and servants, and wives suffer under the anger, and morosity, and peevishnesse, and jealousie of foolish Masters, and Parents, and Husbands, though they must not say so? *David* and *Solomon* have cryed out, That all this world is *vanity,* and *levity;* And (God knowes) all is waight, and burden, and heavinesse, and oppression; And if there were not a waight of future glory to counterpoyse it, we should all sinke into nothing.

I aske not *Mary Magdalen,* whether lightnesse were not a burden; (for sin is certainly, sensibly a burden) But I aske *Susanna* whether even chast beauty were not a burden to her; And I aske *Ioseph* whether personall comelinesse were not a burden to him. I aske not *Dives,* who perished in the next world, the question; but I aske them who are made examples of *Solomons* Rule, of that *sore evill,* (as he calls it) *Riches kept to the owners thereof for their hurt,* whether Riches be not a burden.

All our life is a continuall burden, yet we must not groane; A continuall squeasing, yet we must not pant; And as in the tendernesse of our childhood, we suffer, and yet are whipt if we cry, so we are complained of, if we complaine, and made delinquents if we call the times ill. And that which addes waight to waight, and multiplies the sadnesse of this consideration, is this, That still the best men have had most laid upon them. As soone as I heare God say, that he hath found *an upright man, that feares God, and eschews evill,* in the next lines I finde a Commission to Satan, to bring in

Sabeans and Chaldeans upon his cattell, and servants, and fire and tempest upon his children, and loathsome diseases upon himselfe. As soone as I heare God say, That he hath found *a man according to his own heart,* I see his sonnes ravish his daughters, and then murder one another, and then rebell against the Father, and put him into straites for his life. As soone as I heare God testifie of Christ at his Baptisme, *This is my beloved Sonne in whom I am well pleased,* I finde that Sonne of his *led up by the Spirit, to be tempted of the Devill.* And after I heare God ratifie the same testimony againe, at his Transfiguration, (*This is my beloved Sonne, in whom I am well pleased*) I finde that beloved Sonne of his, deserted, abandoned, and given over to Scribes, and Pharisees, and Publicans, and Herodians, and Priests, and Souldiers, and people, and Judges, and witnesses, and executioners, and he that was called the beloved Sonne of God, and made partaker of the glory of heaven, in this world, in his Transfiguration, is made now the Sewer of all the corruption, of all the sinnes of this world, as no Sonne of God, but a meere man, as no man, but a contemptible worme. As though the greatest weaknesse in this world, were man, and the greatest fault in man were to be good, man is more miserable then other creatures, and good men more miserable then any other men.

But then there is *Pondus Gloriæ, An exceeding waight of eternall glory,* and that turnes the scale; for as it makes all worldly prosperity as dung, so it makes all worldly adversity as feathers. And so it had need; for in the scale against it, there are not onely put temporall afflictions, but spirituall too; And to these two kinds, we may accommodate those words, *He that fals upon this stone,* (upon temporall afflictions) may be bruised, broken, *But he upon whom that stone falls,* (spirituall afflictions) *is in danger to be ground to powder.* And then, the great, and yet ordinary danger is, That these spirituall afflictions grow out of temporall; Murmuring, and diffidence in God, and obduration, out of worldly calamities; And so against nature, the fruit is greater and heavier then the Tree, spirituall heavier then temporall afflictions.

They who write of Naturall story, propose that Plant for the greatest wonder in nature, which being no firmer then a bull-rush, or a reed, produces and beares for the fruit thereof no other but an intire, and very hard stone. That temporall affliction should produce spirituall stoninesse, and obduration, is unnaturall, yet ordinary. Therefore doth God propose it, as one of those greatest blessings, which he multiplies upon his people, *I will take away your stony hearts, and give you hearts of flesh;* And, Lord let mee have a fleshly heart in any sense, rather then a stony heart. Wee finde mention amongst the observers of rarities in Nature, of hairy hearts, hearts of men, that have beene overgrowne with haire; but of petrified hearts, hearts of men growne into stone, we read not; for this petrefaction of the heart, this stupefaction of a man, is the last blow of Gods hand upon the heart of man in this world . . .

Let me wither and weare out mine age in a discomfortable, in an unwholesome, in a penurious prison, and so pay my debts with my bones, and recompence the wastfulnesse of my youth, with the beggery of mine age; Let me wither in a spittle under sharpe, and foule, and infamous diseases, and so recompence the wantonnesse of my youth, with that loathsomnesse in mine age; yet, if God with-draw not his spirituall blessings, his Grace, his Patience, If I can call my suffering his Doing, my passion his Action, All this that is temporall, is but a caterpiller got into one corner of my garden, but a mill-dew fallen upon one acre of my Corne; The body of all, the substance of all is safe, as long as the sould is safe. But when I shall trust to that, which wee call a good spirit, and God shall deject, and empoverish, and evacuate that spirit, when I shall rely upon a morall constancy, and God shall shake, and enfeeble, and enervate, destroy and demolish that constancy; when I shall think to refresh my selfe in the serenity and sweet ayre of a good conscience, and God shall call up the damps and vapours of hell it selfe, and spread a cloud of diffidence, and an impenetrable crust of desperation upon my conscience; when health shall flie from me, and I shall lay hold upon the riches to succour me, and comfort me in my sicknesse, and riches shall flie from me, and I shall snatch after favour, and good opinion, to comfort me in my poverty; when even this good opinion shall leave me, and calumnies and misinformations shall prevaile against me; when I shall need peace, because there is none but thou, O Lord, that should stand for me, and then shall finde, that all the wounds that I have, come from thy hand, all the arrowes that stick in me, from thy quiver; when I shall see, that because I have given my selfe to my corrupt nature, thou hast changed thine; and because I am all evill towards thee, therefore thou hast given over being good towards me; When it comes to this height, that the fever is not in the humors, but in the spirits, that mine enemy is not an imaginary enemy, fortune, nor a transitory enemy, malice in great persons, but a reall, and an irresistible, and an inexorable, and an everlasting enemy, The Lord of Hosts himselfe, The Almighty God himselfe, the Almighty God himselfe onely knowes the waight of this affliction, and except hee put in that *pondus gloriæ*, that exceeding waight of an eternall glory, with his owne hand, into the other scale, we are waighed downe, we are swallowed up, irreparably, irrevocably, irrecoverably, irremediably.

This is the fearefull depth, this is spirituall misery, to be thus fallen from God. But was this *Davids* case? was he fallen thus farre, into a diffidence in God? No. But the danger, the precipice, the slippery sliding into that bottomlesse depth, is, to be excluded from the meanes of comming to God, or staying with God; And this is that that *David* laments here, That by being banished, and driven into the wildernesse of Judah, hee had not accesse to the Sanctuary of the Lord, to sacrifice his part in the praise, and to receive his part in the prayers of the Congregation; for Angels passe not to ends, but by wayes and meanes, nor men to the glory of the triumphant Church, but by participation of the Communion of the Militant. To this note *David* sets his Harpe, in many, many Psalms: Sometimes, that God had suffered his enemies to possess his Tabernacle, (*Hee forsooke the Tabernacle of Shiloh, Hee delivered his strength into captivity, and his glory into the enemies hands*) But most commonly he complaines, that God disabled him from coming to the Sanctuary. In which one thing he had summed up all his desires, all his prayers, (*One thing have I desired of the Lord, that will I looke after; That I may dwell in the house of the Lord, all the dayes of my life, to behold the beauty of the Lord, and to enquire in his Temple*) His vehement desire of this, he expresses againe, (*My soule thirsteth for God, for the living God; when shall I come and appeare before God?*) He expresses a holy jealousie, a religious envy, even to the sparrows and swallows, (yea, *the sparrow hath found a house, and the swallow a nest for her selfe, and where she may lay her yong, Even thine Altars, O Lord of Hosts, my King and my God.*) Thou art my King, and my God, and yet excludest me from that, which thou affordest to sparrows, *And are not we of more value then many sparrows?*

And as though *David* felt some false ease, some halftentation, some whispering that way, That God is *in the wildernesse of Iudah,* in every place, as well as in his *Sanctuary,* there is in the Originall in that place, a patheticall, a vehement, a broken expressing expresses, *O thine Altars;* It is true, (sayes *David*) thou

art here in the wildernesse, and I may see thee here,
and serve thee here, but, *O thine Altars, O Lord of
hosts, my King and my God.* When *David* could not
come in person to that place, yet he bent towards the
Temple, (*In thy feare will I worship towards thy
holy Temple.*) Which was also *Daniels* devotion; when
he prayed, *his Chamber windowes were open towards
Ierusalem;* And so is *Hezekias* turning to the wall to
weepe, and to pray in his sick bed, understood to be
to that purpose, to conforme, and compose himselfe
towards the Temple. In the place consecrated for that
use, God by *Moses* fixes the service, and fixes the Reward; And towards that place, (when they could not
come to it) doth *Solomon* direct their devotion in the
Consecration of the Temple, (*when they are in the
warres, when they are in Captivity, and pray towards
this house, doe thou heare them.*) For, as in private
prayer, when (according to Christs command) we are
shut in our chamber, there is exercised *Modestia fidei,*
The modesty and bashfulnesse of our faith, not pressing upon God in his house: so in the publique prayers
of the Congregation, there is exercised the fervor, and
holy courage of our faith, for *Agmine facto obsidemus
Deum,* It is a Mustering of our forces, and a besieging
of God. Therefore does *David* so much magnifie their
blessednesse, that are in this house of God; (*Blessed
are they that dwell in thy house, for they will be still
praising thee*) Those that looke towards it, may praise
thee sometimes, but those men who dwell in the
Church, and whose whole service lyes in the Church,
have certainly an advantage of all other men (who are
necessarily withdrawne by worldly businesses) in making themselves acceptable to almighty God, if they doe
their duties, and observe their Church-services aright.

Man being therefore thus subject naturally to manifold calamities, and spirituall calamities being incomparably heavier then temporall, and the greatest danger of falling into such spirituall calamities being in

our absence from Gods Church, where onely the outward meanes of happinesse are ministred unto us, certainly there is much tendernesse and deliberation to be used, before the Church doores be shut against any man. If I would not direct a prayer to God, to excommunicate any man from the Triumphant Church, (which were to damne him) I would not oyle the key, I would not make the way too slippery for excommunications in the Militant Church; For, that is to endanger him . . . for, though every Excommunication upon earth be not sealed in Heaven, though it damne not the man, yet it dammes up that mans way, by shutting him out of that Church, through which he must goe to the other; which being so great a danger, let every man take heed of Excommunicating himselfe. The imperswasible Recusant does so; The negligent Libertin does so; The fantastique Separatist does so; The halfe-present man, he, whose body is here, and minde away, does so; And he, whose body is but halfe here, his limbes are here upon a cushion, but his eyes, his eares are not here, does so: All these are selfe-Excommunicators, and keepe themselves from hence. Onely he enjoyes that blessing, the want whereof *David* deplores, that is here intirely, and is glad he is here, and glad to finde this kinde of service here, that he does, and wishes no other.

And so we have done with our first Part, *Davids* aspect, his present condition, and his danger of falling into spirituall miseries, because his persecution, and banishment amounted to an Excommunication, to an excluding of him from the service of God, in the Church. And we passe, in our Order proposed at first, to the second, his retrospect, the Consideration, what God had done for him before, *Because thou hast beene my helpe.*

Through this second part, we shall passe by these three steps. First, That it behoves us, in all our purposes, and actions, to propose to our selves a copy to write by, a patterne to worke by, a rule, or an example to proceed by, Because it hath beene thus heretofore, sayes *David,* I will resolve upon this course for the future. And secondly, That the copy, the patterne, the precedent which we are to propose to our selves, is, The observation of Gods former wayes and proceedings upon us, Because God hath already gone this way, this way I will awaite his going still. And then, thirdly and lastly, in this second part, The way that God had formerly gone with *David,* which was, That he had been his helpe, (*Because thou hast beene my helpe.*)

First then, from the meanest artificer, through the wisest Philosopher, to God himselfe, all that is well done, or wisely undertaken, is undertaken and done according to pre-conceptions, fore-imaginations, designes, and patterns proposed to our selves beforehand. A Carpenter builds not a house, but that he first sets up a frame in his owne minde, what kinde of house he will build. The little great Philosopher *Epictetus,* would undertake no action, but he would first propose to himselfe, what *Socrates,* or *Plato,* what a wise man would do in that case, and according to that, he would proceed. Of God himselfe, it is safely resolved in the Schoole, that he never did any thing in any part of time, of which he had not an eternall pre-conception, an eternall Idea, in himselfe before . . . Of all things in Heaven, and earth, but of himselfe, God had an Idea, a patterne in himselfe, before he made it.

And therefore let him be our patterne for that, to worke after patternes; To propose to our selves Rules and Examples for all our actions; and the more, the more immediately, the more directly our actions concerne the service of God. If I aske God, by what Idea he made me, God produces his *Faciamus hominem ad Imaginem nostram,* That there was a concurrence of the whole Trinity, to make me in *Adam,* according to that Image which they were, and according to that Idea, which they had pre-determined. If I pretend to serve God, and he aske me for my Idea, How I meane to serve him, shall I bee able to produce none? If he ask me an Idea of my Religion, and my opinions, shall I not be able to say, It is that which thy word, and thy Catholique Church hath imprinted in me? If he aske me an Idea of my prayers, shall I not be able to say, It is that which my particular necessities, that which the forme prescribed by thy Son, that which the care, and piety of the Church, in conceiving fit prayers, hath imprinted in me? If he aske me an Idea of my Sermons, shall I not be able to say, It is that which the Analogy of Faith, the edification of the Congregation, the zeale of thy worke, the meditations of my heart have imprinted in me? But if I come to pray or to preach without this kind of Idea, if I come to extemporall prayer, and extemporall preaching, I shall come to an extemporall faith, and extemporall religion; and then I must looke for an extemporall Heaven, a Heaven to be made for me; for to that Heaven which belongs to the Catholique Church, I shall never come, except I go by the way of the Catholique Church, by former Idea's, former examples, former patterns, To beleeve according to ancient beliefes, to pray according to ancient formes, to preach according to former meditations. God does nothing, man does nothing well, without these Idea's, these retrospects, this recourse to pre-conceptions, pre-deliberations.

Something then I must propose to my selfe, to be the rule, and the reason of my present and future actions; which was our first branch in this second Part; And then the second is, That I can propose nothing more availably, then the contemplation of the history of Gods former proceeding with me; which is *Davids* way here, Because this was Gods way before, I will looke for God in this way still. That language in which God spake to man, the Hebrew, hath no present tense; They forme not their verbs as our West-erne Languages do, in the present, *I heare,* or *I see,* or *I reade,* But they begin at that which is past, *I have seene* and *heard,* and *read.* God carries us in his Lan-guage, in his speaking, upon that which he hath done already; I cannot have better security for present, nor future, then Gods former mercies exhibited to me ***.

There is no State, no Church, no Man, that hath not this tie upon God, that hath not God in these bands, That God by having done much for them already, hath bound himselfe to doe more. Men proceed in their former wayes, sometimes, lest they should con-fesse an error, and acknowledge that they had beene in a wrong way. God is obnoxious to no error, and therefore he does still, as he did before. Every one of you can say now to God, Lord, Thou broughtest me hither, therefore enable me to heare; Lord, Thou doest that, therefore make me understand; And that, therefore let me beleeve; And that too, therefore strengthen me to the practise; And all that, therefore continue me to a perseverance. Carry it up to the first sense and apprehension that ever thou hadst of Gods working upon thee, either in thy selfe, when thou camest first to the use of reason, or in others in thy behalfe, in thy baptisme, yet when thou thinkest thou art at the first, God had done something for thee before all that . . . God had thee, before he made thee; He loved thee first, and then created thee, that thou loving him, he might continue his love to thee. The surest way, and the nearest way to lay hold upon God, is the consideration of that which he had done already. So *David* does; And that which he takes knowledge of, in particular, in Gods former proceed-ings towards him, is, Because God had been his helpe, which is our last branch in this part, *Because thou hast beene my helpe.*

From this one word, That God hath been my *Helpe,* I make account that we have both these no-

tions; first, That God hath not left me to my selfe, He
hath come to my succour, He hath helped me; And
then, That God hath not left out my selfe; He hath
been my Helpe, but he hath left some thing for me to
doe with him, and by his helpe. My security for the
future, in this consideration of that which is past, lyes
not onely in this, That God hath delivered me, but in
this also, that he hath delivered me by way of a
Helpe, and Helpe alwayes presumes an endevour and
co-operation in him that is helped. God did not elect
me as a helper, nor create me, nor redeeme me, nor
convert me, by way of helping me; for he alone did all,
and he had no use at all of me. God infuses his first
grace, the first way, meerly as a Giver; intirely, all
himselfe; but his subsequent graces, as a helper; therefore we call them Auxiliant graces, Helping graces;
and we alwayes receive them, when we endevour
to make use of his former grace. *Lord, I beleeve*
(sayes the Man in the Gospel to Christ) *Helpe mine
unbeliefe.* If there had not been unbeliefe, weaknesse,
unperfectnesse in that faith, there had needed no
helpe; but if there had not been a Beliefe, a Faith,
it had not been capable of helpe and assistance, but
it must have been an intire act, without any concurrence on the mans part.

So that if I have truly the testimony of a rectified
Conscience, That God hath helped me, it is in both
respects; first, That he hath never forsaken me, and
then, That he hath never suffered me to forsake my
selfe; He hath blessed me with that grace, that I trust
in no helpe but his, and with this grace too, That I
cannot looke for his helpe, except I helpe my selfe
also. God did not helpe heaven and earth to proceed
out of nothing in the Creation, for they had no possibility of any disposition towards it; for they had no
beeing: But God did helpe the earth to produce grasse,
and herbes; for, for that, God had infused a seminall
disposition into the earth, which, for all that, it could

not have perfected without his farther helpe. As in
the making of Woman, there is the very word of our
Text, *Gnazar,* God made him a *Helper,* one that was
to doe much for him, but not without him. So that
then, if I will make Gods former working upon me, an
argument of his future gracious purposes, as I must
acknowledge that God hath done much for me, so I
must finde, that I have done what I could, by the benefit of that grace with him; for God promises to be but
a helper. *Lord open thou my lips,* says *David;* that
is Gods worke intirely; And then, *My mouth, My
mouth shall shew forth thy praise;* there enters *David*
into the worke with God. And then, sayes God to him,
Dilata os tuum, Open thy mouth, (It is now made
Thy mouth, and therefore doe thou open it) *and I
will fill it;* All inchoations and consummations, beginnings and perfectings are of God, of God alone; but
in the way there is a concurrence on our part, (by a
successive continuation of Gods grace) in which God
proceeds as a Helper; and I put him to more then that,
if I doe nothing. But if I pray for his helpe, and apprehend and husband his graces well, when they come,
then he is truly, properly my helper; and upon that
security, that testimony of a rectified Conscience, I
can proceed to *Davids* confidence for the future, *Because thou hast been my Helpe, therefore in the
shadow of thy wings will I rejoyce;* which is our third,
and last generall part.

   In this last part, which is . . . his prospect, his
confidence for the future, we shall stay a little upon
these two steps; first, That that which he promises
himselfe, is not an immunity from all powerfull enemies, nor a sword of revenge upon those enemies;
It is not that he shall have no adversary, nor that
that adversary shall be able to doe him no harme, but
that he should have a refreshing, a respiration, *In
velamento alarum,* under the shadow of Gods wings.
And then, (in the second place) That this way which

God shall be pleased to take, this manner, this measure of refreshing, which God shall vouchsafe to afford, (though it amount not to a full deliverance) must produce a joy, a rejoycing in us; we must not onely not decline to a murmuring, that we have no more, no nor rest upon a patience for that which remains, but we must ascend to a holy joy, as if all were done and accomplished, *In the shadow of thy wings will I rejoyce.*

First then, lest any man in his dejection of spirit, or of fortune, should stray into a jealousie or suspition of Gods power to deliver him, As God hath spangled the firmament with starres, so hath he his Scriptures with names, and Metaphors, and denotations of power. Sometimes he shines out in the name of a *Sword,* and of a *Target,* and of a *Wall,* and of a *Tower,* and of a *Rocke,* and of a *Hill;* And sometimes in that glorious and manifold constellation of all together, *Dominus exercituum, The Lord of Hosts.* God, as God, is never represented to us, with Defensive Armes; He needs them not. When the Poets present their great Heroes, and their Worthies, they alwayes insist upon their Armes, they spend much of their invention upon the description of their Armes; both because the greatest valour and strength needs Armes, (*Goliah* himselfe was armed) and because to expose ones selfe to danger unarmed, is not valour, but rashnesse. But God is invulnerable in himselfe, and is never represented armed; you finde no shirts of mayle, no Helmets, no Cuirasses in Gods Armory . . . But though God need not, nor receive not defensive armes for himselfe, yet God is to us a Helmet, a Breastplate, a strong tower, a rocke, every thing that may give us assurance and defence; and as often as he will, he can refresh that Proclamation, *Nolite tangere Christos meos,* Our enemies shall not so much as touch us.

But here, by occasion of his Metaphore in this Text, (*Sub umbra alarum, In the shadow of thy wings*) we doe not so much consider an absolute immunity, That we shall not be touched, as a refreshing and consolation, when we are touched, though we be pinched and wounded. The Names of God, which are most frequent in the Scriptures, are these three, *Elohim,* and *Adonai,* and *Iehovah;* and to assure us of his Power to deliver us, two of these three are Names of Power. *Elohim* is *Deus fortis,* The mighty, The powerfull God: And (which deserves a particular consideration) *Elohim* is a plurall Name; It is not *Deus fortis,* but *Dii fortes,* powerfull Gods. God is all kinde of Gods; All kinds, which either Idolaters and Gentils can imagine, (as Riches, or Justice, or Wisdome, or Valour, or such) and all kinds which God himselfe hath called gods, as Princes, and Magistrates, and Prelates, and all that assist and helpe one another) God is *Elohim,* All these Gods, and all these in their height and best of their power; for *Elohim,* is *Dii fortes,* Gods in the plurall, and those plurall gods in their exaltation.

The second Name of God, is a Name of power too, *Adonai.* For, *Adonai* is *Dominus,* The Lord, such a Lord, as is Lord and Proprietary of all his creatures, and all creatures are his creatures***God, as he is *Adonai, The Lord,* may give and take, quicken and kill, build and throw downe, where and whom he will. So then two of Gods three Names are Names of absolute power, to imprint, and re-imprint an assurance in us, that hee can absolutely deliver us, and fully revenge us, if he will. But then, his third Name, and that Name which hee chooses to himselfe, and in the signification of which Name, hee employes *Moses,* for the reliefe of his people under Pharaoh, that Name *Iehovah,* is not a Name of Power, but onely of Essence, of Being, of Subsistence, and yet in the vertue of that Name, God relieved his people. And if, in my afflictions, God vouchsafe to visit mee in that Name, to preserve me in my being, in my subsistence in him, that I be not shaked out of him, disinherited in him, excommunicate from him, devested of him, annihilated towards him, let him, at his good pleasure, reserve his *Elohim,* and his *Adonai,* the exercises and declarations of his mighty Power, to those great publike causes, that more concerne his Glory, then any thing that can befall me; But if he impart his *Iehovah,* enlarge himselfe so far towards me, as that I may live, and move, and have my beeing in him, though I be not instantly delivered, nor mine enemies absolutely destroyed, yet this is as much as I should promise my selfe, this is as much as the Holy Ghost intends in this Metaphor, *Sub umbra alarum, Vnder the shadow of thy wings,* that is a Refreshing, a Respiration, a Conservation, a Consolation in all afflictions that are inflicted upon me.

Yet, is not this Metaphor of *Wings* without a denotation of Power. As no Act of Gods, though it seeme to imply but spirituall comfort, is without a denotation of power, (for it is the power of God that comforts me; To overcome that sadnesse of soule, and that dejection of spirit, which the Adversary by temporall afflictions would induce upon me, is an act of his Power) So this Metaphor, *The shadow of his wings,* (which in this place expresses no more, then consolation and refreshing in misery, and not a powerfull deliverance out of it) is so often in the Scriptures made a denotation of Power too, as that we can doubt of no act of power, if we have this shadow of his wings. For, in this Metaphor of *Wings,* doth the Holy Ghost expresse the *Maritime* power, the power of some Nations at Sea, in Navies, (*Woe to the land shadowing with wings;*) that is, that hovers over the world, and intimidates it with her sailes and ships. In this Metaphor doth God remember his people, of his powerfull deliverance of them, (*You have seene what I did unto the Egyptians, and how I bare you on Eagles wings, and brought you to my selfe.*) In this Metaphor doth God threaten his and their enemies, what hee can doe,

(*The noise of the wings of his Cherubims, are as the noise of great waters, and of an Army.*) So also, what hee will doe, (*Hee shall spread his wings over Bozrah, and at that day shall the hearts of the mighty men of Edom, be as the heart of a woman in her pangs.*) So that, if I have the shadow of his wings, I have the earnest of the power of them too . . . Be it knowne unto thee, O Satan, how long soever God deferre my deliverance, I will not seeke false comforts, the miserable comforts of This world. I will not, for I need not; for I can subsist under this shadow of these Wings, though I have no more.

The Mercy-seat it selfe was covered with the Cherubims Wings; and who would have more then Mercy? and a Mercy-seat; that is, established, resident Mercy, permanent and perpetuall Mercy; present and familiar Mercy; a Mercy-seat. Our Saviour Christ intends as much as would have served their turne, if they had laid hold upon it, when hee sayes, *That hee would have gathered Ierusalem, as a henne gathers her chickens under her wings.* And though the other Prophets doe (as ye have heard) mingle the signification of Power, and actuall deliverance, in this Metaphor of Wings (which are in five or sixe severall Psalmes) still hee rests and determines in that sense, which is his meaning here; That though God doe not actually deliver us, nor actually destroy our enemies, yet if hee refresh us in the shadow of his Wings, if he maintaine our subsistence (which is a religious Constancy) in him, this should not onely establish our patience, (for that is but halfe the worke) but it should also produce a joy, and rise to an exultation, which is our last circumstance, *Therefore in the shadow of thy wings, I will rejoice.*

I would always raise your hearts, and dilate your hearts, to a holy Joy, to a joy in the Holy Ghost. There may be a just feare, that men doe not grieve enough for their sinnes; but there may bee a just jealousie, and suspition too, that they may fall into inordinate griefe, and diffidence of Gods mercy; And God hath reserved us to such times, as being the later times, give us even the dregs and lees of misery to drinke. For, God hath not onely let loose into the world a new spirituall disease; which is, an equality, and an indifferency, which religion our children, or our servants, or our companions professe; (I would not keepe company with a man that thought me a knave, or a traitor; with him that thought I loved not my Prince, or were a faithlesse man, not to be beleeved, I would not associate my selfe; And yet I will make him my bosome companion, that thinks I doe not love God, that thinks I cannot be saved) but God hath accompanied, and complicated almost all our bodily diseases of these times, with an extraordinary sadnesse, a predominant melancholy, a faintnesse of heart, a chearlesnesse, a joylesnesse of spirit, and therefore I returne often to this endeavor of raising your hearts, dilating your hearts with a holy Joy, Joy in the holy Ghost, for *Vnder the shadow of his wings,* you may, you should, *rejoyce.*

If you looke upon this world in a Map, you find two Hemisphears, two half worlds. If you crush heaven into a Map, you may find two Hemisphears too, two half heavens; Halfe will be Joy, and halfe will be Glory; for in these two, the joy of heaven, and the glory of heaven, is all heaven often represented unto us. And as of those two Hemisphears of the world, the first hath been knowne long before, but the other, (that of America, which is the richer in treasure) God reserved for later Discoveries; So though he reserve that Hemisphear of heaven, which is the Glory therof, to the Resurrection, yet the other Hemisphear, the Joy of heaven, God opens to our Discovery, and delivers for our habitation even whilst we dwell in this world. As God hath cast upon the unrepentant sinner two deaths, a temporall, and a spirituall death, so hath he breathed into us two lives; for so, as the word for death is doubled, *Morte morieris, Thou shalt die the death,* so is the word for life expressed in the plurall, *Chaiim, vitarum, God breathed into his nostrils the breath of lives,* of divers lives. Though our naturall life were no live, but rather a continuall dying, yet we have two lives besides that, an eternall life reserved for heaven, but yet a heavenly life too, a spirituall life, even in this world; And as God doth thus inflict two deaths, and infuse two lives, so doth he also passe two Judgements upon man, or rather repeats the same Judgement twice. For, that which Christ shall say to thy soule then at the last Judgement, *Enter into thy Masters joy,* Hee sayes to thy conscience now, *Enter into thy Masters joy.* The everlastingnesse of the joy is the blessednesse of the next life, but the entring, the inchoation is afforded here. For that which Christ shall say then to us, *Venite benedicti, Come ye blessed,* are words intended to persons that are comming, that are upon the way, though not at home; Here in this world he bids us *Come,* there in the next, he shall bid us *Welcome.* The Angels of heaven have joy in thy conversion, and canst thou bee without that joy in thy selfe? If thou desire revenge upon thine enemies, as they are Gods enemies, That God would bee pleased to remove, and root out all such as oppose him, that Affection appertaines to Glory; Let that alone till thou come to the Hemisphear of Glory; There joyne with those martyrs under the Altar, *Vsquequo Domine,* How long O Lord, dost thou deferre Judgement? And thou shalt have thine answere there for that. Whilst thou art here, here joyne with *David,* and the other Saints of God, in that holy increpation of a dangerous sadnesse, *Why art thou cast downe O my sould? why art thou disquieted in mee?* That soule that is dissected and anatomized to God, in a sincere confession, washed in the teares of true contrition, embalmed in the blood of reconciliation, the blood of Christ Jesus, can assigne no reason, can give no just answer to that Interrogatory, *Why art thou cast downe O my soule? why art thou disquieted in me?* No man is so little, as that he can be lost under these wings, no man so great, as that they cannot reach to him***To what temporall, to what spirituall greatnesse soever wee grow, still pray wee him to shadow us under his Wings; for the poore need those wings against oppression, and the rich against envy. The Holy Ghost, who is a Dove, shadowed the whole world under his wings; *Incubabat aquis,* He hovered over the waters, he sate upon the waters, and he hatched all that was produced, and all that was produced so, was good. Be thou a Mother where the Holy Ghost would be a Father; Conceive by him; and be content that he produce joy in thy heart here. First thinke, that as a man must have some land, or els he cannot be in wardship, so a man must have some of the love of God, or els he could not fall under Gods correction; God would not give him his physick, God would not study his cure, if he cared not for him. And then thinke also, that if God afford thee the shadow of his wings, that is, Consolation, respiration, refreshing, though not a present, and plenary deliverance, in thy afflictions, not to thanke God, is a murmuring, and not to rejoyce in Gods wayes, is an unthankfulnesse. Howling is the noyse of hell, singing the voyce of heaven; Sadnesse the damp of Hell, Rejoycing the serenity of Heaven. And he that hath not this joy here, lacks one of the best pieces of his evidence for the joyes of heaven; and hath neglected or refused that Earnest, by which God uses to binde his bargaine, that true joy in this world shall flow into the joy of Heaven, as a River flowes into the Sea; This joy shall not be put out in death, and a new joy kindled in me in Heaven; But as my soule, as soone as it is out of my body, is in Heaven, and does not stay for the

possession of Heaven, nor for the fruition of the
sight of God, till it be ascended through ayre, and
fire, and Moone, and Sun, and Planets, and Firmament, to that place which we conceive to be Heaven,
but without the thousandth part of a minutes stop,
as soone as it issues, is in a glorious light, which is
Heaven, (for all the way to Heaven is Heaven; And
as those Angels, which came from Heaven hither,
bring Heaven with them, and are in Heaven here,
So that soule that goes to Heaven, meets Heaven here;
and as those Angels doe not devest Heaven by comming, so these soules invest Heaven, in their going.)
As my sould shall not goe towards Heaven, but goe
by Heaven to Heaven, to the Heaven of Heavens, So
the true joy of a good soule in this world is the very
joy of Heaven; and we goe thither, not that being
without joy, we might have joy infused into us, but
that as Christ sayes, *Our joy might be full,* perfected,
sealed with an everlastingnesse; for, as he promises,
That no man shall take our joy from us, so neither
shall Death it selfe take it away, nor so much as interrupt it, or discontinue it, But as in the face of Death,
when he layes hold upon me, and in the face of the
Devill, when he attempts me, I shall see the face of
God, (for, every thing shall be a glasse, to reflect God
upon me) so in the agonies of Death, in the anguish of
that dissolution, in the sorrowes of that valediction,
in the irreversiblenesse of that transmigration, I shall
have a joy, which shall no more evaporate, then my
soule shall evaporate, A joy, that shall passe up,
and put on a more glorious garment above, and be
joy super-invested in glory. *Amen.*

SERMON PREACHED AT ST. PAUL'S CATHEDRAL

London, Easter Day, 1625
(John 5:28-29)

V

EDITOR'S PREFACE

The appointment to the Deanery of St. Paul's was more
than a satisfaction to John Donne. It was a fulfillment.
Settling down to his new office, he settled into his
vocation at last. All through his Lincoln's Inn pastor-
ate, in all his early Whitehall preaching he had been
maturing as theologian and as homiletician. But now
he was to grow swiftly into his greatness as a preacher
—which involves something more than theology and
homiletics.

Earlier there had been the repeated sense of a
learned, witty, earnest man working on his sermons,
working at his preaching. Not that the impression was
ever one of disengagement. From the beginning he
was much in his own utterance; Donne always threw
himself into what he said. But in the high years at
St. Paul's the effect is more of sermons being thrown
through John Donne, of sermons not so much worked
at from outside, but working themselves out from
inside the preacher. There is less exterior tinkering,
more emergence whole from an increasingly whole
person. No longer preaching to special groups—
lawyers, courtiers—but to great cross-sectional congregations, Donne spreads his focus, brings into play
more and more of his general learning, experience,
intuitions, sympathies. These are the great, rich
sermons. Poet and preacher are no longer in balance,

each seeking to realize himself in one service. That cordial mutuality between past and present persons in the one person had produced splendid sermons. But now the poet was in glad service of the preacher, and the preacher was in more and more serious service of the Word. From that ordering of extraordinary talents, great art was the issue, splendid sermons, a reverberating Christian witness.

Signs of what was happening show all through the quiet Easter evening sermon Donne preached at St. Paul's in 1625. His royal patron, King James I, had died a fortnight before, March 25. Donne had already preached on command before the new king, Charles I, to general approval. A few days after Easter Donne would preach over the body of King James just before its burial. But now, on Easter, he evidently preaches the sermon he had projected and planned before the excitement of the royal demise. Instead of the emphasis usual in Donne's Easter sermons—and one that would have been especially acceptable to a nation in mourning—on the resurrection of Christ, the accent here is on the positive meaning of the resurrection for this present body.

Note has already been taken of how genuinely, classically and contemporarily Christian this affirmation of the body is. Over against every false asceticism which seeks to sneak an idealistic depreciation of the flesh into the church under the guise of Christian abnegation, John Donne here proceeds from Creation, Incarnation and eschatology to a solid affirmation of the never too solid flesh.

Again, observe him reach back to the first century and ahead to the twentieth when he draws from the doctrine of the resurrection of the body certain strictures on the place of torture in legal practice. Who else in the seevententh century was making ethics consequent to eschatology?

PREACHED AT S. PAULS,
IN THE EVENING,
UPON EASTER-DAY, 1625.

John 5.28 and 29. Marvell Not at This; for the Houre Is Comming, in the Which, All That Are in the Graves, Shall Heare His Voice; and Shall Come Forth, They That Have Done Good, Unto the Resurrection of Life; and They That Have Done Evill, Unto the Resurrection of Damnation.

As the Sun works diversly, according to the diverse disposition of the subject, (for the Sun melts wax, and it hardens clay) so do the good actions of good men: upon good men they work a vertuous emulation, a noble and a holy desire to imitate, upon bad men they work a vicious, and impotent envy, a desire to disgrace, and calumniate. And the more the good is that is done, and the more it works upon good men, the more it disaffects the bad: for so the Pharisees expresse their rancor and malignity against Christ, in this Gospel, *If we let him thus alone, all men will beleeve in him;* And that they foresaw would destroy them in their reputation. And therefore they enlarged their malice, beyond Christ himselfe, to him, upon whom Christ had wrought a Miracle, to *Lazarus, They consulted to put him to death, because by reason of him, many beleeved in Iesus.* Our Text leads us to another example of this impotency in envious men; Christ, in this Chapter had, by his only word, cured a man that had been eight and thirty yeares infirm; and he had done this work upon the Sabbath. They envyed the work in the substance, but they quarrell the circumstance; And they envy Christ, but they turn upon the man, who was more obnoxious to them; and they tell him, *That it was not lawfull for him to carry his bed that day*. He discharges himself upon Christ; I dispute not with you concerning the Law; This satisfies me, *He that made me whole, bad me take up my bed and walk*. Thereupon they put him to finde out Jesus; And when he could not finde Jesus, Jesus found him, and in his behalf offers himself to the Pharisees. Then they direct themselves upon him, and (as the Gospell sayes) *They sought to slay him, because he had done this upon the Sabbath:* And, as the patient had discharged himself upon Christ, Christ discharges himself upon his Father; doth it displease you that I work upon the Sabbath? be angry with God, be angry with the Father, for the Father works when I work. And then this they take worse then his working of Miracles, or his working upon the Sabbath, *That he would say, that God was his Father;* And therefore in the averring of that, that so important point, *That God was his Father,* Christ grows into a holy vehemence, and earnestnesse, and he repeats his usuall oath, *Verily, verily,* three severall times: First, ver. 19. *That whatsoever the Father doth, He, the Son, doth also, And* then ver. 24. *He that beleeveth on me, and him that sent me, hath life everlasting.* And then again, ver. 25. *The houre is comming, and now is, when the dead shall heare the voice of the Son of God, and they that heare it shall live.* At this, that the dead should live, they marvelled; But because he knew that they were men more affected with things concerning the body, then spirituall things, as in another story, when they wondered that he would pretend to forgive sins, because he knew, that they thought it a greater matter to bid that man that had the Palsie, take up his bed and walk, then to forgive him his sins, therefore he took that way which was hardest in their opinion, he did bid him take up his bed and walk; So here, when they wondred at his speaking of a spirituall Resurrection, to heare him say, that at his preaching, the dead (that is, men spiritually dead in their sins) should rise again, to them who more respected the body, and did lesse beleeve a reall Resurrection of the body, then a figurative Resurrection of the soul, he proceeds to that which was, in their apprehension, the more difficult, *Marvel not at this,* sayes he, here in our Text; not at that spirituall Resurrection by preaching, *for the houre is comming, in the which, all that are in the graves, &c.* and so he establishes the Resurrection of the body.

That then which Christ affirmes and avows, is, That he is the Son of God; and that is the first thing, that ever was done in Heaven, The eternall generation of the Son: that, by which, he proves this, to these men, is, That by him, there shall be a resurrection of the body; and that is the last thing, that shall be done in Heaven, for, after that, there is nothing, but an even continuance in equall glory. Before that, saies he, that is, before the resurrection of the body, there shall be another resurrection, a spirituall resurrection of the soule from sin; but that shall be, by ordinary meanes, by Preaching, and Sacraments, and it shall be accomplished every day; but fix not upon that, determin not your thoughts upon that, marvaile not at that, make that no cause of extraordinary wonder, but make it ordinary to you, feele it, and finde the effect thereof in your soules, as often as you heare, as often as you receive, and thereby provide for another resurrection, *For, the houre is comming, in which, all that are in their graves, &c.*

Where we must necessarily make thus many steps, though but short ones. First, the dignity of the Resurrection, marvaile at nothing so much, as at this, nothing is so marvailous, so wonderfull as this; And secondly, the approach of the Resurrection, *The houre*

is comming; And thirdly, The generality, *All that
are in the graves;* and then instrument of the resurrection, *The voice of Christ; that shall be heard;* And
lastly, the diverse end of the resurrection, *They shall
come forth, they that have done good, &c.* God hath a
care of the Body of man, that is first; And he defers it
not, that is next; And he extends it to all, that is a
third; And a fourth is, That he does that last act,
by him, by whom he did the first, The Creation, and
all betweene, the Redemption, that is, by his Son,
by Christ; And then the last is, that this is an everlasting separation and divorce of the good and the
bad, The bad shall never be able to receive good
from the Good, nor to doe harme to the Good, after
that.

First then, Christ saies, *Ne miremini, Marvaile not
at this,* not at your spirituall resurrection, not that a
Sermon should worke upon man, not that a Sacrament
should comfort a man, make it not a miracle, nor
an extraordinary thing, by hearing to come to repentance, and so to such a resurrection. For though
S. *Augustine* say, That to convert a man from sin, is
as great a miracle, as Creation, yet S. *Augustine* speaks
that of a mans first conversion, in which the man himselfe does nothing, but God all; Then he is made of
nothing; but after God hath renewed him, and proposed ordinary meanes in the Church still to worke
upon him, he must not looke for miraculous working,
but make Gods ordinary meanes, ordinary to him.
This is *Panis quotidianus,* The daily bread which God
give you, as often as you meet here, according to his
Ordinances; *Ne miremini,* stand not to wonder, as
though you were not sure, but come to enjoy Gods
goodnesse, in his ordinary way here.

But it is, *Ne miremini hoc, Wonder not at this;*
but yet, there are things, which we may wonder at.
Nil admirari, is but the Philosophers wisdome; He
thinks it a weaknesse, to wonder at any thing, That

any thing should be strange to him: But Christian Philosophy that is rooted in humility, tels us, in the mouth of *Clement* of *Alexandria, Principium veritatis est res admirari,* The first step to faith, is to wonder, to stand, and consider with a holy admiration, the waies and proceedings of God with man: for, Admiration, wonder, stands as in the midst, betweene knowledge and faith, and hath an eye towards both. If I know a thing, or beleeve a thing, I do no longer wonder: but when I finde that I have reason to stop upon the consideration of a thing, so, as that I see enough to induce admiration, to make me wonder, I come by that step, and God leads me by that hand, to a knowledge, if it be of a naturall or civill thing, or to a faith, if it be of a supernaturall, and spirituall thing.

And therefore be content to wonder at this, That God would have such a care to dignifie, and to crown, and to associate to his own everlasting presence, the body of man. God himself is a Spirit, and heaven is his place; my soul is a spirit, and so proportioned to that place; That God, or Angels, or our Soultes, which are all Spirits, should be in heaven, *Ne miremini,* never wonder at that. But since we wonder, and justly, that some late Philosophers have removed the whole earth from the Center, and carried it up, and placed it in one of the Spheares of heaven, That this clod of earth, this body of ours should be carried up to the highest heaven, placed in the eye of God, set down at the right hand of God, *Miramini hoc,* wonder at this; That God, all Spirit, served with Spirits, associated to Spirits, should have such an affection, such a love to this body, this earthly body, this deserves this wonder. The Father was pleased to breathe into this body, at first, in the Creation; The Son was pleased to assume this body himself, after, in the Redemption; The Holy Ghost is pleased to consecrate this body, and make it his Temple, by his sanctification; In that *Faciamus hominem,* Let us, all us, *make man,* that consultation of the whole Trinity in making man, is exercised even upon this lower part of man, the dignifying of his body. So far, as that amongst the ancient Fathers, very many of them, are very various, and irresolved, which way to pronounce, and very many of them cleare in the negative, in that point, That the soule of man comes not to the presence of God, but remaines in some out-places till the Resurrection of the body: That observation, that consideration of the love of God, to the body of man, withdrew them into that error, That the soul it self should lack the glory of heaven, till the body were become capable of that glory too.

They therefore oppose God in his purpose of dignifying the body of man, first, who violate, and mangle this body, which is the Organ in which God breathes; And they also which pollute and defile this body, in which Christ Jesus is apparelled; and they likewise who prophane this body, which the Holy Ghost, as the high Priest, inhabites, and consecrates.

Transgressors in the first kinde, that put Gods Organ out of tune, that discompose, and teare the body of man with violence, are those inhumane persecutors, who with racks, and tortures, and prisons, and fires, and exquisite inquisitions, throw downe the bodies of the true Gods true servants, to the Idolatrous worship of their imaginary Gods; that torture men into hell, and carry them through the inquisition into damnation. S. *Augustine* moves a question, and institutes a disputation, and carries it somewhat problematically, whether torture be to be admitted at all, or no. That presents a faire probability, which he sayes against it: we presume, says he, that an innocent man should be able to hold his tongue in torture; That is no part of our purpose in torture, sayes he, that hee that is innocent, should accuse himselfe, by confession, in torture. And, if an innocent man be able to doe so, why should we not thinke, that a guilty man, who shall save his life, by holding his tongue in torture, should be able to doe so? And then, where is the use of torture? *Res fragilis, & periculosa quaestio,* sayes that Lawyer, who is esteemed the law, alone, *Vlpian:* It is a slippery triall, and uncertaine, to convince by torture: For, many times, sayes S. *Augustine* againe, *Innocens luit pro incerto scelere certissimas poenas;* He that is yet but questioned, whether he be guilty or no, before that be knowne, is, without all question, miserably tortured. And whereas, many times, the passion of the Judge, and the covetousnesse of the Judge, and the ambition of the Judge, are calamities heavy enough, upon a man, that is accused, in this case of torture, *Ignorantia ludicis est calamitas plerumque innocentis,* sayes that Father, for the most part, even the ignorance of the Judge, is the greatest calamity of him that is accused: If the Judge knew that he were innocent, he should suffer nothing; If he knew he were guilty, he should not suffer torture; but because the Judge is ignorant, and knowes nothing, therefore the Prisoner must bee racked, and tortured, and mangled, sayes that Father.

There is a whole Epistle in S. *Hierome,* full of heavenly meditation, and of curious expressions: It is his forty ninth Epistle, *Ad Innocentium:* where a young man tortured for suspition of adultery with a certaine woman, *ut compendio cruciatus vitaret,* sayes he, for his ease, and to abridge his torment, and that he might thereby procure and compasse a present death, confessed the adultery, though false: His confession was made evidence against the woman: and shee makes that protestation, *Tu testis Domine Iesu,* Thou Lord Jesus be my Witnesse, *Non ideo me negare velle, ne peream, sed ideo mentiri nolle, ne peccem:* I doe not deny the fact for feare of death, but I dare not belie my selfe, nor betray mine innocence, for feare of sinning, and offending the God of Truth; And, as it followes in that story, though no torture could draw any Confession, any accusation from her, she was condemned; and one Executioner had three blowes at her with a Sword, and another foure, and yet she could not be killed.

And therefore, because Storie abounds with Examples of this kinde, how uncertaine a way of tryall, and conviction, torture is, though S. *Augustine* would not say, that torture was unlawfull, yet he sayes, It behoves every Judge to make that prayer, *Erue me Domine a necessitatibus meis,* If there bee some cases, in which the Judge must necessarily proceed to torture; O Lord, deliver me, from having any such brought before me.

But what use soever there may be for torture, for Confession, in the Inquisition they torture for a deniall, for the deniall of God, and for the renouncing of the truth of his Gospell: As men of great place, think it concernes their honour, to doe above that which they suffer, to make their revenges, not only equall, but greater then their injuries; so the Romane Church thinks it necessary to her greatnesse, to inflict more tortures now, then were inflicted upon her in the Primitive Church; as though it were a just revenge, for the tortures she received then, for being Christian, to torture better Christians then her selfe, for being so. In which tortures, the Inquisition hath found one way, to escape the generall clamour of the world against them which is to torture to that heighth, that few survive, or come abroad after, to publish, how they have been tortured. And these, first, oppose Gods purpose, in the making, and preserving, and dignifying the body of man.

Transgressors herein, in the second kinde, are they, that defile the garment of Christ Jesus, the body in which he hath vouchsafed to invest and enwrap himselfe, and so apparell a Harlot in Christs cloathes, and make that body, which is his, hers. That Christ should take my body, though defiled with fornication, and make it his, is strange; but that I, in fornication, should take Christs body, and make it hers, is more. *Know ye not,* sayes the Apostle, *that your bodies are the members of Christ?* And againe, *Know you not, that he that is joyned to a harlot, is one body?* Some of the Romane Emperours, made it treason, to carry a Ring, that had their picture engraved in it, to any place in the house, of low Office. What Name can we give to that sin, to make the body of Christ, the body of a harlot? And yet, the Apostle there, as taking knowledge, that we loved our selves better than Christ, changes the edge of his argument, and argues thus, ver. 18. *He that committeth fornication, sinneth against his own body;* If ye will be bold with Christs body, yet favour your own: No man ever hated his own body; and yet, no outward enemy is able so to macerate our body, as our owne licentiousnesse. Christ, who tooke all our bodily infirmities upon him, Hunger, and Thirst, and Sweat, and Cold, tooke no bodily deformities upon him, he tooke not a lame, a blinde, a crooked body; and we, by our intemperance, and licentiousnesse, deform that body which is his, all these wayes. The licentious man, most of any, studies bodily handsomenesse, to be comely, and gracious, and acceptable, and yet, soonest of any, deformes, and destroyes it, and makes that loathsome to all, which all his care was to make amiable: And so they oppose Gods purpose of dignifying the body.

Transgressors in a third kinde are they, that sacrilegiously prophane the Temple of the Holy Ghost, by neglecting the respect and duties, belonging to the dead bodies of Gods Saints, in a decent and comely accompanying them to convenient Funerals. Heires and Executors are oftentimes defective in these offices, and pretend better employments of that, which would be, (say they) vainly spent so. But remember you, of whom (in much such a case) that is said in S. *Iohn,*

This he said, not because he cared for the poore, but because he was a Thiefe, and had the bagge, and bore that which was put therein: This Executors say, not because they intend pious uses, but because they beare, and beare away the bagges. Generally, thy opinion must be no rule for other mens actions; neither in these cases of Funerals, must thou call all too much, which is more then enough; That womans Ointment poured upon Christs feet, that hundred pound waight of perfumes to embalme his one body, was more then enough, necessarily enough; yet it was not too much, for the dignity of that person, nor for the testimony of their zeale, who did it, in so abundant manner.

Now, as in all these three waies, men may oppose the purpose of God, in indignifying the body, so in concurring with Gods purpose, for the dignifying thereof, a man may exceed, and goe beyond Gods purpose, in all three. God would not have the body torne, and mangled with tortures, in those cases; but then, hee would not have it pampered with wanton delicacies, nor varnished with forraigne complexion. It is ill, when it is not our own blood, that appeares in our cheekes; It may doe some ill offices of blood, it may tempt, but it gives over, when it should doe a good office of blood, it cannot blush. If when they are filling the wrinkles, and graves of their face, they would remember, that there is another grave, that calls for a filling with the whole body, so, even their pride would flow into a mortification. God would not have us put on a sad countenance, nor disfigure our face, not in our fastings, and other disciplines; God would not have us marre his work; nor God would not have us goe about to doe his last work, which he hath reserved to himselfe in heaven, here upon earth, that is, to glorifie our bodies, with such additions here, as though we would need no glorification there.

So also in the second way of giving due respect to the body of man, a man may exceed Gods purpose. God would not have the body corrupted and attenuated, shrunk and deformed with incontinency, and licentiousnesse; But God would not have that sparing of the body, to dishonour, or undervalue, or forbeare mariage, nor to frustrate that, which was one of Gods purposes, in the institution of mariage, procreation of children. Mariage without possibility of children, lacks one halfe of Gods purpose in the institution of mariage; for, the third reason of mariage, after the other two, (which two were, for a Helper, and for Children) which is, that mariage should be for a Remedy, that third came in after; for at the time of the institution of mariage, man was not fallen into any inordinate concupiscencies, and so, at that time, needed no remedy. Mariage without possibility of children, lacks one of Gods two reasons for children; but mariage with a contract against children, or a practice against children, is not (sayes S. *Augustine*) a mariage, but a solemne, an avowed, a daily Adultery. To choose to be ill in the sight of God, rather then to look ill, in the sight of men, is a perverse, and a poysonous Physick. The sin of *Er,* and *Onan,* in maried men; the sin of procured abortions, in maried women, doe, in many cases, equall, in some, exceed, the sin of Adultery; To rob a husband, or a wife, of a future child, may be in the wife, or husband, as great a sin, as to bring a supposititious, or a spurious child, into the Fathers inheritance. God would not have the comelinesse, the handsomenesse of the body defaced by incontinency, and intemperance, but he would not have the care of that comelinesse, and handsomenesse frustrate his purpose of children in mariage.

And as in those two, (God would not have the body tortured, nor mangled, God would not have the body deformed by licentiousnesse) so, in his third respect to mans body, God would not have the bodies of his dead Saints neglected, Gods purpose may be exceeded too. Gods purpose therein is, that all men should be Decently, and Honourable persons, Honourably buried; but his purpose herein is exceeded, when any ragge of their skin, or chip of their bones, or lock of their haire, is kept for a Relique, and made an Universall balme, and Amulet, and Antidote, against all temporall, and all spirituall diseases, and calamities, not onely against the rage of a Feaver, but of hell it selfe. What their counterfait Reliques may doe, against their counterfait hell, against their Purgatory, I know not: That powerfull, and precious, and onely Relique, which is given to us, against hell it selfe, is onely the Communion of the body, and blood of Christ Jesus, left to us by him, and preserved for us, in his Church, though his body be removed out of our sight.

To end this, *Miramini hoc,* marvell at this, at the wonderfull love of God to the body of man, and thou wilt favour it so, as not to macerate thine owne body, with uncommanded and inhumane flagellations, and whippings, nor afflict their bodies, who are in thy charge, with inordinate labour; thou wilt not dishonour this body, as it is Christs body, nor deforme it, as it is thine owne, with intemperance, but thou wilt behave thy selfe towards it so, as towards one, whom it hath pleased the King to honour, with a resurrection, (which was our first) and not to deferre that resurrection long, which is our next step, *Venit hora, The houre is comming.*

Non talem Deum tuum putes, qualis nec tu debes esse, is excellently said by S. *Augustine:* Never presume upon any other disposition in God, then such as thou findest in thine own heart, that thou art bound to have in thy selfe; for we finde in our hearts, a band of conformity, and assimilation to God, that is, to be as like God as we can. Therefore whatsoever thou findest thy selfe bound to doe to another, thou maist expect at Gods hand. Thou art bound to help up another that is fallen, therefore thou maist assure thy selfe, that God will give thee Resurrection: so, thou findest in thy heart, that the soule of an almes, the soule of a benefit, that that gives it life, is the speedy, the present doing of it; Therefore thou maist be sure, that God will make speed to save thee, that he will not long deferre this thy resurrection, *hora venit.* S. *Augustine* comparing the former resurrection, which is the spirituall resurrection of the soule, ver. 25, with this in the Text, which is the resurrection of the body, observes, that there Christ sayes, *Hora venit, & nunc est, the houre is comming, and now is;* because in every private inspiration of the Holy Ghost, in every Sermon, in every meeting of the Congregation, the dead may heare, and live; *nunc est,* they may doe it now. But that in this resurrection in the Text, the resurrection of the body, it is not said, *nunc est,* that the houre is now; for, the Son of Man who sayes it, (as hee is the Son of Man) knowes not when it shall bee; But hee sayes *Hora venit, It is comming,* and comming apace, and comming quickly, shortly.

As soone as God had made man, he gave him his patent, *Dominamini,* Dominion over the Creature; As soone as Man was fallen, God gave him the promise of a Messias; And of his second comming, himselfe, sayes, *Ecce, venio cito, Behold, I come speedily: Venit,* he comes, he is upon the way; and *Ecce, venit, Behold he comes,* he is within sight, you may see him in his fore-running tokens; and *Ecce cito,* as little way as he hath to goe, he makes haste, And there is a Jesuit that makes the haste so great, as that he sayes, Howsoever S. *Augustine* make use of that note, that it is not said in the Text, *Nunc est,* That the houre of the Resurrection is now, yet he does beleeve, that Christ did say so, though the Euangelist left it out. We need not say so; we doe not; so much lesse liberty doe we take in departing from the Fathers, then the

Romane Authors doe: But yet, so as S. *Iohn* speaks, *Hora novissima,* This is the last time, (*Now there are many Antichrists, whereby we know that this is the last time*) And so, as S. *Peter* speaks, *Be not ignorant of this one thing, that one day is with the Lord as a thousand yeares, and a thousand yeares as one day:* So as this *Nunc* may signifie *Vltimum statum,* The last course of times, the time not of Nature, nor of Law, but of Grace; so we admit that addition in this Resurrection too, *Hora venit, & nunc est, The houre is comming, and now is,* because there are no other meanes to be hereafter instituted for the attaining of a happy Resurrection, then those that now are established in the Church, especially at a mans death, may we very properly say, *Nunc est,* Now is the Resurrection come to him, not onely because the last Judgement is involved in the first, (for that Judgement which passeth upon every man at his death, stands for ever without Repeal, or Appeal, or Error) but because after the death of the Body, there is no more to be done with the Body, till the Resurrection; for as we say of an Arrow, that it is over shot, it is gone, it is beyond the mark, though it be not come to the mark yet, because there is no more to be done to it till it be; so we may say, that he that is come to death, is come to his Resurrection, because he hath not another step to make, another foot to goe, another minute to count, till he be at the Resurrection.

The Resurrection then, being the Coronation of man, his Death, and lying downe in the grave, is his enthroning, his sitting downe in that chayre, where he is to receive that Crown. As then the Martyrs, under the Altar, though in heaven, yet doe cry out for the Resurrection; so let us, in this miserable life, submit our selves cheerfully to the hand of God, in death, since till that death we cannot have this Resurrection, and the first thing that we shall doe after this death, is to rise againe. To the child that is now borne, we may say, *Hora venit,* The day of his Resurrection is comming; To him that is old, we may say, The hour is come; but to him that is dead, The minute is come, because to him there are no more minutes till it doe come.

Miramini hoc, Marvail at this, at the descent of Gods love, He loves the Body of Man, And *Miramini hoc,* Mervaile at his speed, He makes haste to expresse this love, *Hora venit,* And then *Miramini hoc,* Marvaile at the Generality, it reaches to all, all that are in the Grave; *All that are in the graves shall heare his voice, &c.* God hath made the Body as a House for the soule, till he call her out, and he hath made the Grave as a House for the body, till he call it up. The misery, and poore estate that Christ submitted himselfe unto for man, was not determined in that, *That foxes had holes, but he no where to lay his head,* while he lived; but he had no grave that he could claime, when he was dead. It is some discontinuance of the Communion of Saints, if I may not be buried with the Saints of God. Every man that hath not devested Humanity, hath a desire to have his bones lie at rest, and we cannot provide for that so well, any way, as to bury them in Consecrated places, which are, in common entendment, safest from prophane violences. Even that respect, that his bones might lye at rest, seems to have mov'd one Prophet, to enjoyne his Sons, to bury him, in the Sepulcher, where the other Prophet was buried. He knew that *Iosiah* would burne the bones of all the other graves, upon the Altar of *Bethel,* as was prophecied; and he presum'd that he would spare the bones of that Prophet, and so his bones should be safe, if they were mingled with the other. God expressed his love to *Moses,* in that particular, *That he buried him;* And, to deliver, and remove him, from the violence of any that lov'd him not, and so might dishonor his memory, and from the superstition of any that over-lov'd him, and so might over-honour his memory, God buried him in secret. In more then one place doth *David* complaine, *That there was none to bury Gods Saints;* And the Dignity that is promised here in the Text, is appropriated to them, *who are in the graves,* who are buried.

But then, was that generall? Is it simply, plainly, literally of them, and them onely, who are in graves, who are buried? Shall none enjoy a Resurrection, that have not enjoy'd a Grave? Still I say, it is a comfort to a dying man, it is an honour to his memory, it is a discharge of a duty in his friends, it is a piece of the Communion of Saints, to have a consecrated grave: But the word here is, *In monumentis,* All that are in Monuments; that is, in Receptacles of Bodies, of what kind soever they be: wheresoever the hand of God layes up a dead Body, that place is the Receptacle, so the monument, so the grave of that Body. *God keeps all the bones of the righteous, so that none of them are broken:* Though they be trod to dust in our sight, they are intire in his, because he can bid them be whole againe in an instant. Some Nations burnt their dead, there the fire is the grave; some drowned their dead, there the sea is the grave; some hung them up upon trees, and there the ayre is their grave: Some Nations eat their dead themselves, and some maintained dogs to eat the dead; and as they called those dogs, *Canes Sepulchrales,* Sepulchrall dogs, so those men were sepulchrall men, those men and those dogs were graves. *Death and hell shall deliver up their dead,* sayes S. *Iohn:* That is, the whole state, and mansion of the dead, shall be emptied: The state of the dead is their grave, and upon all that are in this state, shall the testimony of Gods love, to the body of man, fall; And that is the Generality, *All that are in the grave, &c.*

Our next step, is, The Instrument, the Means, by which, this, first so speedy, and then so generall love of God, to man, to man in his lowest part, his body, is accomplished unto him; These, All these that are in graves, in all these kinds of graves, *shall heare his voice,* and that is the Meanes. First, whose voice? That is expressed immediately before. *The Son of man.* In the other Resurrection, in that of the dead soule, *ver.* 25. there it is said, *The dead shall heare the voyce of the Son of God.* In this, which is the Resurrection to Judgement, it is *The Son of man.* The former Resurrection (that of a sinner to repentance by preaching) is wrought by a plaine, and ordinary meanes here in the Church; where you doe but heare a man in a Pew, read prayers, and pronounce Absolution, and a man in a Pulpit preach a Sermon, and a man at a Table consecrate, and administer a Sacrament; And because all this, though it be the power of life, and the meanes of your spirituall resurrection, is wrought by the Ministery of man, who might be contemptible in your eye, therefore the whole worke is referred to God, and not the son of man, but *the Son of God,* is said to do it.

In this Resurrection of the Text, which is a Resurrection to Judgement, and to an account with God, that God whom we have displeased, exasperated, violated, wounded in the whole course of our life, lest we should be terrified, and dejected at the presence of that God, the whole worke is referred to *the Son of Man,* which hath himselfe formerly felt all our infirmities, and hath had as sad a soule at the approach of death, as bitter a Cup in the forme of Death, as heavy a feare of Gods forsaking him in the agony of death, as we can have: And for sin it self, I would not, I do not extenuate my sin, but let me have fallen, not seven times a day, but seventy seven times a minute, yet what are my sins, to all those sins that were upon Christ? The sins of all men, and all women, and all children, the sins of all Nations, all the East and West, and all the North and South, the sins of all times and ages, of Nature, of Law, of Grace, the sins of all natures, sins of the body, and sins of the mind, the sins of all growth, and all extentions, thoughts, and words, and acts, and habits, and delight, and glory, and contempt, and the very sin of boasting, nay of our belying our selves in sin; All these sins, past, present and future, were at once upon Christ, and in that depth of sin, mine are but a drop to his Ocean; In that treasure of sin, mine are but single money to his Talent; And therefore, that I might come with a holy reverence to his Ordinance, in this place, though it be but in the Ministery of man, that first Resurrection is attributed to the Son of God, to give a dignity to that Ministery of man, which otherwise might have beene under-valued, that thereby we might have a consolation, and a cheerfulnesse towards it; It is He, that is, the Son of God, and the Son of man, Christ; which remembers us also, that all that belongs to the expressing of the Law of God to man, must be received by us, who professe our selves Christians, in, and by, and for, and through Christ.

We use to ascribe the Creation to the Father, but the Father created by the Word, and his Word, is his Son, Christ; *When he prepared the Heavens, I was there,* (saies Christ, of himselfe in the person of Wisdome) *and when he appointed the foundations of the earth, then was I by him, as one brought up with him;* It is not, as one brought in to him, or brought in by him, but with him; one as old, that is, as eternall, as much God as he. We use to ascribe Sanctification to the Holy Ghost; But the Holy Ghost sanctifies in the Church, And the Church was purchased by the blood of Christ, and Christ remaines Head of the Church, *usque in consummationem,* till the end of the world. I looke upon every blessing that God affords me, and I consider whether it be temporall, or spirituall; and that distinguishes the metall; the temporall is my silver, and the spirituall is my Gold; but then I looke againe upon the Inscription, *Cujus Imago,* whose Image, whose inscription it beares, and whose Name; and except I have it, in, and for, and by Christ Jesus, Temporall, and Spirituall things too, are but imaginary, but illusory shadows; for God convayes himselfe to us, no other way, but in Christ.

The benefit then in our Text, the Resurrection, is by him; but it is limited thus, It is by hearing him, *They that are in their Graves shall heare, &c.* So it is in the other Resurrection too, the spirituall resurrection, *v.* 25. There, they must *heare* him, that will *live.* In both resurrections, That in the Church, now, by Grace, And that in the Grave hereafter, by Power, it is said, *They shall heare him.* They shall, which seemes to imply a necessity, though not a coaction; But that necessity, not of equall force, not equally irresistible in both: In the Grave, *They shall;* Though they be dead, and senslesse as the dust, (for they are dust it selfe) though they bring no concurrence, no cooperation, *They shall heare,* that is, They shall not chuse but heare, In the other resurrection, which is, in the Church, by Grace, in Gods Ordinance, *They shall heare too,* that is, There shall be a voice uttered so, as that they may heare, if they will, but not whether they will or no, as in the other case, in the grave. Therefore when God expresses his gathering of his Church, in this world, it is *Sibilabo & congregabo, I will hisse, or chirpe for them, and so gather them:* He whispers in the voyce of the Spirit, and he speaks a little louder, in the voice of a man; Let the man be a *Boanerges,* a Son of thunder, never so powerfull a speaker, yet no thunder is heard over all the world. But for the voyce that shall be heard at the Resurrection, *He shall send his Angels, with a great sound of a Trumpet;* A great sound, such as may be made by a Trumpet, such as an Angell, all his Angels can make in a Trumpet, and more then all that, *The Lord himselfe shall descend from Heaven,* and that, *with a shout, and with the voice of an Archangel,* that is, saies S. *Ambrose,* of Christ himselfe, *And in the Trumpet of God,* that is also, Christ himselfe.

So then, you have the Person, Christ; The meanes, A Voyce, And the powerfulnesse of that voyce, in the Name of an Archangell, which is named but once more in all the Scriptures: And therefore, let no man, that hath an holy anhelation and panting after the Resurrection, suspect that he shall sleepe in the dust, for ever; for, this is a voyce that will be heard, he must rise. Let no man, who because he hath made his course of life like a beast, would therefore be content his state in death might be like a beast too, hope that he shall sleepe in the dust, for ever, for this is a voice, that must be heard, *And all that heare shall come forth, they that have done good, &c.*

He shall come forth; even he that hath done ill, and would not, shall come forth. You may have seene morall men, you may have seen impious men, go in confidently enough: not afrighted with death, not terrified with a grave; but when you shall see them come forth againe, you shall see them in another complexion. That man that dyed so, with that confidence, thought death his end; It ends his seventy yeares, but it begins his seventy millions of generations of torments, even to his body, and he never thought of that: Indeed, *Iudicii, nisi qui vitae aeternae praedestinatus est, non potest reminisci,* saies S. *Ambrose,* No man can, no man dares thinke upon the last Judgement, but he that can thinke upon it with comfort, he that is predestinated to eternall life. Even the best, are sometimes shaked with the consideration of the Resurrection, because it is impossible to separate the consideration of the Resurrection, from the consideration of the Judgement; and the terrors of that may abate the joy of the other: *Sive comedo, sive bibo,* saies S. *Hierom,* Whether I eate, or drink, still me thinks I heare this sound, *Surgite mortui, & venite ad Iudicium,* Arise you dead, and come to Judgement: When it cals me up from death, I am glad, when it cals me to Judgement, that impaires my joy. Can I thinke that God will not take a strict account; or, can I be without feare, if I thinke he will? *Non expavescere requisiturum est dicere, non requiret,* is excellently said by S. *Bernard,* If I can put off all feare of that Judgement, I have put off all imagination, that any such Judgement shall be. But, when I begin this feare, in this life, here, I end this feare, in my death, and passe away cheerefully: But the wicked begin this feare, when the Trumpet sounds to the Resurrection, and then shall never end it; but, as a man condemned to be halfe hang'd, and then quartered, hath a fearfull addition in his quartering after, and yet had no ease in his hanging before; so they that have done ill, when they have had their hanging, when they have suffered in soule, the torments of Hell, from the day of their death, to the day of Judgement, shall come to that day with feare, as to an addition to that, which yet, was infinite before. And therefore the vulgat Edition hath rendered this well, *Procedent, They shall proceed,* they shall go farther and farther in torment.

But this is not the object of our speculation, the subject of our meditation, now: we proposed this Text, for the Contemplation of Gods love to man, and therefore we rather comfort our selves with that branch, and refresh our selves with the shadow of that, *That they who have done good, shall come forth unto the Resurrection of life.* Alas, the others shall live as long as they; *Lucifer* is as immortall as *Michael,* and *Iudas* as immortall as S. *Peter:* But *Vita damnatorum, mors est,* That which we call immortality in the damned, is but a continuall dying; howsoever it must be called life, it hath all the qualities of death, saving the ease, and the end, which death hath, and damnation hath not. They must come forth; they that have done evill, must do so too: Neither can stay in their house, their grave; for, their house (though that house should be the sea) shall be burnt downe; all the world dissolv'd with fire. But then, They who have done evill, shall passe from that fire, into a farther heat, without light, They who have done good, into a farther light, without heat.

But fix upon the Conditions, and performe them; They must *have done Good;* To have knowne Good, to have beleeved it, to have intended it, nay to have preached it to others, will not serve, They must have done good. They must be rooted in faith, and then bring forth fruit, and fruit in season; and then is the season of doing good, when another needs that good at thy hands. God gives the evening raine, but he gave the morning rain before; A good man gives at his death, but he gives in his life time too. To them belongs this Resurrection of the body to life; upon which, since our Text inclines us to marvell rather then to discourse, I will not venture to say with David, *Narrabo omnia mirabilia tua, I will shew all thy wondrous works,* (an Angels tongue could not shew them) but I will say with him, *Mementote mirabilium, Remember the marvellous works he hath done,* And by that, God will open your eyes, that you may behold the wondrous things that he will do: Remember with thankfulnesse the severall resurrections that he hath given you; from superstition and ignorance, in which, you, in your Fathers lay dead; from sin, and a love of sin, in which, you, in the dayes of your youth, lay dead; from sadnesse, and dejection of spirit, in which, you, in your worldly crosses, or spirituall tentations, lay dead; And assure your self, that that God that loves to perfect his own works, when you shall lye dead in your graves, will give you that Resurrection to life, which he hath promised to all them that do good, and will extend to all them, who having done evill, do yet truly repent the evill they have done.

SERMON PREACHED AT THE FUNERAL OF SIR WILLIAM COKAYNE

December 26, 1626 (John 11:21)

VI

EDITOR'S PREFACE

The greatest preachers may not be disputatious but they are disputants. Their proclamation is never from a void into a void. They are aware of the important alternatives to their statements on every subject and, though rarely belligerent, they seek to deal availingly with such alternatives. Even when a preacher does not woodenly line up opposing sides and set them to combat in his sermon, he can by word and reference make effective argument in his preaching. So does he meet at least part of the preacher's important teaching obligation.

John Donne was such a disputant. Because the literarily noteworthy and easily memorable passages in his sermons are usually the unqualified, direct statements of his own deepest conviction, it is easy to overlook the large element of dialectic in his preaching.

That element is there from preaching design, of course, but quite as much it is a consequence of the preacher's character and practice. John Donne's earliest prose work was, in the fashion of his time, a set of artificial and brittle trifles called *Paradoxes and Problems* in which he cracked his wits, crossing arguments, proving or disproving certain frivolous fancies. *Biathanatos* was another youthful work, this one a labored and casuistic examination and refutation of every law—civil or ecclesiastical—against suicide.

Pseudo Martyr is a tedious piece of elaborate scholastic reasoning in defense of the oath of allegiance to the King. There is evidence of Donne's early having done a vast amount of reading, analyzing and evaluating in the torrents of published controversy between Anglican and Roman champions.

The give and take of argument was then part of the exercise as well as part of the personality of the singularly dialectical Dean. Even in a funeral sermon like the one following, the cerebral preacher keeps a sharp eye on the controversial ground across which his comfortable words pick their way. The very first sentences of the sermon, as a matter of fact, are a roundly phrased, but pointedly put, refutation of the doctrine of the transmigration of souls. Much earlier, poet Donne had used the doctrine to good effect in the satirical *Progress of the Soule*. But now he makes clear its rejection for its incompatibility with the Christian conviction of the resurrection of the dead.

A few pages later the preacher crosses swords over the coffin with the Puritans. Always eager to keep the English church exactly halfway between Rome and Geneva, neither Roman Catholic nor ultra-Reformed, Donne through most of his ministry, pressed hardest against the Romanists who pressed the hardest attack on Anglicanism. But now, with the low church Puritans daily more demanding and obstreperous, Donne began to shift his weight. So in this sermon he is discovered maintaining Church and sacraments against all enthusiasts who in the name of direct and even ecstatic individual communion with God jeopardize the institutional communion of saints.

But the preacher is still more a pastor than a contraversialist. There is no evidence that the Sir William Cokayne over whom he preached was any intimate or long time acquaintance of Donne's. As Dean of the cathedral, though, he pours himself into a sermon for the funeral of this presumably distinguished alderman of the City of London.

As usual, the thought of death powerfully activates John Donne. Head, heart and mouth warm quickly to the occasion. There is long eloquence on the impermanence and instability of all that lies this side of the last mystery. And then at last, when that mystery itself, death, is confronted, the preacher is thrust as near as he ever comes in any sermon to the poet's orbit. Jezebel and Goliath and Dives are the names with auras that a poet needs. Subtle but definite rhythms are set pulsing. Even rhyme is involved.

At the end there is admiring tribute to the admirable alderman. In the course of those closing remarks a fair picture of a prosperous businessman, a model husband and father, a devout churchman is invoked. That Astrid Friis, in a 1929 study called *Alderman Cokayne's Project and the Cloth Trade,* came up with a less impressive account of the honored dead's sharp practice, would probably not have surprised John Donne at all. Or any other preacher.

PREACHED AT THE FUNERAL
OF SIR WILLIAM COKAYNE, KNIGHT,
ALDERMAN OF LONDON,
DECEMBER 12, 1626.

Joh. 11.21. Lord, If Thou Hadst Been Here, My Brother Had Not Died.

God made the first Marriage, and man made the first Divorce; God married the Body and Soule in the Creation, and man divorced the Body and Soule by death through sinne, in his fall. God doth not admit, not justifie, not authorize such Super-inductions upon such Divorces, as some have imagined; That the soule departing from one body, should become the soule of another body, in a perpetuall revolution and transmigration of soules through bodies, which hath been the giddinesse of some Philosophers to think; Or that the body of the dead should become the body of an evill spirit, that that spirit might at his will, and to his purposes informe, and inanimate that dead body; God allowes no such Super-inductions, no such second Marriages upon such divorces by death, no such disposition of soule or body, after their dissolution by death. But because God hath made the band of Marriage indissoluble but by death, farther then man can die, this divorce cannot fall upon man; As farre as man is immortall, man is a married man still, still in possession of a soule, and a body too; And man is for ever immortall in both; Immortall in his soule by Preservation, and immortall in his body by Reparation in the Resurrection. For, though they be separated *à Thoro & Mensa,* from Bed and Board, they are

172

not divorced; Though the soule be at the *Table of the Lambe,* in Glory, and the body but at the table of *the Serpent, in dust;* Though the soule be *in lecto florido,* in that bed which is alwayes green, in an ever-lasting spring, in *Abrahams bosome;* And the body but in that green-bed, whose covering is but a yard and a halfe of Turfe, and a Rugge of grasse, and the sheet but a winding sheet, yet they are not divorced; they shall returne to one another againe, in an insep-arable re-union in the Resurrection. To establish this assurance of a Resurrection in us, God does some-times in this life, that which he hath promised for the next; that is, he gives a Resurrection to life, after a bodily death here. God hath made two Testaments, two Wills; And in both, he hath declared his Power, and his Will, to give this new life after death, in this world. To the Widows sonne of *Zarephtha,* he be-queaths new life; and to the Shunamites sonne, he gives the same legacy, in the Old Testament. In the New Testament, to the widow of *Naims* sonne, he bequeaths new life; And to *Iairus* daughter he gives the same legacy: And out of the surplusage of his in-exhaustible estate, out of the overflowing of his Power, he enables his Executors to doe as he did; for *Peter* gives *Dorcas* this Resurrection too. Divers examples hath he given us, of the Resurrection of every particu-lar man, in particular Resurrections; such as we have named; And one of the generall Resurrection, in the Resurrection of Christ himselfe; for, in him, we all rose; for, he was All in All . . . They that are not faln yet by any actuall sinne, (children newly bap-tized) are risen already in him; And they that are not dead yet, nay, not alive yet, not yet borne, have a Resurrection in him, who was not onely the Lambe *slaine* from the beginning, but from before all begin-nings was *risen* too; and all that shall ever have part in the second Resurrection, are risen with him from that time. Now, next to that great Propheticall action, that type of the generall Resurrection, in the Resurrection of Christ, the most illustrious Evidence, of the Resurrection of particular men, is this Resuscitation of *Lazarus;* whose sister *Martha,* directed by faith, and yet transported by passion, seeks to entender and mollifie, and supple him to impressions of mercy and compassion, who was himselfe the Mold, in which all mercy was cast, nay, the substance, of which all mercy does consist, Christ Jesus, with this imperfect piece of Devotion, which hath a tincture of Faith, but is deeper dyed in Passion, *Lord, if thou hadst been here, my brother had not dyed.*

This Text which you Heare, *Martha's* single words, complicated with this Text which you See, The dead body of this our Brother, makes up between them this body of Instruction for the soule; first, That there is nothing in this world perfect; And then, That such as it is, there is nothing constant, nothing permanent. We consider the first, That there is nothing perfect, in the best things, in spirituall things; Even *Martha's* devotion and faith hath imperfections in it; And we consider the other, That nothing is permanent in temporall things; Riches prosperously multiplied, Children honorably bestowed, Additions of Honor and Titles, fairly acquired, Places of Command and Government, justly received, and duly executed; All testimonies, all evidences of worldly happinesse, have a Dissolution, a Determination in the death of this, and of every such Man: There is nothing, no spirituall thing, perfect in this world; Nothing, no temporall thing, permanent and durable; And these two Considerations shall be our two parts; And then, these the branches from these two roots; First, in the first, we shall see in generall, The weaknesse of Mans best actions; And secondly, more particularly, The weaknesses in *Martha's* Action; And yet, in a third place, the easinesse, the propensnesse, the largenesse of Gods goodnesse towards us, in the acceptation of our imperfect Sacrifices; for, Christ does not refuse, nor discourage *Martha,* though her action have these imperfections; And in this largenesse of his Mercy, which is the end of all, we shall end this part. And in our second, That as in spirituall things nothing is perfect, so in temporall things nothing is permanent, we shall, by the same three steps, as in the former, looke first upon the generall consideration, the fluidnesse, the transitorinesse of all such temporall things; And then, consider it more particularly, in Gods Master-piece, amongst mortall things, the body of man, That even that flowes into putrefaction; And then lastly, returne to that, in which we determined the former part, The largenesse of Gods goodnesse to us, in affording even to mans body, so dissolved into putrefaction, an incorruptible and a glorious state. So have you the frame set up, and the roomes divided; The two parts, and the three branches of each; And to the furnishing of them, with meditations fit for this Occasion, we passe now.

In entring upon the first branch of our first part, That in spirituall things nothing is perfect, we may well afford a kinde of spirituall nature to knowledge; And how imperfect is all our knowledge? What one thing doe we know perfectly? Whether wee consider Arts, or Sciences, the servant knows but according to the proportion of his Masters knowledge in the Art, and the Scholar knows but according to the proportion of his Masters knowledge in that Science; Young men mend not their sight by using old mens Spectacles; and yet we looke upon Nature, but with *Aristotles* Spectacles, and upon the body of man, but with *Galens,* and upon the frame of the world, but with *Ptolomies* Spectacles. Almost all knowledge is rather like a child that is embalmed to make a Mummy, then that is nursed to make a Man; rather conserved in the stature of the first age, then growne to be greater; And if there be any addition to knowledge, it is rather

a new knowledge, then a greater knowledge; rather a
singularity in a desire of proposing something that was
not knowne at all before, then an emproving, an ad-
vancing, a multiplying of former inceptions; and by
that meanes, no knowledge comes to be perfect. One
Philosopher thinks he is dived to the bottome, when
he sayes, he knows nothing but this, That he knows
nothing; and yet another thinks, that he hath expressed more knowledge then he, in saying, That he
knows not so much as that, That he knows nothing.
S. *Paul* found that to be all knowledge, To know
Christ; And Mahomet thinks himselfe wise therefore,
because he knows not, acknowledges not Christ, as S.
Paul does. Though a man knew not, that every sin
casts another shovell of Brimstone upon him in Hell,
yet if he knew that every riotous feast cuts off a year,
and every wanton night seaven years of his seventy
in this world, it were some degree towards perfection
in knowledge. He that purchases a Mannor, will
thinke to have an exact Survey of the Land: But who
thinks of taking so exact a survey of his Conscience,
how that money was got, that purchased that Mannor?
We call that a mans meanes, which he hath; But that
is truly his meanes, what way he came by it. And yet
how few are there, (when a state comes to any great
proportion) that know that; that know what they
have, what they are worth? We have seen great Wills,
dilated into glorious uses, and into pious uses, and
then too narrow an estate to reach to it; And we have
seen Wills, where the Testator thinks he hath be-
queathed all, and he hath not knowne halfe his own
worth. When thou knowest a wife, a sonne, a servant,
a friend no better, but that that wife betrayes thy bed,
and that sonne thine estate, and that servant thy
credit, and that friend thy secret, what canst thou
say thou knowest? But we must not insist upon this
Consideration of knowledge; for, though knowledge
be of a spirituall nature, yet it is but as a terrestriall

Spirit, conversant upon Earth; Spirituall things, of a more rarified nature then knowledge, even faith it selfe, and all that grows from that in us, falls within this Rule, which we have in hand, That even in spirituall things, nothing is perfect.

We consider this therefore in *Credendis,* In things that we are bound to Beleeve, there works our faith; And then, *in Pretendis,* In things that we are bound to pray for, there works our hope; And lastly, *in Agendis,* In things that we are bound to doe, and there works our charity; And there is nothing in any of these three perfect. When you remember who they were, that made prayer***That the Apostles themselves prayed, that their faith might receive an encrease, *Lord increase our faith,* you must necessarily second that consideration with a confession, That no mans faith is perfect. When you heare Christ so often upbraid, sometimes whole Congregations***And sometimes his Disciples alone, with the same reproach, *Modicæ fidei, O yee of little faith;* . . . and when . . . he spoke plainly to his owne Disciples . . . *Because of your unbeliefe you cannot doe this;* In which Disciples of his, he denies also, that there is such a proportion of faith, as a graine of Mustard-seed, can ye place a perfectnesse of faith in any? When the Apostle takes knowledge of the good estate and condition of the Thessalonians, and gave God thanks for their *Workes of faith,* for *their labours of love,* for their *patience of hope, in our Lord Iesus Christ:* does he conclude them to be perfect? No; for after this he sayes, *Night and day we pray exceedingly, that we may perfect that which is lacking in your faith* . . . There are men that are said to be *Rich in faith;* men that are come from the *weake and beggarly elements of Nature, or of the Law,* to the knowledge of the precious and glorious *Gospell,* and so are *Rich in faith,* enriched, emproved by faith. There are men that *Abound in faith;* that is, in comparison of the empti-

nesse of other men, or of their owne emptinesse before
they embraced the Gospell, they abound now; But
still it is, *As God hath given the measure of faith to
every man;* Not as of his Manna, a certaine measure,
and an equall measure, and a full measure to every
man; no man hath such a measure of faith, as that he
needs no more, or that he may not lose at least some
of that. When Christ speakes so doubtfully, *When the
Son of man commeth, shall he finde faith upon earth?*
Any faith in any way? If the Holy Ghost be come into
this presence, into this Congregation, does he find
faith in any? A perfect faith he does not.

Deceive not your selves then, with that new charme
and flattery of the soule, That if once you can say to
your selves you have faith, you need no more, or that
you shall alwaies keepe that alive; The Apostle sayes,
All boasting, that is, all confidence, *is excluded; By
what Law?* sayes he, *by the Law of faith,* Not by faith,
but by the Law of faith; There is a Law of faith; a
rule that ordinates, and regulates our faith; by which
law and rule, the Apostle cals upon us, To examine
our selves whether we be in the faith, or no; not onely
by the internall motions, and private inspirations of
his blessed Spirit, but by the Law and the Rule, which
he hath delivered to us in the Gospell. The Kings
pardon flowes from his meere grace, and from his
brest; but we must have the writing and the Seale,
that we may plead it: So does faith from God; But
we must see it our selves, and shew it to others, or else
we doe not observe the Law of faith . . . it is not
enough to say, I feele the inspiration of the Spirit of
God, He infuses faith, and faith infused cannot be
withdrawne; but, as there is a Law of faith, and a
practise of faith, a Rule of faith, and an example of
faith, apply thy selfe to both; Regulate thy faith by
the Rule, that is, the Word, and by Example, that is,
Beleeve those things which the Saints of God have
constantly and unanimely beleeved to be necessary to

salvation: The Word is the Law, and the Rule, The Church is the Practise, and the Precedent that regulates thy faith; And if thou make imaginary revelations, and inspirations thy Law, or the practise of Sectaries thy Precedent, thou doest but call Fancie and Imagination, by the name of Reason and Understanding, and Opinion by the name of Faith, and Singularity, and Schisme, by the name of Communion of Saints. The Law of thy faith is, That that that thou beleevest, be Universall, Catholique, beleeved by all; And then, that the Application be particular, To beleeve, that as Christ dyed sufficiently for all, so he dyed effectually for thee. And of this effectuall dying for thee, there arises an evidence from thy selfe, in thy conformity to him; Thy conformity consists in this, That thou art willing to live according to his Gospell, and ready to dye for him, that dyed for thee. For, till a man have resisted unto blood, he cannot know experimentally what degrees towards perfection his faith hath: And though he may conceive in himselfe a holy purpose to dye for Christ, yet till he have dyed for Christ, or dyed in Christ, that is, as long as we are in this valley of tentations, there is nothing, no not in spirituall things, not in faith it selfe, perfect.

It is not *In credendis,* in our embracing the object of faith; we doe not that perfectly; It is not *In petendis,* in our directing our prayers faithfully neither; we doe not that; our faith is not perfect, nor our hope is not perfect; for, so argues the Apostle, *Ye aske, and receive not, because ye aske amisse;* you cannot hope constantly, because you doe not pray aright: And to make a Prayer a right Prayer, there go so many essentiall circumstances, as that the best man may justly suspect his best Prayer: for, since Prayer must bee of faith, Prayer can be but so perfect, as the faith is perfect; and the imperfections of the best faith we have seene. Christ hath given us but a short Prayer; and yet we are weary of that. Some of the old Heretiques of the Primitive Church abridged that Prayer, and some of our later Schismatiques have annihilated, evacuated that Prayer: The Cathari then, left out that one Petition, *Dimitte nobis, Forgive us our trespasses,* for they thought themselves so pure, as that they needed no forgivenesse, and our new men leave out the whole Prayer, because the same Spirit that spake in Christ, speakes in their extemporall prayers, and they can pray, as well as Christ could teach them. And (to leave those, whom we are bound to leave, those old Heretiques, those new Schismatiques) which of us ever, ever sayes over that short Prayer, with a deliberate understanding of every Petition as we passe, or without deviations, and extravagancies of our thoughts, in that halfe-minute of our Devotion? We have not leasure to speake of the abuse of prayer in the Roman Church; where they wil antidate and postdate their prayers; Say to morrows prayers to day, and to dayes prayers to morrow, if they have other uses and employments of the due time betweene; where they will trade, and make merchandise of prayers by way of exchange, My man shall fast for me, and I will pray for my man; or my Atturney, and Proxy shall pray for us both, at my charge; nay, where they will play for prayers, and the loser must pray for both; To this there belongs but a holy scorne, and I would faine passe it over quickly. But when we consider with a religious seriousnesse the manifold weaknesses of the strongest devotions in time of Prayer, it is a sad consideration. I throw my selfe downe in my Chamber, and I call in, and invite God, and his Angels thither, and when they are there, I neglect God and his Angels, for the noise of a Flie, for the ratling of a Coach, for the whining of a doore; I talke on, in the same posture of praying; Eyes lifted up; knees bowed downe; as though I prayed to God; and, if God, or his Angels should aske me, when I thought last of God in that prayer, I cannot tell: Sometimes I finde that I had forgot what I was about, but when I began to forget it, I cannot tell. A memory of yesterdays pleasures, a feare of to morrows dangers, a straw under my knee, a noise in mine eare, a light in mine eye, an any thing, a nothing, a fancy, a Chimera in my braine, troubles me in my prayer. So certainely is there nothing, nothing in spirituall things, perfect in this world.

Not *In credendis,* In things that belong to Faith; not *In petendis,* In things that belong to Hope; nor *In agendis,* In things that belong to Action, to Workes, to Charity, there is nothing perfect there neither. I would be loath to say, That every good is a sin; That were to say, That every deformed, or disordered man were a beast, or that every corrupt meat were poyson; It is not utterly so; not so altogether; But it is so much towards it, as that there is no worke of ours so good, as that wee can looke for thanks at Gods hand for that worke; no worke, that hath not so much ill mingled with it, as that wee need not cry God mercy for that worke. There was so much corruption in the getting, or so much vaine glory in the bestowing, as that no man builds an Hospitall, but his soule lies, though not dead, yet lame in that Hospitall; no man mends a high-way, but he is, though not drowned, yet mired in that way; no man relieves the poore, but he needs reliefe for that reliefe. In all those workes of Charity, the world that hath benefit by them, is bound to confesse and acknowledge a goodnesse, and to call them good workes; but the man that does them, and knows the weaknesses of them, knows they are not good works. It is possible to Art, to purge a peccant humour out of a sick bodie; but not possible to raise a dead bodie to life. God, out of my Confession of the impuritie of my best actions, shall vouchsafe to take off his eyes from that impurity, as though there were none; but no spirituall thing in us, not Faith, not Hope, not Charitie, have any puritie, any perfection in themselves; which is the generall Doctrine wee proposed at first; And our next Consideration is, how this weakenesse appeares in the Action, and in the Words of *Martha* in our Text, *Lord, if thou hadst beene here, my brother had not dyed.*

Now lest we should attribute this weakenesse, onely to weake persons, upon whom we had a prejudice, to *Martha* alone, we note to you first, that her sister *Mary,* to whom in the whole Story very much is ascribed, when she comes to Christ, comes also in the same voice of infirmity, *Lord, if thou hadst beene here, my brother had not died.* No person so perfect, that hath not of these imperfections; Both these holy Sisters, howsoever there might be differences of degrees in their holinesse, have imperfections in all three, in the consideration of their Faith, and their Hope, and their Charity; though in all three they had also, and had both, good degrees towards perfection. Looke first upon their Faith; they both say, *Lord, if thou hadst beene here, our brother had not died.* We cannot say so to any Consultation, to any Colledge of Physitians; not to a *Chiron,* to an *Esculapius,* to a God of Physicke, could any man say, If you had beene here, my friend had not died? though surely there be much assistance to be received from them, whom God had endowed with knowledge to that purpose. And yet there was a weakenesse in these Sisters, in that they said but so, and no more to Christ. They thought Christ to be the best amongst good men; but yet they were not come to the knowledge that he was God. *Martha* saies, *I know, that even now, whatsoever thou askest of God, God will give it thee;* but she does not know him to be God himselfe. I doe not here institute a confutation, but here, and every where I lament the growth, and insinuation of that pestilent Heresie of Socinianisme; That Christ was a holy, a thrice-holy man, an unreproachable, an irreprehensible, an admirable, an incomparable man; A man, to whom, he that should equall any other man, were worse then a

Devill; A man worthy to bee called God, in a farre higher sense then any Magistrate, any King, any Prophet; But yet hee was no God, say they, no Son of God; A Redeemer, by way of good example; but no Redeemer, by way of equivalent satisfaction, say those Heretiques. S. *Paul* sayes, *He is an Atheist, that is without Christ;* And he is as much an Atheist still, that pretends to receive Christ, and not as God; For if the receiving of Christ must redeeme him from being an Atheist, there can no other way be imagined, but by receiving him as God, for that onely, and no other good opinion of Christ, overcomes, and removes his Atheisme. After the last day, whatsoever is not Heaven, is Hell; Hee that then shall be where the Sunne is now, (if he be not then in heaven) shall be as farre from heaven, as if hee were where the Center of the earth is now; Hee that confesses not all Christ, confesses no Christ. *Horribile dictu, dicam tamen,* sayes S. *Augustine* in another case; There belongs a holy trembling to the saying of it, yet I must say it, *If Christ were not God, hee was a devill that durst say he was God.* This then was one weaknesse in these Sisters faith, that it carried them not up to the consideration of Christ as God; And then another rose out of that, That they insisted so much, relied so much, upon his corporall, and personall presence, and promised themselves more from that, then hee had ever given them ground for; which was that which Christ diverted *Mary* from, when after his Resurrection manifesting himselfe to her, and shee flying unto him with that impatient zeale, and that impetuous devotion, *Rabboni, Master, My Master,* Christ said to her, *Touch mee not, for I am not ascended to my Father;* that is, Dwell not upon this passionate consideration of my bodily, and personall presence, but send thy thoughts, and thy reverence, and thy devotion, and thy holy amorousnesse up, whither I am going, to the right hand of my Father, and consider

me, contemplate mee there. S. *Peter* had another holy
distemper of another kinde, upon the personall presence of Christ; He was so astonished at his presence
in the power of a Miracle, that he fell downe at his
feet, and said, *Depart from me, for I am a sinfull man,
O Lord.* These Sisters longed for him, and S. *Peter*
longed as much to be delivered of him; both out of
weaknesse and error. So is it an error, and a weaknesse
to attribute too much, or too little to Christs presence
in his Sacraments, or other Ordinances. To imprison
Christ *in Opere operato,* to conclude him so, as that
where that action is done, Christ must necessarily bee,
and necessarily work, this is to say weakly with these
Sisters, *Lord, if thou hadst beene here, our brother
had not died.* As long as we are present at thine Ordinance, thou art present with us. But to banish Christ
from those holy actions, and to say, That he is no
otherwise present, or works no otherwise in those actions, then in other times, and places, this is to say
with *Peter,* in his astonishment, *Exi à me Domine, O
Lord depart from me;* It is enough that thy Sacrament
be a signe; I do not look that it should be a Seal, or a
Conduit of Grace; This is the danger, this is the distemper, to ascribe too much or too little to Gods visible Ordinances, and Institutions, either to say with
those holy Sisters, *Lord, if thou hadst been here, our
brother had not died,* If we have a Sacrament, if we
have a Sermon all is well, we have enough; or else with
Peter, Exi à me, Leave me to my selfe, to my private
motions, to my bosome inspirations, and I need no
Churchwork, no Sermons, no Sacraments, no such assistances.

So there was weaknesse in their Faith, there was so
too in their Hope, in their confidence in Christ, and in
their manner of expressing it. For, they did not goe
to him, when their brother was sick, but sent. *Nico-
demus* came in person for his sick soule; And the
Centurion in person, for his sick servant; And *Iairus*

in person, for his sick daughter; And the woman with
the bloddy Issue in person, for her sick selfe. These
sisters did but send, but piously, and reverendly; Their
Messenger was to say to Christ, not *Lazarus,* not *Our
Brother,* but *He whom thou lovest, is sick;* And they
left this intimation to work upon Christ; But that
was not enough, we must bring Christ and our necessities neerer together then so . . . I must not wrap up
all my necessities in generall termes in my prayers,
but descend to particulars; For this places my devotion
upon particular considerations of God, to consider
him in every Attribute, what God hath done for me in
Power, what in Wisedome, what in Mercy; which is
a great assistance, and establishing, and propagation
of devotion. As it is a degree of unthankfulnesse, to
thank God too generally, and not to delight to insist
upon the waight, and measure, and proportion, and
the goodnesse of every particular mercy: so is it an
irreverent, and inconsiderate thing, not to take my
particular wants into my thoughts, and into my
prayers, that so I may take a holy knowledge, that I
have nothing, nothing but from God, and by prayer.
And as God is an accessible God, as he is his owne
Master of Requests, and is ever open to receive thy
Petitions, in how small a matter soever: so is he an
inexhaustible God, he can give infinitely, and an inde-
fatigable God, he cannot be pressed too much. Therefore hath Christ given us a Parable of getting *Bread
at midnight* by *Importunity,* and not otherwise; And
another of a *Iudge* that heard the widows cause by
Importunity, and not otherwise; And, not a Parable,
but a History, and a History of his own, of a woman
of *Canaan,* that overcame him in the behalfe of her
daughter, by *Importunity;* when, but by importunity,
she could not get so much as an answer, as a deniall
at his hands. Pray personally, rely not upon dead nor
living Saints; Thy Mother the Church prayes for thee,
but pray for thy selfe too; Shee can open her bosome,

and put the breast to thy mouth, but thou must draw, and suck for thy selfe. Pray personally, and pray frequently; *David* had many stationary times of the day, and night too, to pray in. Pray frequently, and pray fervently; God took it not ill, at *Davids* hands, to be *awaked,* and to be called upon, *to pull his hand out of his bosome,* as though he were slack in relieving our necessities. This was a weaknesse in those Sisters, that they solicited not Christ in person; still get as neare God as you can; And that they declared not their case particularly; It is not enough to pray, nor to confesse in generall termes; And, that they pursued not their prayer earnestly, thorowly; It is not enough to have prayed once; Christ does not onely excuse, but enjoine Importunity.

And then a weaknesse there was in their Charity too, even towards their dead brother. To lament a dead friend is naturall, and civill; and he is the deader of the two, the verier carcasse, that does not so. But inordinate lamentation implies a suspition of a worse state in him that is gone; And if I doe beleeve him to be in heaven, deliberately, advisedly to wish him here, that is in heaven, is an uncharitable desire. For, for me to say, He is preferred by being were he is, but I were better, if he were againe where I am, were such an indisposition, as if the Princes servant should not hold the same place with him, being King, as he did when he was Prince. Not to hope well of him that is gone, is uncharitablenesse; and at the same time, when I beleeve him to be better, to wish him worse, is uncharitablenesse too. And such weaknesses were in those holy and devout Sisters of Lazarus; which establishes our Conclusion, There is nothing in this world, no not in spirituall things, not in knowledge, not in faith, not in hope, not in charity perfect. But yet, for all these imperfections, Christ doth not refuse, nor chide, but cherish their piety, which is also another circumstance in that Part.

There is no forme of building stronger then an Arch, and yet an Arch hath declinations, which even a flat-roofe hath not; The flat-roofe lies equall in all parts; the Arch declines downwards in all parts, and yet the Arch is a firme supporter. Our Devotions doe not the lesse beare us upright, in the sight of God, because they have some declinations towards natural affections: God doth easilier pardon some neglectings of his grace, when it proceeds out of a tendernesse, or may be excused out of good nature, then any presuming upon his grace. If a man doe depart in some actions, from an exact obedience of Gods will, upon infirmity, or humane affections, and not a contempt, God passes it over oftentimes . . . When we consider that weaknesse, that went through the Apostles, even to Christs Ascension, that they looked for a temporall Kingdome, and for preferment in that; when we consider that weaknesse in the chiefe of them, S. *Peter,* at the *Transfiguration,* when, as the Text sayes, *He knew not what to say;* when we consider the weaknesse of his action, that for feare of death, he renounced the Lord of Life, and denied his Master; when in this very story, when Christ said that *Lazarus* was *asleepe,* and that *he would goe to awake him,* they could understand it so impertinently, as that Christ should goe such a journey, to come to the waking of a man, asleep at that time when he spoke; All these infirmities of theirs, multiply this consolation upon us, That though God look upon the Inscription, he looks upon the metall too, Though he look that his Image should be preserved in us, he looks in what earthen vessels this Image is put, and put by his own hand; and though he hate us in our rebellions, yet he pities us in our grievances; though he would have us better, he forsakes us not for every degree of illnesse. There are three great dangers in this consideration of perfectnesse, and purity; First to distrust of Gods mercy, if thou finde not this purity in thy selfe, and this perfect-

nesse; And then to presume upon God, nay upon thine
own right, in an overvaluing of thine own purity, and
perfectnesse; And againe, to condemne others, whom
thou wilt needs thinke lesse pure, or perfect then thy
selfe. Against this diffidence in God, to thinke our
selves so desperately impure, as that God will not look
upon us; And this presumption in God, to thinke
our selves so pure, as that God is bound to look upon
us; And this uncharitablenesse towards others, to think
none pure at all, that are not pure our way; Christ
armes us by his Example, He receives these sisters of
Lazarus, and accomplishes as much as they desired,
though there were weaknesses in their Faith, in their
Hope, in their Charity, expressed in that unperfect
speech, *Lord, if thou hadst been here, my brother had
not dyed:* for, there is nothing, not in spirituall things
perfect. This we have seen out of the Text we have
Heard; And now out of the Text, which we See, we
shall see the rest, That as in spirituall things, there is
nothing Perfect, so in temporall, there is nothing Permanent.

I need not call in new Philosophy, that denies a
settlednesse, an acquiescence in the very body of the
Earth, but makes the Earth to move in that place,
where we thought the Sunne had moved; I need not
that helpe, that the Earth it selfe is in Motion, to
prove this, That nothing upon Earth is permanent;
The Assertion will stand of it selfe, till some man assigne me some instance, something that a man may
relie upon, and find permanent. Consider the greatest
Bodies upon Earth, The Monarchies; Objects, which
one would thinke, Destiny might stand and stare at,
but not shake; Consider the smallest bodies upon
Earth, The haires of our head, Objects, which one
would thinke, Destiny would not observe, or could
not discerne; And yet Destiny, (to speak to a naturall
man) And God, (to speake to a Christian) is no more
troubled to make a Monarchy ruinous, then to make

a haire gray. Nay, nothing needs be done to either, by God, or Destiny; A Monarchy will ruine, as a haire will grow gray, of it selfe. In the Elements themselves, of which all sub-elementary things are composed, there is no acquiescence, but a vicissitudinary transmutation into one another; Ayre condensed becomes water, a more solid body, And Ayre rarified becomes fire, a body more disputable, and in-apparant. It is so in the Conditions of men too; A Merchant condensed, kneaded and packed up in a great estate, becomes a Lord; And a Merchant rarified blown up by a perfidious Factor, or by a riotous Sonne, evaporates into ayre, into nothing, and is not seen. And if there were any thing permanent and durable in this world, yet we got nothing by it, because howsoever that might last in it selfe, yet we could not last to enjoy it; If our goods were not amongst Moveables, yet we our selves are; if they could stay with us, yet we cannot stay with them; which is another Consideration in this part.

The world is a great Volume, and man the Index of that Booke; Even in the body of man, you may turne to the whole world; This body is an Illustration of all Nature; Gods recapitulation of all that he had said before, in his *Fiat lux,* and *Fiat firmamentum,* and in all the rest, said or done, in all the six dayes. Propose this body to thy consideration in the highest exaltation thereof; as it is the *Temple of the Holy Ghost:* Nay, not in a Metaphor, or comparison of a Temple, or any other similitudinary thing, but as it was really and truly the very body of God, in the person of Christ, and yet this body must wither, must decay, must languish, must perish. When *Goliah* had armed and fortified this body, And *Iezabel* had painted and perfumed this body, And *Dives* had pampered and larded this body, As God said to *Ezekiel,* when he brought him to the *dry bones, Fili hominis, Sonne of Man, doest thou thinke these bones can live?* They said in their hearts to all the world, Can these

bodies die? And they are dead. *Iezabels* dust is not
Ambar, nor *Goliahs* dust *Terra sigillata,* Medicinall;
nor does the Serpent, whose meat they are both, finde
any better relish in *Dives* dust, then in *Lazarus.* But
as in our former part, where our foundation was,
That in nothing, no spirituall thing, there was any
perfectnesse, which we illustrated in the weaknesses
of Knowledge, and Faith, and Hope, and Charity, yet
we concluded, that for all those defects, God accepted
those their religious services; So in this part, where our
foundation is, That nothing in temporall things is
permanent, as we have illustrated that, by the decay
of that which is Gods noblest piece in Nature, The
body of man; so we shall also conclude that, with this
goodnesse of God, that for all this dissolution, and
putrefaction, he affords this Body a Resurrection.

The Gentils, and their Poets, describe the sad state
of Death so, *Nox una obeunda,* That it is one everlasting Night; To them, a Night; But to a Christian,
it is *Dies Mortis,* and *Dies Resurrectionis,* The day
of Death, and The day of Resurrection; We die in the
light, in the sight of Gods presence, and we rise in the
light, in the sight of his very Essence. Nay, Gods corrections, and judgements upon us in this life, are still
expressed so, *Dies visitationis,* still it is a Day, though
a *Day of visitation;* and still we may discerne God to
be in the action. The *Lord of Life* was the first that
named *Death; Morte morieris,* sayes God, Thou shalt
die the Death. I doe the lesse feare, or abhorre Death,
because I finde it in his mouth; Even a malediction
hath a sweetnesse in his mouth; for there is a blessing
wrapped up in it; a mercy in every correction, a Resurrection upon every Death. When *Iezabels* beauty, exalted to that height which it had by art, or higher then
that, to that height which it had in her own opinion,
shall be infinitely multiplied upon every Body; And
as God shall know no man from his own Sonne, so
as not to see the very righteousnesse of his own Sonne

upon that man; So the Angels shall know no man from Christ, so as not to desire to looke upon that mans face, because the most deformed wretch that is there, shall have the very beauty of Christ himselfe; So shall *Goliahs* armour, and *Dives* fulnesse, be doubled, and redoubled upon us. And every thing that we can call good, shall first be infinitely exalted in the goodnesse, and then infinitely multiplied in the proportions, and againe infinitely extended in the duration. And since we are in an action of preparing this dead Brother of ours to that state, (for the Funerall is the Easter-eve, The Buriall is the depositing of that man for the Resurrection) As we have held you, with Doctrine of Mortification, by extending the Text, from *Martha* to this occasion; so shall we dismisse you with Consolation, by a like occasionall inverting the Text, from passion in *Martha's* mouth, *Lord, if thou hadst been here, my Brother had not dyed,* to joy in ours, *Lord, because thou wast here, our Brother is not dead.*

The Lord was with him in all these steps; with him in his life; with him in his death; He is with him in his funerals, and he shall be with him in his Resurrection; and Therefore, because the Lord was with him, our Brother is not dead. He was with him in the beginning of his life, in this manifestation, That though he were of Parents of a good, of a great Estate, yet his possibility and his expectation from them, did not slacken his own industry; which is a Canker that eats into, nay that hath eat up many a family in this City, that relying wholly upon what the Father hath done, the Sonne does nothing for himselfe. And truly, it falls out too often, that he that labours not for more, does not keepe his own. God imprinted in him an industrious disposition, though such hopes from such parents might have excused some slacknesse, and God prospered his industry so, as that when his Fathers estate came to a distribution by death, he needed it not. God was with him, as with *David* in a Dilatation, and then in a Repletion; God enlarged him, and then he filled him; He gave him a large and a comprehensive understanding, and with it, A publique heart; And such as perchance in his way of education, and in our narrow and contracted times, in which every man determines himselfe in himselfe, and scarce looks farther, it would be hard to finde many Examples of such largenesse . . . This man hath God accompanied all his life; and by performance thereof seemes to have made that Covenant with him, which he made to *Abraham, Multiplicabo te vehementer, I will multiply thee exceedingly*. He multiplied his extate so, as was fit to endow many and great Children; and he multiplied his Children so, both in their number, and in their quality, as they were fit to receive a great Estate. God was with him all the way, In a *Pillar of Fire,* in the brightnesse of prosperity, and in the *Pillar of Clouds* too, in many darke, and sad, and heavy crosses: So great a Ship, required a great Ballast, So many blessings, many crosses; And he had them, and sailed on his course the steadier for them; The *Cloud* as well as the *Fire,* was a *Pillar* to him; His crosses, as well as his blessings established his assurance in God; And so, in all the course of his life, *The Lord was here,* and therefore *our Brother is not dead;* not dead in the evidences and testimonies of life; for he, whom the world hath just cause to celebrate, for things done, when he was alive, is alive still in their celebration.

The Lord was here, that is, with him, at his death too. He was served with the Processe here in the City, but his cause was heard in the Country; Here he sickned, There he languished, and dyed there. In his sicknesse there, those that assisted him, are witnesses, of his many expressings, of a religious and a constant heart towards God, and of his pious joyning with them, even in the holy declaration of kneeling, then, when they, in favour of his weakenesse, would disswade him from kneeling. I must not defraud him of this testimony from my selfe, that into this place where we are now met, I have observed him to enter with much reverence, and compose himselfe in this place with much declaration of devotion . . . His last Commandement to Wife and Children was Christs last commandement to his Spouse the Church, in the Apostles, *To love one another.* He blest them, and the Estate devolved upon them, unto them: And by Gods grace shall prove as true a Prophet to them in that blessing, as he was to himselfe, when in entring his last bed, two dayes before his Death, he said, *Help me off with my earthly habit, and let me go to my last bed.* Where, in the second night after, he said, *Little know ye what paine I feele this night, yet I know, I shall have joy in the morning;* And in that morning he dyed . . . And his last and dying words were the repetition of the name of Jesus; And when he had not strength to utter that name distinctly and perfectly, they might heare it from within him, as from a man a far off; even then, when his hollow and remote naming of Jesus, was rather a certifying of them, that he was with his Jesus, then a prayer that he might come to him. And so *The Lord was here,* here with him in his Death; and because *the Lord was here, our Brother is not dead;* not dead in the eyes and eares of God; for as the blood of *Abel* speaks yet, so doth the zeale of Gods Saints; and their last prayers (though we heare them not) God continues still; and they pray in Heaven, as the Martyrs under the Altar, even till the Resurrection.

He is with him now too; Here in his Funerals. Buriall, and Christian Buriall, and Solemne Buriall are all evidences, and testimonies of Gods presence. God forbid we should conclude, or argue an absoence of God, from the want of Solemne Buriall, or Christian Buriall, or any Buriall; But neither must we deny it, to be an evidence of his favour and presence, where he is pleased to afford these. So God makes that the seale of all his blessings to *Abraham, That he should be buried* in a good age; God established *Iacob* with that promise, *That his Son Ioseph should have care of his Funerals:* And *Ioseph* does cause his servants, *The Physitians, to embalme him, when he was dead.* Of Christ it was Prophecied, *That he should have a glorious Buriall;* And therefore Christ interprets well that profuse, and prodigall piety of the Woman that poured out the Oyntment upon him, *That she did it to Bury him;* And so shall *Ioseph* of Arimathea be ever celebrated, for his care in celebrating Christs Funerals. If we were to send a Son, or a friend, to take possession of any place in Court, or forraine parts, we would send him out in the best equipage: Let us not grudge to set downe our friends, in the Anti-chamber of Heaven, the Grave, in as good manner, as without vaine-gloriousnesse, and wastfulnesse we may; And, in inclining them, to whom that care belongs, to expresse that care as they doe this day, *The Lord is with him,* even in this Funerall; And because *The Lord is here, our brother is not dead;* Not dead in the memories and estimation of men.

And lastly, that we may have God present in all his Manifestations, *Hee that was, and is, and is to come,* was with him, in his life and death, and is with him in this holy Solemnity, and shall bee with him againe in the Resurrection. God sayes to *Iacob, I will goe downe with thee into Egypt, and I will also surely bring thee up againe.* God goes downe with a good man into the Grave, and will surely bring him up againe. When? The Angel promised to returne to *Abraham* and *Sarah,* for the assurance of the birth of *Isaac, according to the time of life;* that is, in such time, as by nature a woman may have a childe. God will returne to us in the Grave, *according to the time of life;* that is, in such time, as he, by his gracious Decree, hath fixed for the Resurrection. And in the meane time, no more then the God-head departed from the dead body of our Saviour, in the grave, doth his power, and his presence depart from our dead bodies in that darknesse; But that which *Moses* said to the whole Congregation, I say to you all, both to you that heare me, and to him that does not, *All ye that did cleave unto the Lord your God, are alive, every one of you, this day;* Even hee, whom we call dead, is alive this day. In the presence of God, we lay him downe; In the power of God, he shall rise; In the person of Christ, he is risen already. And so into the same hands that have received his soule, we comment his body; beseeching his blessed Spirit, that as our charity enclines us to hope confidently of his good estate, our faith may assure us of the same happinesse, in our owne behalfe; And that for all our sakes, but especially for his own glory, he will be pleased to hasten the consummation of all, in that kingdome which that Son of God hath purchased for us, with the inestimable price of his incorruptible blood. *Amen.*

SERMON PREACHED AT WHITEHALL

Probably February 11, 1626/7 (Isaiah 65:20)

VII

EDITOR'S PREFACE

The high years of Donne's preaching career were not as turbulent as the earlier decades of his life. The horrors of the 1625 plague paled in the next two years. Slowly the trauma of his wife's death in 1617 had healed. Donne's grown daughters were an aid and comfort to him. He was in favor with the king and counted the greatest nobles among his friends. New, younger men like poet George Herbert replaced older intimates as they aged or died out of the inner circle around Donne. The Dean of St. Paul's entertained graciously and was entertained grandly. His ample income now permitted regular gifts to poor scholars who were thus helped through school, and to prisoners who were thus released from debtor's prison.

Dean Donne's principal exercise was now the preparation and delivery of his sermons. The order which he always followed in this enterprise was by now a deep-grooved and familiar way. As soon as one sermon was delivered, he chose the text for the next one. By evening of the same day he had "divided" the text, outlining the whole sermon. The following days were given to reading in the Fathers for illumination on and illustration of his thesis. Then full notes were prepared and memorized. By Friday evening preparations were complete. Saturday was reserved for relaxation and refreshment. And on Sunday that sermon was delivered and the next one begun. No sermons were written out until after delivery—sometimes many years after delivery.

By 1627, however, the quiet evenness of this life is ruffled once more by history and by family. England was at war again with France and Spain. Donne's son George, something of a favorite with his father, was a prisoner of the Spanish for more than two years. King and Parliament fell out over the military budget. And then Donne's eldest unmarried daughter, Lucy, left in charge of the deanery when Constance married a few years before, died shortly after her eighteenth birthday.

Old wounds suddenly bled again. There is, in ensuing sermons, ever stronger emphasis on the communion of saints. For Donne the images which best expressed his hope were all of openness and continuity between heaven and earth. In the sermon which he preached just before the one printed hereafter, Donne insists that

. . . for this world and the next world, are not, to the pure in heart, two houses, but two roomes, a Gallery to passe through, and a Lodging to rest in, in the same House, which are both under one roofe, Christ Jesus; The Militant and the Triumphant, are not two Churches, but this the Porch, and that the Chancell of the same Church, which are under one Head, Christ Jesus; so the Joy, and the sense of Salvation, which the pure in heart have here, is not a joy severed from the Joy of Heaven, but a Joy that begins in' us here, and continues, and accompanies us thither, and there flowes on, and dilates it selfe to an infinite expansion . . . though the fulness of the glory thereof be reserved to that which is expressed in the last branch, *Videbunt Deum, They shall see God* . . .

In an Easter sermon at the end of the Lent which was introduced by our next sermon, Donne returned to the figure of two rooms under a single roof:

He was but a Heathen that said, If God love a man, *Iuvenis tollitur,* He takes him young out of this world; And they were but Heathens, that observed that custome, To put on mourning when their sons were born, and to feast and triumph when they dyed. But thus much we may learne from these Heathens, That if the dead, and we, be not upon one floore, nor under one story, yet we are under one roofe. We think not a friend lost, because he is gone into another roome, nor because he is gone into another Land; And into another world, no man is gone; for that Heaven, which God created, and this world, is all one world. If I had fixt a Son in Court, or married a daughter into a plentifull Fortune, I were satisfied for that son and that daughter. Shall I not be so, when the King of Heaven hath taken that son to himselfe, and maried himselfe to that daughter for ever? . . .

This is the faith that sustaines me, when I lose by the death of others, or when I suffer by living in misery my selfe, That the dead, and we, are now all in one Church, and at the resurrection, shall be all in one Quire.

Between those two sermons comes the grand and gentle one preached to the King on the first Sunday of Lent, 1627. It is as melodious a statement of the gospel, of the good news of the love and mercy of God—"the Mercy, the early Mercy, the everlasting Mercy of yours, and my God"—that we have from Donne. Here is a faith sustaining the preacher, not a preacher sustaining a faith. This is the gospel which defends Donne before he defends it.

Not that there are no shadows in the sermon. "If there were any other way to be saved and to get to Heaven, then by being born into this life, I would not wish to have come into this world. And now that God hath made this life a *Bridge* to Heaven; it is but a giddy, and a vertiginous thing, to stand long gazing upon so narrow a bridge, and over so deep and roaring waters, and desperate whirlpools, as this world abounds with . . ." There are heavy words about the eternity of God's judgment. There is a sudden prayer in the middle of the sermon, Donne abruptly reaching out through his outline to thrust himself upon God, and in so doing thrusting himself startlingly, palpitantly upon us through the printed lines: "Forgive me *O Lord, O Lord* forgive me my sinnes, the sinnes of my youth, and my present sinnes . . . Forgive me my crying sins, and my whispering sins . . ."

But the bulk of the sermon, studded with its shining sentences, is an affirmation of the all-embracing love of God. It is a useful reminder to all who hurriedly shudder past the darker lines of the Church's gravest preachers that it is as much the brightness of the light as size of the obstruction that makes a shadow dark.

PREACHED TO THE KING, AT WHITE-HALL THE FIRST SUNDAY IN LENT (PROBABLY FEBRUARY 11, 1626/7).

Esaiah 65.20. For the Child Shall Die a Hundred Years Old: but the Sinner, Being a Hundred Years Old, Shall Be Accursed.

Peace is in Sion; Gods whole Quire is in tune; Nay, here is the musick of the Sphears; all the Sphears (all Churches) all the Stars in those Sphears (all Expositours in all Churches) agree in the sense of these words; and agree the words to be a Prophesie, of the Distillation, nay Inundation, of the largenesse, nay the infinitenesse of the blessings, and benefits of Almighty God, prepared and meditated before, and presented, and accomplisht now in the Christian Church. The Sun was up betimes, in the *light of nature,* but then the Sun moved but in the *winter Tropick,* short and cold, dark and cloudy dayes; A *Diluculum* and a *Crepusculum, a Dawning* and *a Twilight,* a little *Traditionall* knowledge for the past, and a little *Conjucturall* knowledge for the future, made up their day. The Sunne was advanced higher to the *Jewes* in the *Law;* But then the Sunne was but in *Libra;* as much day as night: There was as much *Baptisme,* as *Circumcision* in that Sacrament; and as much Lamb as Christ, in that Sacrifice; The Law was their *Equinoctiall,* in which they might see both the Type, and that which was figured in the Type; But in the Christian Church the Sun is in a *perpetuall Summer Solstice;* which are high degrees, and yet there is a higher, the Sun is

in a perpetuall *Meridian* and *Noon,* in that Summer
solstice. There is not onely a *Surge Sol,* but a *Siste sol:*
God hath brought the Sunne to the height, and fixt
the Sun in that height in the Christain Church;
where he is in his own Sonne by his Spirit hath
promised to dwell, *usque ad consummationem,* till
the end of the world. Here is *Manna;* and not in
Gomers, but in *Barns;* and *Quails;* and not in *Heaps,*
but in *Hills;* the waters above the Firmament, and
not in drops of Dew, but in showers of former and
latter Rain; and the Land of *Canaan;* not in *Promise*
onely, nor onely in performance, and *Possession,* but
in Extention and *Dilatation.* The Graces, and blessings of God, that is, means of salvation, are so abound-
antly poured upon the Christian Church, as that the
triumphant Church if they needed means, might
fear they should want them. And of these means
and blessings, *long life,* as it is a *Modell* and abridge-
ment of *Eternity,* and a *help* to *Eternitie,* is one; and
one in this Text, *The childe shall die 100. yeares old.*
But shall we receive good from God, and not receive
evill too? shall I shed upon you *Lumen visionis,* the
light of that vision, which God hath afforded me in
this Prophecie, the light of his countenance, and his
gracious blessings upon you, and not lay upon you
Onus visionis, as the *Prophets* speak often, The
burthen of that vision which I have seen in this Text
too? . . . Christ promises of the *Holy Ghost,* that he
should lead them into *all Truth:* And the Apostles
discharge in his office was, that he had spoken to them
all Truth: And therefore lest I should be defective in
that integritie, I say with Saint *Augustine****I will
not be so bold with you as flatter you, I will not presume so much upon your weaknesse, as to go about to
deceive you, as though there were nothing but blessing in God, but shew you the Commination, and
judgement of this Text too, that though *the childe
should die a hundred years old, yet the sinner being a*

hundred years old shall be accursed. If God had not lengthened his childes, life, extended my dayes, but taken me in the sinnes of my youth, where had I been, may every soul here say? And where would you be too, if no man should tell you, that though *The childe should die a hundred years old, yet the sinner being a hundred years old shall be accursed?* What can be certain in this world, if even the mercy of God admit a variation? what can be endlesse here, if even the mercy of God receive a determination? and *sin* doth vary the nature, *sin* doth determine even the infinitenesse of the mercy of God himself, for though *The childe shall die a hundred yeares old,* yet *the sinner being a hundred years old shall be accursed.* Disconsolate soul, dejected spirit, bruised and broken, ground and trodden, attenuated, evaporated, annihilated heart come back; heare thy *reprieve,* and sue for thy *pardon;* God will not take thee away in thy sins, thou shalt have time to repent, *The childe shall die a hundred years old.* But then lame and decrepit soul, gray and inveterate sinner, behold the full ears of corn blasted with a mildew, behold this long day shutting up in such a night, as shall never see light more, the night of death; in which, the deadliest pang of thy *Death* will be thine *Immortality:* In this especially shalt thou die, that thou canst not die, when thou art dead; but must live dead for ever: for *The sinner being a hundred yeers old, shall be accursed,* he shall be so for ever.

In his discovery from this Red *Sea,* to this *dead Sea;* from the mercy of God, in the blood of his Son, to the malediction of God, in the blood of the sinner, be pleased to name these the points of your Compasse, and your Land-marks by the way, in those, the two parts of this exercise. First, in the first, consider the *precedencie,* and *primogeniture* of *Mercy;* God begins at *Mercy,* and not at *Judgement:* God's method here, is not, *The sinner shall be accursed,* but *The childe*

shall have long life: but first, the blessing, and then
the malediction. And then *secondly,* we shall see, in
what form the particular blessing is given here; In
long life; The childe shall die a hundred years old.
And then also, because we find it in the company of
Mercies, in the region of Mercies, in this first part
of the Text, which is the *Sphear of Mercy;* we shall
look also how this very *dying* is a Mercy too: The
mercy is especially plac'd in the long life: *The childe
shall live a hundred yeares;* but the Holy Ghost
would not leave out that, that he should *die; The
childe shall die* a hundred yeares old. And in these
three, first the precedencie, and primogeniture of
God's mercy, and then the specification of that mercy
in long life, and lastly, the association of mercy, that
death as well as life is a blessing to the Righteous; we
shall determine that first part. And in the second, *But
the sinner being a hundred years old, shall be accursed,* we shall see first, that the malediction of God
hath no object but a *sinner:* God antidates no malediction: Till there be a sinner, there is no malediction;
nay not till there be an *inveterate* sinner: *A sinner of
a hundred yeares,* at least, such a sinner, as would be
so, if God would spare him a hundred yeares here. And
upon such a sinner, God thunders out this Prosterna-
tion, this Consternation, in this one word of our Text,
which involves and inwraps all kinds of miseries, fee-
blenesse in body, infatuation in mind, evacuation of
power, dishonour in fame eclipses in favour, ruine in
fortune, dejection in spirit, *He shall be accursed.*
Where, because in this second part we are in the Region and Sphear of maledictions, we cannot consider
this future, *He shall be,* as a future of favour, a
prorogation, a deferring of the malediction: *He shall
be,* is not, he shall be hereafter, but not yet: but it is
a future of continuation; He shall be accursed, that is,
he shall be so *for ever.* And so have you the frame,
and partitions of this *Bethel,* this House of God in

which he dwells, which is both *Iosuah's Beth-hagla,* the house of Joy, and *John's Bethania,* his house of affliction too; and we passe now to the furnishing of these roomes, with such stuff as I can have laid together.

First, in our first part, we consider the *precedency,* and *primogeniture* of *Mercy.* It is a good thing to be descended of the eldest Brother; To descend from God, to depend upon God, by his eldest Son, the Son of his love, the Sonne of his right hand, Mercy, and not to put God to his second way, his sinister way, his way of judgement. *David* prophesies of God's exaltation of *Solomon* so, *Ponam in Primogenitum,* I will make him my first-born: Though *Solomon* were not so, God would make him so. And in that Title, the Wiseman makes his prayer for *Israel; Quem coæquasti Primogenito,* whom thou hast nam'd thy first-born; for so God had in *Exodus. Israel* is my Sonne, even my *first-born:* and in *Job,* the fiercest terrour of death is exprest so, *Primogenitus mortis, the first-born of Death shall devour his strength:* Still the exaltation, the Superlative is called so; *The first-born.* And in such a sense; if we could think of more degrees of goodnesse in God, of an exaltation of God himself in God, of more God in God, of a Superlative in God, we must necessarily turn upon his mercy, for that *Mercie* must be the *Superlative:* So is it too, if we consider Gods first action, or Gods first thought towards Man; Mercy was the first-born by every Mother; by that Understanding, by that Will, by that Power, which we conceive in God; Mercy was the first-born, and first-mover in all. We consider a *preventing Grace* in God; and that preventing Grace is before all . . . And we consider an *Antecedent-Will* in God, and that *Antecedent Will* is before all; for by that Will, God would have *all* men *saved* . . .

When God gives me accesse into his Library, leave to consider his proceedings with man, I find the first

book of Gods making to be the *Book of Life.* The
Book where all their names are written that are elect
to Glory. But I find no such *Book of Death:* All that
are not written in the Book of Life, are certainly the
sonnes of Death: To be pretermitted there, there to be
left out, wraps them up, at least leaves them wrapt up,
in death. But God hath not wrought so positively, nor
in so primary a consideration in a book of Death, as in
the Book of Life. As the aftertimes made a Book of
Wisdome out *of the Proverbs,* of *Salomon,* and out
of his *Ecclesiastes;* but yet it is not the same Book,
nor of the same certainty: So there is a Book of Life
here, but that is not the same book that is in *Heaven,*
nor of the same certainty: For in this Book of Life,
which is the Declaration and Testimony which the
Church gives of our Election, by those marks of the
Elect, which she seeth in the Scriptures, and believeth
that she seeth in us, a man may be *Blotted out of the
Book of the living* . . . Intimating that in some cases,
and in some Book of Life, a man may have been
written in, and *blotted* out, and written in again.
The Book of Life in the Church, The Testimony of
our Election here, admits such expunctions, and such
redintegrations: but Gods first Book, his *Book of
Mercy;* (for this Book in the Church, is but his *Book
of Evidence*) is inviolable in it self, and all the names
of that Book indelible.

In Gods first Book, the Book of Life, Mercy hath so
much a precedency, and primogeniture, as that there
is nothing in it, but Mercy. In Gods other Book, his
Book of Scripture, in which he is put often to denounce judgements, as well as to exhibite mercies, still
the Tide sets that way, still the Biass leads on that
hand, still his method directs us *ad Primogenitum,*
to his first-born, to his Mercy. So he began in that
Book: *He made man to his Image, and then he blest
him.* Here is no malediction, no intermination
mingled in Gods first Act, in Gods first purpose upon

man: In *Paradise* there is, That if he eat the forbidden fruit, if he will not forbear that, that one Tree, *He shall die.* But God begins not there: before that, he had said, of every tree in the Garden thou maist freely eat; neither is there more vehemency in the punishment, then in the libertie. For as in the punishment there is an ingemination, *Morte morieris,* Dying thou shalt die; that is, thou shalt surely die; so in the liberty, there was an ingemination too, *Comedendo comedes,* Eating thou shalt eat; that is, thou maist freely eat. In *Deuteronomy* we have a fearfull *Chapter of Maledictions;* but all the former parts of that Chapter, are blessings in the same kind: And he that reads that Chapter, will beginne at the beginning, and meet Gods first-born, his Mercy first. And in those very many places of that Book where God divides the condition, *If you obey you shall live, if you rebell you shall die,* still the better Act, and the better condition, and the better reward, is placed in the first place, that God might give us possession, *In jure Primogeniti,* in the right of his first-born, his mercy . . . There are elder pictures in the world of Water, then there are any of oyl; but those of oyl have got above them, and shall outlive them. *Water* is a frequent embleme of *Affliction,* in the Scriptures; and so is *oyl* of *Mercy;* If at any time in any place of Scripture, God seemed to begin with water, with a judgement, yet the oyl will get to the top: in that very judgement, you may see that God had first a mercifull purpose in inflicting that medicinall judgement; for his mercy is his first-born. *His Mercy is new every morning,* saith the Prophet; not onely *every day,* but *as soon as it is day.*

Trace God *in thy self,* and thou shalt find it so. If thou beest drowzie now, and unattentive, curious or contentious, or quarrelsome now, now God leaves thee in that indisposition, and that is a judgement: But it was his Mercy that brought thee hither before.

In every sinne thou hast some remorse, some *relucta-tion,* before thou do that sinne; and that *pre-relucta-tion,* and *pre-remorse* was Mercy. If thou hadst no such remorse in thy last sinne, before the sinne, and hast it now, this is the effect of Gods former mercy, and former good purpose upon thee, to let thee see that thou needest the assistance of his Minister, and of his Ordinance, to enable thee to lay hold on Mercy when it is offered thee. Can any calamity fall upon thee, in which thou shalt not be bound to say, I have had blessings in a greater measure then this? If thou have had losses, yet thou hast more, out of which God took that. If all be lost, perchance thou art but where thou begunst at first, at nothing. If thou begunst upon a good heighth, and beest fallen from that, and fallen low, yet as God prepared a *Whale* to transport *Jonas,* before *Jonas* was cast into the Sea, God pre-pared thee a holy *Patience,* before he reduced thee to the exercise of that Patience. *If thou* couldest ap-prehend nothing done for thy self, yet all the mercies that God hath exhibited to others, are former mercies to thee, in the *Pattern,* and in the *Seal,* and in the *Argument* thereof: They have had them, therefore thou shalt. All Gods *Prophecies,* are thy *Histories:* whatsoever he hath promised others, he hath done in his purpose for thee: And all Gods *Histories* are thy *Prophesies;* all that he hath done for others, he owes thee. Hast thou a *hardnesse* of heart? knowest thou not that Christ hath wept before to entender that hardnesse? hast thou a *palenesse* of soul, in the appari-tion of God in fire, and in judgement? knowest thou not, that Christ hath *bled* before, to give a vigour, and a vegetation, and a verdure to that palenesse? is thy sinne *Actuall* sinne? knowest thou not, that there is a Lamb bleeding before upon the Altar, to expiate that? Is thy terrour from thy inherence, and encom-brance of *Originall* sinne? knowest thou not, that the effect of *Baptism* hath blunted the sting of that sinne

before? art thou full of sores, putrid and ulcerous sores?
full of wounds, through and through piercing wounds?
full of diseases, namelesse and complicate diseases?
knowest thou not that there is a holy Charm, a blessed
Incantation, by which thou art, though not invulnerable, yet invulnerable *unto death,* wrapt up in the
eternall Decree of thine *Election?* that's thy pillar,
the assurance of thine Election: If thou shake that,
if thou cast down that Pillar, if thou distrust thine
Election, with *Samson,* who pulled down pillars in
his blindnesse, in thy blindnesse thou destroyest thy
self. Begin where thou wilt at any Act in thy self, at
any act in God, yet there was mercy before that, for
his mercy is eternall, eternall even towards thee . . .
Earth cannot receive, Heaven cannot give such another universall soul to all: all persons, all actions,
as Mercy. And were I *the childe of this Text,* that
were to live *a hundred yeares,* I would ask no other
marrow to my bones, no other wine to my heart, no
other light to mine eyes, no other art to my understanding, no other eloquence to my tongue, then the
power of apprehending for my self, and the power
of deriving and conveying upon others by my Ministery, the Mercy, the early Mercy, the everlasting Mercy
of yours, and my God. But we must passe to the consideration of this immense *Light,* in that one *Beam,*
wherein it is exhibited here, that is, long life: *The
childe shall die a hundred yeares old.*

Long life is a blessing, as it is an image of eternity:
as Kings are blessings, because they are Images of God.
And as to speak properly, a King that possest the
whole earth, hath no proportion at all to God, (he
is not a dramme, not a grain, not an atome to God)
so neither if a thousand *Methusalems* were put in
one life, had that long life any proportion to eternity;
for *Finite* and *Infinite* have no proportion to one another. But yet when we say so, That the King is
nothing to *God,* we speak then between God and

the King; and we say that, onely to assist the Kings
Religious humiliation of himself in the presence of
God. But when we speak between the King and our
selves his Subjects, there we raise our selves to a
just reverence of him, by taking knowledge that he
is the Image of God to us. So though *long life* be
nothing to eternity, yet because we need such *Glasses*
and such *Images,* as God shews us himself in the King,
so he shewes us his eternitie in a long life. *In this,*
that the *Patriarchs* complain every where of the
shortnesse of life, and neernesse of death; *(Jacob* at
a hundred and thirtie yeares tells *Pharaoh,* that his
dayes were *few,)* In this, that God threatens the
shortnesse of life for a punishment to *Eli,* God saies,
There shall not be an old man in thy house for ever:
In this, that God brings it into Promise, and enters
it, as into his Audite, and his revenue, *(With long life
will I satisfie him, and shew him my salvation,)* That
God would give him long life, and make that long
life a Type of Eternity; In this, that God continues
that promise into performance, and brings it to execution, in some of his chosen servants . . . In all these
and many others, we receive so many testimonies that
God brings long life out of his Treasurie, as an
immediate blessing of his. And therefore . . . let us
reverence this blessing of long life . . . and let us not
make this blessing of long life, impossible to our
selves, by disappointing Gods purpose of long life
upon us, by our surfets, our wantonnesse, our quarrels,
which are all *Goths,* and *Vandals,* and *Giants,* called
in by our selves to fight with God against us. But yet,
so receive we long life, as a blessing, as that we may
also find a blessing in departing from this life: For
so manifold, and so multiform are his blessings, as
even *death* it self hath a place in this Sphear of
blessings, *The childe shall live a hundred yeares,* but
yet *The childe shall die.*

When *Paradise* should have extended, as man

should have multiplied, and every holy family, every religious Colony have constituted a new Paradise . . . when all affections should have been subjects, and all creatures servants, and all wives helpers, then life was a sincere blessing. But, but a mixt blessing now, when all these are so much vitiated; onely a possible blessing; a disputable, a conditionable, a circumstantiall blessing now. If there were any other way to be saved and to get to Heaven, then by being born into this life, I would not wish to have come into this world. And now that God hath made this life a *Bridge* to Heaven; it is but a giddy, and a vertiginous thing, to stand long gazing upon so narrow a bridge, and over so deep and roaring waters, and desperate whirlpools, as this world abounds with: *So teach us to number our dayes,* saith *David, that we may apply our hearts unto wisedome:* Not to number them so, as that we place our happinesse, in the increase of their number. What is this *wisedome?* he tells us there; *He asked life of thee, and thou gavest it him:* But was that this life? It was *Length of dayes for ever and ever,* the dayes of Heaven.

As houses that stand *in two Shires,* trouble the execution of Justice, the house of death that stands in two worlds, may trouble a good mans resolution. As death is a sordid *Postern,* by which I must be thrown out of this world, I would decline it: But as death is the gate, by which I must enter into Heaven, would I never come to it? certainly now, now that *Sinne* hath made life so miserable, if God should deny us death, he multiplied our misery. We are in this Text, upon blessings appropriated to the Christian Church, and so to these times. And in *these Times,* we have not so long life, as the Patriarchs had before. They were to multiply children for replenishing the world, and to that purpose had long life. We multiply sinnes, and the children and off-spring of sinnes, miseries, and therefore may be glad to get from this generation of

Vipers. God gave his Children *Manna* and *Quails,* in the Wildernesse, where nothing else was to be had; but when they came to the Land of Promise, that Provision ceas'd: God gave them long life in the times of *Nature,* and long, (though shorter then before) in the times of the Law; because in nature especially, but in the Law also, it was hard to discern, hard to attain the wayes to Heaven. But the wayes to Heaven are made so manifest to us in the Gospel, as that for that use, we need not long life; and that is all the use of our life here. He that is ready for Heaven, hath lived to a blessed age; and to such an intendment, a childe newly baptized may be elder then his Grandfather. Therefore we receive long life for a blessing, when God is pleased to give it; though *Christ* entered it into no *Petition of his Prayer,* that God would give it: and so though we enter it into no Petition, nor Prayer, we receive it as a blessing too, when God will afford us a deliverance, a manumission, an emancipation from the miseries of this life. Truely I would not change that joy and consolation, which I proposed to my hopes, upon my *Death-bed,* at my passage out of this world, for all the joy that I have had in this world over again. And so very a part of the Joy of Heaven is a joyful transmigration from hence, as that if there were no more reward, no more recompence, but that, I would put my self to all that belongs to the duty of an honest Christian in the world, onely for a joyfull, a cheerful passage out of it. And farther we shall not exercise your patience, or your devotion, upon these three pieces which constitute our first part: The Primogeniture of Gods Mercy, which is first in all; The specification of Gods Mercy, long Life, as it is a figure of, and a way to eternity; and then the association of Gods Mercy; that Death, as well as Life, is a blessing to the Righteous.

So then we have brought our Sunne to his *Meridi-*

anall height, to a full Noon, in which all shadows are removed: for even the *shadow of death,* death it self is a blessing, and in the number of his Mercies. But the *Afternoon shadows* break out upon us, in our second part of the Text. And as afternoon shadowes do, these in our Text do also; they grow greater and greater upon us, till they end in night, in everlasting night, *The sinner being a hundred yeares old shall be accursed.* Now of shadowes it is appliably said, *Vmbræ non sunt tenebræ sed densior lux,* shadowes are not utter darknesse, but a thicker light; shadowes are thus much nearer to the nature of light then darkness is, that shadowes presume light, which darknesse doth not; shadowes could not be, except there were light. The first shadowes in this dark part of our Text, have thus much light in them, that it is but the *sinner,* onely the sinner that is accursed. The Object of Gods malediction, is not *man,* but *sinfull man.* If God make a man sinne, God curses the man; but if sinne make God curse, God curses but the sinne. *Non talem Deum tuum putes, qualis nec tu debes esse* (Augustine), Never propose to thy self such a God, as thou wert not bound to imitate: Thou mistakest God, if thou make him to be any such thing, or make him to do any such thing, as thou in thy proportion shouldst not be, or shouldst not do. And shouldst thou curse any man that had never offended, never transgrest, never trespast thee? Can God have done so? Imagine God, as the Poet saith, *Ludere in humanis,* to play but a *game at Chesse* with this world; to sport himself with making little things great, and great things nothing: Imagine God to be but at play with us, but a gamester; yet will a gamester *curse,* before he be in danger of losing any thing? Will God curse man, before man have sinned? In the Law there are denuntiations of *curses* enjoyned and multiplied: There is *maledictus* upon *maledictus;* but it is *maledictus homo,* cursed be the man; He was not curst by God, *before* he was a man; nor curst by God, *because* he was a man; but if that man commit *Idolatry, Adultery, Incest, Beastiality, Bribery, Calumny,* (as the sinnes are reckoned there) there he meets a paricular *curse,* upon his particular sinne. The book of Life is but names written in Heaven; all the Book of Death, that is, is but that in the Prophet, when *names are written in the Earth.* But whose names are written in the Earth there? *They that depart from thee, shall be written in the Earth:* They shall be, when they depart from thee. For saith he, *They have forsaken the Lord, the Fountain of Living water:* They did not that, because their names were written in the Earth, but they were written there, because they did that. *Our Saviour Christ* came hither to do all his Fathers will; and he returned cheerfully to his Father again, as though he had done all, when he had taken away the sinnes of the world by dying for all sinnes, and all sinners. But if there were an *Hospitall* of miserable men, that lay under the *reprobation* and malediction of *Gods decree,* and not for sinne; the blood of that Lamb is not sprinkled upon the Postills of that doore. Forgive me *O Lord, O Lord* forgive me my sinnes, the sinnes of my youth, and my present sinnes, the sinne that my Parents cast upon me, Originall sinne, and the sinnes that I cast upon my children, in an ill example; Actuall sinnes, sinnes which are manifest to all the world, and sinnes which I have so laboured to hide from the world, as that now they are hid from mine own conscience, and mine own memory; Forgive me my crying sins, and my whispering sins, sins of uncharitable hate, and sinnes of unchaste love, sinnes against *Thee* and *Thee,* against thy Power O Almighty Father, against thy Wisdome, O glorious Sonne, against thy Goodness, O blessed Spirit of God; and sinnes against *Him* and *Him,* against Superiours and Equals, and Inferiours; and sinnes against *Me* and *Me,* against mine own soul, and against my body,

which I have loved better then my soul; Forgive me
O Lord, O Lord in the merits of thy *Christ* and my
Jesus, thine Anointed, and my Saviour; Forgive me my
sinnes, all my sinnes, and I will put *Christ* to no
more cost, nor thee to more trouble, for any reprobation or malediction that lay upon me, otherwise then
as a sinner. I ask but an application, not an extention
of that Benediction, *Blessed are they whose sinnes are
forgiven;* Let me be but so blessed, and I shall envy
no mans Blessednesse: say thou to my sad soul, *Sonne
be of good comfort, thy sinnes are forgiven thee,* and
I shall never trouble thee with Petitions, to take any
other Bill off of the fyle, or to reverse any other Decree, by which I should be accurst, before I was
created, or condemned by thee, before thou saw'st me
as a sinner; For the object of malediction is but a
sinner, (which was our first) and an *Invetrate sinner,
A sinner of a hundred yeares,* which is our next consideration.

First, *Quia centum annorum,* because he is so old;
so old in sinne, *He shall be accursed.* And then,
Quamvis centum annorum, though he be so old,
though God have spared him so long he shall be
accursed. *God is not a Lion in his house, nor frantick
amongst his servants,* saith the Wiseman; God doth
not rore, not tear in pieces for every thing that dis-
pleaseth him. But *when God is prest under us, as a
cart is prest that is full of sheaves;* the Lord will
grone under that burthen a while, but he will cast it
off at last. That which is said by *David,* is, if it be well
observed, spoken of God himself, *Cum perverso per-
vertêris;* from our frowardnesse, God will learn to be
froward: But he is not so, of his own nature. *If you
walk contrary unto me, I will walk contrary unto you,*
saith God. But this is not said of one, first, wry step;
but it is a *walking,* which implies a long, and a con-
siderate continuance. And if man come to sinne so,
and will not walk with *God, God* will walk with that

man in his own pace, and overthrow him in his own
wayes. Nay, it is not onely in that place, *If you walk
contrary* to me, *In occursu,* as *Calvin* hath it***
which implies an *Actuall* Opposition against the
wayes of God: but the word is but *Chevi,* and *Chevi*
is but *In accidente, in contingente;* if you walk *negli-
gently, inconsiderately;* if you leave out God, pretermit, and slight God; if you come to call Gods
Providence *Fortune,* to call Gods Judgements *Accidents,* or to call the Mercies of God, *favours of great
Persons,* if you walk in this *neglect* of *God, God* shall
proceed to a *neglect* of you; and then though God be
never the worse for your leaving him out, (for if it
were in your power to annihilate this whole world,
God were no worse, then before there was a World)
yet if God neglect you, forget, pretermit you, it is a
miserable annihilation, a fearfull malediction. But
God begins not before sinne, nor at the first sinne.
God did not curse *Adam* and *Eve* for their sinne;
it was their first, and God foresaw they would not be
sinners of a hundred yeares. But him that was in the
Serpent, that inveterate sinner, him, who had sinned
in Gods Court, in Heaven, before, and being banished
from thence, fell into this *transmarine treason,* in *another land,* to seduce Gods other Subjects there, him
God accurs'd. Who amongst us can say, that he had
a *Fever* upon his *first excesse,* or a *Consumption* upon
his first *wantonnesse,* or a *Commission* put upon him
for his first *Briberie?* Till he be a *sinner of a hundred
yeares,* till he have brought age upon himself, by his
sinne, before the time, and thereby be *a hundred
yeares old at fourtie,* and so a *sinner of a hundred
yeares,* till he have a *desire* that he might, and a *hope*
that he *shall be* able to sinne *to a hundred yeares;*
and so be a sinner of a hundred yeares; Till he sinne
hungerly and thirstily, and ambitiously, and swiftly,
and commit the sinnes *of a hundred yeares in ten,*
and so be *a sinner of a hundred yeares;* till he infect

and poyson that age, and spoile that time that he lives
in by his exemplary sinnes . . . till in his actions he
have been, or in his desires be, or in the *fore-knowledge of God would be a sinner of a hundred yeares,*
an inveterate, an incorrigible, an everlasting sinner,
God comes not to curse him.

But then *Quamvis centum annorum,* though he
have lived a hundred yeares, though God have multiplied upon him Evidences, and Seals, and Witnesses,
and Possessions, and Continuances, and prescriptions
of his favour, all this hath not so riveted God to that
man, as that God must not depart from him. God
was crucified for him, but will not be crucified to
him; still to hang upon this Crosse, this perversnesse
of this habituall sinner, and never save himself and
come down, never deliver his own Honour, by delivering that sinner to malediction. It is true, that
we can have no better Title to *Gods future Blessings,*
then his Blessings formerly exhibited to us; Gods
former blessings are but his *marks* set up there, that
he may know that place, and that man the better
against another time, when he shall be pleased to
come thither again with a supply of more Blessings:
God gives not Blessings as *payments,* but as *obligations;* and becomes a debtor by giving. If I can produce that, *Remember thy mercies of old,* I need ask
now now; for even that is a *Specialty* by which God
hath bound himself to me for more. But yet not so,
if I abuse his former Blessings, and make them occasions of sinne. *How often would I have gathered you
as a hen gathers her chickens,* saith *Christ,* I know not
how often; surely very often; for *many hundreds of
yeares:* But yet, how often soever, God left them open
to the *Eagle, the Romane Eagle* at last. God gives thee
a *recovery* from sicknesse, that doth not make thee
Immortall. God gives thee a good interpretation of
thine actions from a gracious Prince, this doth not
make thee impeccable in thy self. God gives thee titles

of *Honour* upon thy self, this doth not alwayes give thee honour, and respect from others. For as it is God that *Raiseth up the poore out of the dust,* and *lifteth the needy out of the dunghill, that he may set him with Princes;* so it is God that *Cuts off the Spirit of Princes,* and is *terrible to the Kings of the Earth . . .* And so with the same unwillingnesse, that God comes to the execution, we come to the denunciation of this malediction. They, They, these inveterate, incorrigible sinners, *Quamvis centum annorum,* though God have spared them so long, yet *Quia centum annorum,* because they have imployed all that time in sinne, *They shall be accursed.*

Accursing is *malediction, malediction* is literally but *maledicence;* and that is but *evill speaking.* Now all kinds of evill speaking do not inwrap a man within the curse of this Text; For, though it be a shrewd degree of this curse of God, to be generally ill spoken of by sad, sober, and discreet, and dispassioned, and dis-interested *Men,* yet we are fallen into times, when men will speak ill of men, in things which they do not know, nor should not know, and out of credulity and easie beleeving of men, whom they should not beleeve; men distempered and transported with passion: So men speak evill out of passion, and out of compassion; out of humour, and out of rumour. But malediction in our Text, is an Imprecation of evil, by such men as would justly inflict it if they could, and because they cannot, they pray to God that he would, and he doth: When God seconds the Imprecations of good men, that is this curse. The Person that is curst here is *Peccator centum annorum;* an habituall, an incorrigible sinner. If you put me to assigne, *in what rank of men,* Magistrates or Subjects, rich or poore, Judges or prisoners, *All.* If you put me to assigne, for *what* sinnes, sins of *complexion* and constitution, sinnes of societie and *conversation,* sinnes of our *profession,* and *calling,* sinnes of the particular *place,* or of the

whole *times,* that we live in, sins of *profit,* or sins of
pleasure, or sins of *glory;* (for we all do some sins
which are sins *merely* of *glory;* sins that we make no
profit by, nor take much pleasure in, but do them
onely out of a mis-imagined necessity, lest we should
go too much lesse, and sink in the estimation of the
World, if we did them not;) if I must say which of
these sinnes put us under this curse, *All;* If he be
centum annorum, Inveterate, Incorrigible, *He is accursed.* But then who curses him? God put an extraordinary spirit, and produc'd extraordinary effects
from *curses,* in the mouths of his Prophets which have
been since the World began. So *Elizeus* curses, and
two Bears destroy fourty two persons. These curses
are deposited by God, in the Scriptures, and then inflicted by the *Church,* in her ordinary jurisdiction,
by *excommunications,* and other censures. But this
may be but matter of *form* in the *Church,* or matter
of indignation in the Prophet. Not so, but as God
saith, *That the rod in Ashurs hand is his rod,* and
the *sword in Babylons hand his sword,* so the curse
deposited in the Scripture, and denounced by the
Church, is his *curse.* For as the Prophet saith, *Non
est malum,* all the evill (that is, all the *penall* ill,
all plagues, a warre, all famine,) that is *done* in the
World, God doth; so all the evill that is spoken, all
the curses deposited in the Scriptures, and denounced
by the Church, God speaks. But be all this so; *there
is* a curse deposited, denounced, seconded by God;
yet, all this is but malediction, but *a speaking,* here
is no *execution* spoken of: yes, there is, for as the sight
of God is Heaven, and to be banisht from the sight
of God, is Hell in the World to come, so the blessing
of God, is Heaven, and the curse of God is Hell and
damnation, even in this Life. The *Hieroglyphique* of
silence, is the hand upon the mouth; If the hand of
God be gone from the mouth, it is gone to strike . . .
Solomon puts both *hand* and *tongue* together;***

saith he, *Death and Life are in the hand of the tongue:* Gods *Tongue* hath a *hand;* where his Sentence goeth before, the execution followeth. Nay, in the execution of the last sentence, we shall feel the Hand, before we heare the Tongue, the execution is before the sentence; It is, *Ite maledicti,* go ye accursed: First, you must *Go, go out of the presence of God;* and by that being gone, you shall know, that you are accursed; Whereas in other proceedings, the sentence denounces the execution, here the execution denounces the sentence. But be all this allowed to be thus; There is a malediction deposited in the Scriptures, denounced by the Church, ratified by God, brought into execution, yet it may be born, men doe bear it. How men do bear it, we know not; what passes between God and those men, upon whom the curse of God lieth, in their dark *horrours at midnight,* they would not have us know, because it is part of their curse, to envy God that glory. But we may consider in some part the insupportablenesse of that weight, if we proceed but so farre, as to accomodate to God, that which is ordinarily said of naturall things, *Corruptio optimi pessima;* when the best things change their nature, they become worst. When God, who is all sweetnesse, shall have learned frowardnesse from us, as *David* speaks; and being all rectitude, shall have learned perversenesse and crookednesse from us, as *Moses* speaks; and being all providence, shall have learned negligence from us, and being of himself spread as an universall Hony-combe over All, takes in an impression, a tincture, an infusion of gall from us, what extraction of Wormwood can be so bitter, what exaltation of fire can be so raging, what multiplying of talents can be so heavy, what stiffnesse of destiny can be so inevitable, what confection of gnawing worms, of gnashing teeth, of howling cries, of scalding brimstone, of palpable darknesse, can be so, so insupportable, so inexpressible, so in-imaginable, as

the curse and malediction of God? *And therefore* let
not us by our works provoke, nor by our words teach
God to curse. Lest if *with the same tongue that we
blesse God, we curse Men;* That is, seem to be in
Charity in our Prayers here, and carry a ranckerous
heart, and venemous tongue home with us God come
to say (and Gods *saying* is *doing*) **As** *he loved cursing,
so let it come unto him; as he clothed himself with
cursing, as with a garment, so let it be as a girdle,
wherewith he is girded continually:* When a man
curses out of *Levity,* and makes a loose habit of that
sinne, God shall so gird it to him, as he shall never
devest it. The Devils grammar is *Applicare Activa
Passivis,* to apply Actives to Passives; where he sees
an inclination, to subminister a temptation; where
he seeth a froward choler, to blow in a curse. And
Gods grammar is to *change* Actives into Passives:
where a man delights in cursing, to make that man
accursed. And if God do this to them who do but
curse men, will he do lesse to them, who blaspheme
himself? where man wears out *** his own eternity,
his own hundred yeares; that is, his whole life, in cursing and blaspheming, God shall also extend his curse,
In æterno suo, in his eternity, that is, for *ever.* Which
is that, that falls to the botomme, as the heaviest of
all, and is our last consideration; that all the rest, that
there is a curse deposited in the Scriptures, denounced
by the Church, avowed by God, reduced to execution,
and that insupportable in this life, is infinitely aggravated by this, that he shall be *accursed for ever.*

This is the *Anathema Maran-atha,* accursed *till the
Lord come;* and when the Lord cometh, he cometh
not to reverse, nor to alleviate, but to ratifie and aggravate that curse. As soon as Christ curst the *fig-tree,*
it withered, and it never recovered: for saith that
Gospell, he curst it *In æternum,* for ever. In the course
of our sinne, the *Holy Ghost* hath put here a number
of yeares, a hundred yeares: We sinne long, as long as

we can, but yet sinne hath an end. But in this curse of God in the Text, there is no number; it is an *indefinite* future; *He shall be accursed:* A mile of cyphers or figures, added to the former hundred, would not make up a minute of this eternity. Men have calculated how many particular graines of sand, would fill up all the vast space between the Earth and the Firmament: and we find, that a few lines of cyphers will designe and expresse that number. But if every grain of sand were that number, and multiplied again by that number, yet all that, all that inexpressible, inconsiderable number, made not up one minute of this eternity; neither would this curse, be a minute the shorter for having been indured so many Generations, as there were grains of sand in that number. Our *Esse,* our *Being,* is from Gods saying *Dixit & facti,* God spoke, and we were made: our *Bene esse,* our *Well-being,* is from Gods saying too; *Bene-dicit* God blesses us, in speaking gratiously to us. Even our *Ill-being,* our condemnation is from Gods saying also: for *Malediction* is *Damnation.* So far God hath gone with us that way, as that our Being, our well-being, our ill-being is from his saying: But God shall never come to a *Non esse,* God shall never say to us, *Be nothing,* God shall never succour us with an *annihilation,* nor give us the ease of resolving into nothing, for this curse flowes on into an *everlasting* future, *He shall be accurst,* he shall be so for *ever.* In a true sense we may say, that Gods *fore-knowledge* growes lesse and lesse every day; for his fore-knowledge is of *future* things, and many things which were future heretofore are past, or present now; and therefore cannot fall under his fore-knowledge: His fore-knowledge in that sense, growes lesse, and decaieth. But his eternity decayeth in no sense; and as long as his eternity lasts, as long as God is God, God shall never see that soul, whom he hath accurst, delivered from that curse, or eased in it.

But we are now in the work of an houre, and no more. If there be a minute of sand left, (There is not) If there be a minute of patience left, heare me say, This minute that is left, is that eternitie which we speake of; upon this minute dependeth that eternity: And this minute, God is in this Congregation, and puts his eare to every one of your hearts, and hearkens what you will bid him say to your selves: whether he shall blesse you for your acceptation, or curse you for your refusall of him this minute: for this minute makes up your *Century,* your hundred yeares, your eternity, because it may be your last minute. We need not call that a *Fable,* but a *Parable,* where we heare, That a Mother to still her froward childe told him, she would cast him to the Wolf, the Wolf should have him; and the Wolf which was at the doore, and within hearing, waited, and hoped he should have the childe indeed: but the childe being still'd, and the Mother pleased, then she saith, so shall we kill the Wolf, the Wolf shall have none of my childe, and then the Wolf stole away. No Metaphor, no comparison is too high, none too low, too triviall, to imprint in you a sense of Gods everlasting goodnesse towards you. God bids your Mother the Church, and us her Servants for your Souls, to denounce his judgements upon your sinnes, and we do it; and the executioner *Satan,* beleeves us, before you beleeve us, and is ready on his part. Be you also ready on your part, to lay hold upon those conditions, which are annext to all Gods maledictions, Repentance of former, *preclusion* against *future sinnes,* and we shall be alwayes ready, on our part to assist you with the *Power* of our *Intercession,* to deliver you with the *Keies* of our *Absolution,* and to establish you with the *seales* of *Reconciliation,* and so disappoint that *Wolf,* that roaring *Lion,* that seeks whom he may devour: Go in Peace, and be this your Peace, to know this *** God hath laid the whole curse belonging to us upon him, that hangs upon the Crosse; But *** To all them that hang upon him, that hangeth there, God offereth now, all those blessings, which he that hangeth there hath purchased with the inestimable price of his Incorruptible blood; And to this glorious Sonne of God, who hath suffered all this, and to the most Almighty *Father*, who hath *done* all this, and to the *blessed Spirit of God*, who offereth now to *apply* all this, be ascribed by us, and by the whole Church, All power, praise, might, majesty, glory, and dominion, now and for evermore *Amen*.

SERMON PREACHED AT WHITEHALL

February 29, 1627
(Acts 7:60)

VIII

EDITOR'S PREFACE

John Donne's preoccupation with death was sufficient
to justify titling a recent study of the poet-preacher
"The Death Wish of John Donne" (D. R. Roberts).
From his first prose writing, through poems and letters, to his last sermons, Donne worked over the fact
of death and traced out its implications. As the sermons in this selection should affirm, death was never
the morbid preoccupation in his preaching which un-
informed comment has sometimes suggested. Death
was only one concern of the preacher, and even it was
always seen in the context of a larger life.

But as Donne's own health faltered, and as long
time friends died in ever swifter succession (the
Countess of Bedford, Lady Danvers, Sir Henry Goodyer, all within ten months in 1627-1628), his sermons
turned ever oftener to a contemplation of death. The
last two sermons in this volume, therefore, are properly meditations on that theme. But agreement on subject is their only similarity.

The sermon before us is mainly a meditation on a
good death, on the Christian testimony of a death
trustingly approached. It is therefore as much a reflection on the good life lived in awareness of death
as it is a study of the good death. It is like almost
no other Donne sermon left to us. Donne was not always blazing and flashing in the pulpit. He had quiet

pasages, some wholly low-keyed sermons. These were probably not always intended, but there are more than enough tedious, flat stretches everywhere.

The present sermon, though, is obviously intended to be a humming, poetic musing on the death of Stephen and the life of the Christian. Beginning with still another version of Donne's favorite and most familiar symbol—"He that will dy with Christ upon Good-Friday, must hear his own bell toll all Lent"— the preacher quietly describes the pictures that shift before his mind's eye.

This is one of those very few late sermons which Mrs. Simpson describes as having "a queer haunting beauty, an excellent strangeness that makes them memorable. They are full of symbolism and ambiguity, so that one should read them again and again in order to discover their full meaning."

A SERMON PREACHED
AT WHITE-HALL,
FEBRUARY 29, 1627 (1627/28).

*Acts. 7:60. And When He Had Said This, He Fell
a Sleep.*

He that will dy with Christ upon Good-Friday, must
hear his own bell toll all Lent; he that will be partaker of his passion at last, must conform himself to
his discipline of prayer and fasting before. Is there
any man, that in his chamber hears a bell toll for
another man, and does not kneel down to pray for
that dying man? and then when his charity breaths
out upon another man, does he not also reflect upon
himself, and dispose himself as if he were in the
state of that dying man? We begin to hear Christ's bell
toll now, and is not our bell in the chime? We must
be in his grave, before we come to his resurrection,
and we must be in his death-bed before we come to
his grave: we must do as he did, fast and pray, before wee can say as he said, that *In manus tuas,* Into
thy hands O Lord I commend my Spirit. You would
not go into a Medicinal Bath without some preparatives; presume not upon that Bath, the blood of
Christ Jesus, in the Sacrament then, without preparatives neither. Neither say to your selves, we shall have
preparatives enough, warnings enough, many more
Sermons before it come to that, and so it is too soon
yet; you are not sure you shall have more; not sure
you shall have all this; not sure you shall be affected
with any. If you be, when you are, remember that as
in that good Custome in these Cities, you hear cheer-

231

ful street musick in the winter mornings, but yet
there was a sad and doleful bell-man, that wak'd you,
and call'd upon you two or three hours before that
musick came; so for all that blessed musick which the
servants of God shall present to you in this place,
it may be of use, that a poor bell-man wak'd you before, and though but by his noyse, prepared you for
their musick. And for this early office I take Christs
earliest witness, his Proto-Martyr, his first witness
St. *Stephen*, and in him that which especially made
him his witness, and our example, his death, and our
preparation to death, what he suffered, what he did,
what he said, so far as is knit up in those words, *When
he had said this, he fell a sleep.*

From which example, I humbly offer to you these
two general considerations; first, that every man is
bound to do something before he dye; and then to
that man who hath done those things which the duties
of his calling bind him to, death is but a sleep. In
the first, we shall stop upon each of those steps; first
there is a *sis aliquid*, every man is bound to be something, to take some calling upon him. Secondly there
is a *hoc age;* every man is bound to do seriously and
scedulously, and sincerely the duties of that calling.
And thirdly there is a *sis aliquis;* the better to performe those duties, every man shall do well to propose
to himself some person, some pattern, some example
whom he will follow and imitate in that calling. In
which third branch of this first part we shall have just
occasion to consider some particulars in him who is
here propos'd for our Example, St. *Stephen;* and in
these three, *sis aliquid*, be something profess something; and then *hoc age*, do truly the duties of that
profession; and lastly, *sis aliquis*, propose some good
man, in that profession to follow, and in the things
intended in this text, propose St. *Stephen*, we shall
determine our first part. And in the other we shall
see that to them that do not this, that do not settle

their consciences so, death is a bloody conflict, and
no victory at last, a tempestuous sea, and no harbor
at last, a slippery heighth, and no footing, a desperate
fall and no bottom. But then to them that have done
it, their pill is gilded, and the body of the pill hony
too; *mors lucrum,* death is a gain, a treasure, and this
treasure brought home in a calm too; they do not only
go to heaven by death, but heaven comes to them in
death; their very manner of dying is an inchoative act
of their glorified state: therefore it is not call'd a
dying but a sleeping; which one metaphor intimates
two blessings, that because it is a sleep it gives a
present rest, and because it is a sleep, it promises a
future waking in the resurrection.

First, Then for our first branch of our first part,
we begin with our beginning, our birth; *man is born
to trouble;* so we read it, *to trouble.* The original is
a little milder then so; yet there it is, *Man is born
unto labor,* God never meant less then labor to any
man. Put us upon that which we esteem the honora-
blest of labors, the duties of martial discipline, yet
where it is said, that man is appointed to a warfare
upon earth, it is seconded with that, *His dayes are
like the dayes of an hireling.* How honorable soever
his station be, he must do his daies labor in the day,
the duties of the place in the place. How far is he from
doing so, that never so much as considers why he was
sent into this world; who is so far from having done
his errand here, that he knows not, considers not
what his errand was; nay knows not, considers not,
whether he had any errand hither or no. But as
though that God, who for infinite millions of millions
of generations, before any creation, any world, contented himself with himself, satisfied, delighted himself with himself in heaven, without any creatures,
yet at last did bestow six daies labor upon the Creation and accommodation of man, as though that God
who when man was sour'd in the whole lump, poy-

soned in the fountain, perished at the chore, withered
in the root, in the fall of *Adam,* would then in that
dejection, that exinanition, that evacuation of the
dignity of man, and not in his former better estate,
engage his own Son, his only, his beloved Son, to
become man by a temporary life, and then to become no man by a violent, and yet a voluntary death;
as though that God who (when) he was pleased to
come to a creation, might yet have left thee where
thou wast before, amongst privations, a nothing; or
if he would have made thee something, a creature,
yet he might have shut thee up in the close prison
of a bare being and no more, without life or sense,
as he hath done earth and stones; or if he would
have given thee life and sense, he might have left thee
a toad, without the comeliness of shape, without that
reasonable and immortal Soul, which makes thee a
man; or if he had made thee a man, yet he might
have lost thee upon the common amongst the Heathen,
and not have taken thee into his inclosures, by giving
thee a particular form of religion; or if he would have
given thee a religion, He might have left thee a Jew;
or if he would have given thee Christianity, He might
have left thee a Papist; as though this God who had
done so much more for thee, by breeding thee in a
true Church, had done all this for nothing; thou
passest through this world as a flash, as a lightning of
which no man knows the beginning or the ending, as
an *ignis fatuus* in the air, which does not only give
light for any use, but does not so much as portend
or signifie any thing; and thou passest out of the
world, as a hand passes out of a bason, or a body out
of a bath, where the water may be the fouler for
thy having washed in it, else the water retains no impression of thy hand or body; so the world may be
the worse for thy having liv'd in it, else the world
retains no marks of thy having been there. When
God plac'd *Adam* in the world, God enjoyned *Adam*

to fill the world, to subdue the world, and to rule the world; when God plac'd him in Paradise, He commanded him to dress Paradise, and to keep Paradise; when God plac'd his children in the land of promise, he enjoyned them to fight his battails against Idolatry, and to destroy Idolators; to every body some errand, some task for his glory; and thou commest from him into this world, as though he had said nothing to thee at parting, but go and do as thou shalt see cause, go and do as thou seest other men do, and serve me so far, and save thine own Soul so far, as the times, and the places, and the persons, with whom thou doest converse, will conveniently admit. Gods way is positive and thine is privative: God made every thing something, and thou mak'st the best of things, man, nothing; and because thou canst not annihilate the world altogether, as though thou hadst God at an advantage, in having made an abridgment of the world in man, there in that abridgment thou wilt undermine him, and make man, man, as far as thou canst, man in thy self nothing. He that qualifies himself for nothing, does so; He whom we can call nothing, is nothing: this whole world is one intire creature, one body; and he that is nothing may be excremental nailes, to scratch and gripe others, he may be excremental hairs for ornament, or pleasurableness of meeting; but he is no limb of his intire body, no part of Gods universal creature, the world. Gods own name is *I am: Being*, is Gods name, and nothing is so contrary to God as to be nothing. Be something, or else thou canst do nothing; and till thou have said this, saies our text, that is, done something in a lawful calling, thou canst not sleep *Stephens* sleep, not die in peace. *Sis aliquid*, propose something, determine thy self upon something, be, profess something, that was our first; and then our second consideration is, *hoc age*, do seriously, do scedulously, do sincerely the duties of that calling.

He that stands in a place and does not the duty of

that place, is but a statue in that place; and but a statute without an inscription; Posterity shall not know him, nor read who he was. In nature the body frames and forms the place; for the place of the natural body is that *proxima aëris superficies,* that inward superficies of the air, that invests and clothes, and apparals that body, and obeys, and follows, and succeeds to the dimensions thereof. In nature the body makes the place, but in grace the place makes the body: The person must actuate it self, dilate, extend and propagate it self according to the dimensions of the place, by filling it in the execution of the duties of it. *Plinie* delivers us the history of al the great Masters in the art of painting: He tels us who began with the extremities and the out lines at first, who induc'd colors after that, and who after super-induc'd shadows; who brought in *Argutias vultus* as he cals them, not only the countenance, but the meaning of the countenance, and all that so exquisitely, that (as he saies there) *Divinantes diem mortis dixerunt,* Physiognomers would tell a mans fortune as well by the picture as by the life; he tels us, *quis pinxit quæ pingi non possunt,* who first adventured to express inexpressible things; *Tonitrua, perturbationes animæ;* they would paint thunder which was not to be seen, but heard: and affections, and the mind, the Soul which produc'd those affections. But for the most part he tels us all the way, in what places there remained some of their pieces to be seen, and copied in his time. This is still that that dignifies all their works, that they wrought so, as that posterity was not only delighted, but improv'd and better'd in that art by their works: For truly thats one great benefit that arises out of our doing the duties of our own places, in our own time, that as a perfume intended only for that room, where the entertainment is to be made, breaths upward and downward, and round about it; so the doing of the duties of the place, by men that move in middle

Sphears, breath upwards and downwards, and about
too, that is, cast a little shame upon inferiors if they
doe not so, and a little remembrance upon Superiors
that they should doe so, and a thanksgiving to Almighty God for them that doe so: And so it is an
improvement of the present, and an Instruction and
a Catechisme to future times. The duty in this Text
is expressed and limited in speaking. *Cum dixisset,
When hee had said this he fell a sleepe,* and truly
so, literally so, in speaking, and no more, it stretches
far: Many duties, in many great places consist in
speaking; Ours doe so: And therefore, when Vices
abound in matter of Manners, and Schismes abound
in matter of Opinions, *Antequam dixerimus hoc,* till
wee have said this, that is, that that belongeth to that
duty, wee cannot sleepe *Stephen's* sleepe, wee cannot
die in peace. The Judges duty lies much in this too,
for hee is bound not only to give a hearing to a Cause,
but to give an End, a Judgement in the Cause too:
And so, for all them whose duty lies in speaking, from
him who is to counsell his friend, to him who is to
counsell his Master in the family (for *Job* professes
that hee never refused the counsell of his Servant)
Antequam dixerint, till they have said this, that is
still, that that belongs to that duty, they cannot sleep
Stephen's sleepe, they cannot die in peace: and when
wee ascent to the consideration of higher Persons,
they and wee speake not one language, for our speaking is but speaking, but with great Persons, *Acta
Apothegmata,* their Apothegms are their Actions, and
wee heare their words in their deeds. God, whose
Image and Name they beare does so: If wee consider
God; as a second Person in the Godhead, the Sonne
of God, God of God, so God is *Logos, Sermo, Verbum,
Oratio;* The Word, Saying, Speaking; But God considered primarily and in himself so, is *Actus purus,*
all Action, all doing. In the Creation there is a *Dixit*
in Gods mouth, still God sayes something; but ever-

more the *Dixit* is accompanied with a *Fiat*, Something was to be done, as well as said. The Apostles are Apostles in that capacity as they were sent to preach, that's Speaking; But, when wee come to see their proceeding, it is *in Praxi*, in the Acts of the Apostles. In those Persons whose duty lies in speaking, there is an *Antequam dixerint;* in those where it lies in Action, there is an *Antequam fecerint;* till that be said, and done, which belongs to their particular callings, they cannot sleepe *Stephen's* sleepe, they cannot die in peace; and therefore, *Non dicas de Deo tuo gravis mihi est*, say not of thy God, that he lies heavy upon thee, if he exact the duties of thy place at thy hands; *Nec dicas de loco tuo, inutilis mihi est*, say not of thy place, that it is good for nothing, if thou must be put to doe the duties of the place, in the place; for it is good for this, that when thou hast done that, thou mayst sleepe *Stephen's* sleepe, die in Peace. *Sis aliquid*, Be something, that was our first, and then *hoc age*, doe truly the duties of that place without pretermitting thine own, without intermedling with others, which was our second; and then our third consideration is, *Sis aliquis*, Be sombody, be like somebody, propose some good example in thy calling and profession to imitate.

It was the counsell of that great little Philosopher *Epictetus*, whensoever thou undertakest any action, to consider what a *Socrates*, or a *Plato*; what a good and a wise man would doe in that Case, and to doe conformably to that. One great Orator, *Latinus Rufus*, proposed to himselfe *Cicero* for his example, and *Cicero* propounded *Demosthenes*, and hee *Pericles*, and *Pericles*, *Pisistratus;* and so there was a concatenation, a genealogie, a pedegree of a good Orator; *Habet unumquodque propositum principes suos:* In every Calling, in every Profession, a man may finde some exemplar, some leading men to follow. The King hath a *Josias*, and the beggar hath a *Job*, and every man hath some: But here wee must not pursue particulars, but propose to all, him whom our Text proposes, Saint *Stephen;* and in him wee offer you first his name, *Stephen. Stephen, Stephanos* is a leading, an exemplar name, a Significative, a Propheticall, a Sacramentall, a Catechisticall name; a Name that carries much instruction with it. Our Countryman *Bede* takes it to be an Hebrew name, and it signifies (saith hee) *Norman vestram,* Your Rule, Your Law: To obey the Law, to follow, to embrace the Law is an acceptable service to God, especially invariable Law, the Law of God himselfe: But wee are sure that this name *Stephen, Stephanos* signifies a Crowne; to obey the Crowne, to follow, to serve the Crowne, is an acceptable service to God, especially the immarcessible Crown, the Crown of Glory. *Nomen Omen;* scarce any man hath a name, but that name is Legal and Historicall to him: His very name remembers him of some good men of the same name; and so his name is historicall. *Nomina Debita:* In the old formularies of the Civill Law, if a man left so many names to his Executors, they were so many specialties for debts. Our Names are Debts, every man owes the world the signification of his name, and of all his names; every addition of honour, or of office, layes a new Debt, a new Obligation upon him; and his first name, his Christian-Name above all. For, when new names are given to men in the Scriptures, that doth not abolish or extinguish the old: *Jacob* was called *Jacob* after God had called him *Israel:* and *Gedeon Gedeon* after he was called *Jerubaal,* and *Simon* when he was *Peter* too, was called *Simon.* Changes of Office and additions of Honour must not extinguish our Christian Name; The duties of our Christianity, and our Religion must preponderate and weigh down the duties of all other places, and for all together. Saint *Gregory* presents us a good use of this diligence to answere our Names, *Quo quis timet magis, ne quod dicitur non esset, eo plus quam dicitur erit;* The more a man is afraid that hee is not worthy of the name hee beares, whether the name of office or his Christian-Name, the better Officer and the better Christian he will be for that feare, and that solicitude; and therefore it is an usefull and an applyable Prayer for great Persons, which that Father makes in their behalfe, *Præsta, quæsumus Domine, ut quod in ore hominum sumus, in conspectu tuo esse valeamus:* Grant, O Lord, that wee may alwayes be such in thine eyes, as wee are in their tongues that depend upon us, and justifie their acclamations with thy approbations. And so far *Stephens* name, as his name signifies the Law, and as his name signifies the reward of fulfilling the Law, a Crown; hath carried us to the consideration of the duty of answering the signification of our names; But then there are other passages in his History and Actions that carries us farther.

First then we receive Saint *Stephen* to have been Saint *Paul's* kinsman in the flesh, and to have been his fellow pupill under Gamaliel, and to have been equall to him, at least in the foundations, in natural faculties, and in the super-edifications too, in learnings of acquisition and study; And then to have had this great advantage above him, That hee applied himselfe as a Disciple to Christ before Saint *Paul* did; and in that profession became so eminent (for all the Sects, the Libertines themselves taking the liberty to dispute against him, they were not able to resist the wisedome and the Spirit by which hee spake) as that his Cosin *Paul,* then but *Saul,* envied him most, and promov'd and assisted at his execution: For upon those words but two verses before our Text, That *they that stoned* Stephen, *laid down their clothes at* Saul's *feet,* Saint *Augustine* sayes, *In manu omnium eum lapidavit,* That it was *Saul* that stoned *Stephen,* though by the hands of other executioners. Men of the best extraction and families, Men of the best parts and

faculties, Men of the best education and proficiencies,
owe themselves to God by most obligations. Him that
dyes to day, God shall not only aske, where it that
Soule? Is it as cleane as I made it at first? No stayn
of Sin? or is it as clean as I wash'd it in Baptisme?
No sting? No venome of original sinne in it? Or is it
as clean as I left it when wee met last at the Sacrament? No guiltinesse of actuall sinne in it? God shall
not only aske this, Where is that Soul? Nor only aske
where is that Body? Is it come back in that Virginal
integrity in which I made it? Or is it no farther departed from that then Marriage, which I made for it,
hath made it? Are those *Maritales ineptiæ* (that we
may put *Luther's* words into God's mouth) the worst
that is faln upon that body? God shall not only ask for
that Soul and that Body but aske also, Where is that
Wit, that Learning, those Arts, those languages which
by so good education I afforded thee? Truly when a
weake and ignorant man departs into any vicious way,
though in that case he doe adhere to the Enemy, and
doe serve the Devill against God, yet he carries away
but a single Man, and serves but as a common Soul-
dier: But he that hath good parts, and good education,
carries a Regiment in his person, and Armies and mu-
nition for a thousand in himself. Though then thy
kinsmen in the flesh, and thy fellow pupils under
Gamaliel, men whom thou hast accompanied heretofore in other waies, think thy present fear of God, but
a childishness and pusilanimity, and thy present zeal
to his service but an infatuation and a melancholy,
and thy present application of thy self to God in
prayer, but an argument of thy Court-dispaire, and of
thy falling from former hopes there; yet come thou
early, if it be early yet; and if it be not early, come
apace to Christ Jesus: how learned soever thou are,
thou art yet to learn thy first letters, if thou know not
that Christ Jesus is *Alpha* and *Omega,* he in whom
thou must begin and determine every purpose: Thou

hast studied thy self but into a dark and damnable ignorance, if thou have labored for much learning only to prove that thou canst not be sav'd, only to dispute against the person and the Gospel of Christ Jesus. But propose to thine imitation *Stephen,* who though enriched with great parts, and formerly accustomed to the conversation of others of a different perswasion, applied himself early to Christ as a Disciple, and more then in that general application, in a particular function and office as a Deacon, as is expressed in the former Chapter.

The Roman Church that delights in irresolutions and gains, and makes profit in holding things in suspence, holds up this question undetermind, whether that office and function which Stephen took of Deacon, be so *è sacris,* a part of holy Orders, as that it is a Sacrament, or any part of the Sacrament of Orders. *Durand,* a man great in matter of Ceremony, *Cajetan,* a man great in matter of substance, do both deny it; and divers, many, very many besides them; and they are let alone, and their Church saies nothing against them, or in determination of the opinion. But yet howsoever the stronger opinion even in that Church lead the other way, and the form of giving that office by imposition of hands, and the many and great capacities that they receive, that receive it, carry it to a great heighth, yet the use that we make of it here shall be but this, that even *Stephen,* who might have been *inter Doctores, Doctor,* (as *Chrysologus* saies of him) a Doctor to teach Doctors; and *inter Apostolos Apostolus,* an Apostole to lead Apostles, contented himself with a lower degree in the service of Christ in his Church, the service of a Deacon, which very name signifies service, and ministration. It is a diminution of regal dignity, that the Roman Church accounts the greatest Kings, but as Deacons, and assigns them that rank and place in all their Ecclesiastical Solemnities, in their Ceremonials. But *Constantine* knew his own

place without their marshalling: In the midst of
Bishops, and Bishops met in Council, he cals himself
Bishop, and Bishop of Bishops: and the greatest
Bishop of this land, in his time, professed his Master
the King, to be *Pastor Pastorum,* a Shepheard of
Shepheards. It is a name due to the King, for it signifies inspection and superintendency; as the name of
Priest is also given to secular Magistrates that had no
part in Ecclesiastical function in the Scriptures; particularly, in *Putipher,* and to divers others in divers
other places. But yet though that name of super-in-
tendancy be due unto him, let him who is crown'd in
his office as *Stephen* was in his name, accept this name
and office of ministration of Deacon, since the holy
Ghost himself hath given him that name, *The Minister of God for good,* (ther's the word of ministration,
the name *Diaconos* imprinted upon the King) and
since our Super-Supream Ordinary, our Super-Sover-
aign head of the Church, Christ Jesus himself cals
himself, by that name, *The Son of man came not to
be ministred unto, but to minister;* ther's this word of
ministration, the office, the name of Deacon imprinted
upon Christ himself. And though in our interest in
him who is also a King and a Priest, we are all *regale
Sacerdotium,* Kings and Priests too, yet let us accept
the name, and execute the office of Deacon, of ministration, especially upon our selves: for as every man
is a world in himself, so every man is a Church in himself too: and in the ancient Church, it was a part of
the Deacons office, to call out to the Church, to the
Congregation, *Nequis contra aliquem, nequis in Hi-
pocrisi;* let no man come hither to Church, (indeed
no whether, for every place, because God is present in
every place, is a Church,) either in uncharitableness
towards others, or in Hypocrisie and in dissimulation
in himself: Bring alwaies a charitable opinion towards
other men, and sincere affections in thy self, and thou
hast done the right office of a Deacon, upon the right

subject, thou hast ministred to thine own Soul. But then the height of *Stephens* exemplariness, (which is the consideration that we pursue in this branch of this first part) is not so much in his active as in his passive part; not so much in that he did, as in that he suffered; not as he answered and discharged the duties of his name; so we have proposed him to you; nor as he was an early Disciple, and came to Christ betimes, we have proposed him so too; nor as he made his ambition only to serve Christ, and not to serve him in a high place, but only as a Deacon; for in that line also we have proposed him to you; But as he was a constant and chearful Martyr, and laid down his life for Christ, and in that qualification propose him to your selves, and follow him as a Martyr.

Eusebius the Bishop of *Cæsarea,* was so in love with *Pamphilus* the Martyr, as a Martyr, that he would needs take his name, before he could get his addition; and though he could not be call'd Martyr then, yet he would be called *Pamphilus* and not *Eusebius.* The name of *Stephen* hath enough in it to serve not only the vehementest affection, but the highest ambition; for there is a Coronation in the Name as we told you before. And therefore in the Ecclesiastical story and Martyrologes of the Church, there are (I think) more Martyrs of this name *Stephen,* then of any other Name; indeed they have all that Name, for the Name is a Coronation. And therefore the Kingdome of heaven, which is express'd by many precious Metaphors in the Gospel, is never call'd a Crown, till after *Stephens* death, till our Coronation was begun in his Martyrdome, but after in the Epistles often, and in the *Revelation* very often. For to suffer for God, man to suffer for God, I to suffer for my Maker, for my Redeemer, is such a thing, as no such thing, excepting only Gods sufferings for man can fall into the consideration of man. Gods suffering for man was the Nadir, the lowest point of Gods humiliation, mans suffering for God is the Zenith, the highest point of mans exaltation: That as man needed God, and God would suffer for man, so God should need man, and man should suffer for God; that after Gods general Commission, *fac hoc & vives,* do this and thou shalt live, I should receive and execute a new Commission, *Patere hoc & vives abundantius,* suffer this and you shall have life, and life more abundantly, as our Saviour speaks in the Gospel; that when I shall ask my soul *Davids* question, *Quid retribuam,* what shall I render to the Lord, I shall not rest in *Davids* answer, *Accipiam Calicem,* I will take the cup of salvation, in applying his blood to my soul, but proceed to an *Effundam Calicem,* I will give God a Cup, a cup of my blood, that whereas to me the meanest of Gods servants it is honor enough to be believed for Gods sake: God should be believed for my sake, and his Gospel the better accepted, because the seal of my blood is set to it; that that dew which should water his plants, the plants of his Paradise, his Church, should drop from my veines, and that sea, that red sea, which should carry up his bark, his Ark, to the heavenly Jerusalem, should flow from me: This is that that poures joy even into my gladness, and glory even into mine honor, and peace even into my security; that exaltes and improves every good thing, every blessing that was in me before, and makes even my creation glorious, and my redemption precious; and puts a farther value upon things inestimable before, that I shall fulfil the sufferings of Christ in my flesh, and that I shall be offerd up for his Church, though not for the purchasing of it, yet for the fencing of it, though not by way of satisfaction as he was, but by way of example and imitation as he was too. Whether that be absolutely true or no, which an Author of much curiosity in the Roman Church saies, that *Inter tot millia millium,* amongst so many thousand thousands of Martyrs in the Primitive Church, it cannot be said that ever one lack'd burial, (I know not whence he raises that) certainly no Martyr ever lack'd a grave in the wounds of his Saviour, no nor a tomb, a monument, a memorial in this life, in that sense wherein our Saviour speaks in the Gospel, That no man shall leave house, or Brother, or wife for him, but he shall receive an hundred fold in this life; Christ does not mean he shall have a hundred houses, or a hundred wives, or a hundred Brethren; but that that comfort which he lost in losing those things shall be multiplied to him in that proportion even in this life. In which words of our Saviour, as we see the dignity and reward of Martyrdome, so we see the extent and latitude, and compass of Martyrdome too; that not only loss of life, but loss of that which we love in this life; not only the suffering of death, but the suffering of Crosses in our life, contracts the Name, and entitles us to the reward of Martyrdome. All Martyrdome is not a *Smithfeild* Martyrdome, to burn for religion. To suffer injuries, and upon advantages offerd, not to revenge those injuries is a Court Martyrdome. To resist outward tentations from power, and inward tentations from affections, in matter of Judicature, between party and party, is a *Westminster* Martyrdome. To seem no richer then they are, not to make their states better, when they make their private bargains with one another, and to seem so rich, as they are, and not to make their states worse, when they are call'd upon to contribute to publick services, this is an Exchange-Martyrdome. And There is a Chamber-Martyrdome, a Bosome-Martyrdome too; *Habet pudicitia servata Martyrium suum,* Chastity is a dayly Martyrdome; and so all fighting of the Lords battails, all victory over the Lords Enemies, in our own bowels, all chearful bearing of Gods Crosses, and all watchful crossing of our own immoderate desires is a Martyrdome acceptable to God, and a true copy of our patters *Stephen,* so it be inanimated with that which was

even the life and soul and price of all *Stephens* actions
and passions, that is, fervent charity, which is the last
contemplation, in which we propose him for your
Example; that as he, you also may be just paymasters
in discharging the debt, which you owe the world in
the signification of your Names; and early Disciples
and appliers of your selves to Christ Jesus, and humble
servants of his, without inordinate ambition of high
places; and constant Martyrs, in dying every day as
the Apostle speaks, and charitable intercessors, and
Advocates and Mediators to God, even for your heaviest Enemies.

We have a story in the Ecclesiastical story of *Nicephorus* and *Sapricius,* formerly great friends, and
after as great Enemies: *Nicephorus* relented first, and
sued often for reconciliation to *Sapricius,* but was still
refused: he was refused even upon that day, when
Sapricius being led out to execution, as a Martyr for
the Christian religion, *Nicephorus* upon the way, put
himself in his way, and upon his knees beg'd a reconciliation, and obtained it not. The effect of his uncharitableness was this: *Sapricius,* when he came to
the stake, recanted, and renounced the christian religion, and lost the crown of Martyrdome, and *Nicephorus* who came forth upon another occasion professed Christ, and was receiv'd to the Coronation of
Martyrdome. Though I give my body to be burned
and have not charity, it profiteth me nothing, saies
the Apostle; but if I have not charity I shall not be
admitted to that Sacrifice, to give my body to be
burnt. St. *Augustine* seems to have delighted himself
with that saying (for he saies it more then once) *Si
Stephanus non orasset,* if St. *Stephen* had not praid
for *Saul,* the Church had had no *Paul:* and may we
not justly add to that, If *Stephen* had not praid for
Saul, Heaven had had no *Stephen,* or *Stephen* had had
no Heaven: suffering it self is but a stubborness, and a
rigid and stupid standing under an affliction; it is not

a humiliation, a bending under Gods hand, if it be not done in charity. *Stephen* had a pattern, and he is a pattern; Christ was his, and he is our Example; *ut hoc dicam tibi, at te primo audivi,* saies St. *Augustine* in *Stephen's* person to Christ, Lord thou taughtest me this prayer upon the cross; receive it now from me, as the Father receiv'd it from thee then. He prayed for his enemies as for himself; and thus much more earnestly for them then for himself, that he prayed for himself standing, and kneeling for them. *Stephen* was the Plaintiff, and when he comes to his *Nolo prosequi,* and to release, what hath the Judg to say to the Defendant? If a potent adversary oppress thee to ruine, to death, if thou pass away uncharitably towards him, thou raisest an everlasting Trophee for thine enemy, and prepar'st him a greater triumph then he proposed to himself; he meant to triumph over thy body, and thy fortune, and thou hast provided him a triumph over thy Soul too by thy uncharitableness; and he may survive to repent, and to be pardoned at Gods hands, and thou who are departed in uncharitableness canst not; he shall be saved that ruind thee unjustly, and thou who wast unjustly ruind by him, shalt perish irrecoverably. And so we have done with all those peeces which constitute our first part, *Sis aliquid,* profess something, *Hoc age,* do seriously the duties of that profession, and then *Sis aliquis,* propose some good man in that profession for thine imitation; as we have proposed *Stephen* for general duties, falling upon all professions. And we shall pass now to our other part, which we must all play, and play in earnest, that conclusion in which we shall but begin our everlasting state, our death, *When he had said this he fell asleep.*

Here I shall only present to you two Pictures, two pictures in little: two pictures of dying men; and every man is like one of these, and may know himself by it; he that dies in the Bath of a peaceable, and he that dies upon the wrack of a distracted conscience. When the devil imprints in a man, a *mortuum me esse non curo,* I care not though I were dead, it were but a candle blown out, and there were an end of all: where the Devil imprints that imagination, God will imprint an *Emori nolo,* a loathness to die, and fearful apprehension at his transmigration: As God expresses the bitterness of death, in an ingemination, *morte morietur,* in a conduplication of deaths, he shall die, and die, die twice over; So *ægrotando ægrotabit,* in sicknesse he shall be sick, twice sick, body-sick and soul-sick too, sense-sick and conscience-sick together; when, as the sinnes of his body have cast sicknesses and death upon his Soule, so the inordinate sadnesse of his Soule, shall aggravate and actuate the sicknesse of his body. His Physitian ministers, and wonders it works not; He imputes that to flegme, and ministers against that, and wonders again that it works not: He goes over all the humors, and all his Medicines, and nothing works, for there lies at his Patients heart a dampe that hinders the concurrence of all his faculties, to the intention of the Physitian, or the virtue of the Physick. Loose not, O blessed Apostle, thy question upon this Man, *O Death where is thy sting? O Grave where is thy victory?* for the sting of Death is in every limb of his body, and his very body is a victorious grave upon his Soule: And as his Carcas and his Coffin shall lie equally insensible in his grave, so his Soule, which is but a Carcas, and his body, which is but a Coffin of that Carcas, shall be equally miserable upon his Death-bed; And Satan's Commissions upon him shall not be signed by Succession, as upon Job, first against his goods, and then his Servants, and then his children, and then himselfe; but not at all upon his life; but he shall apprehend all at once, Ruine upon himselfe and all his, ruine upon himselfe and all him, even upon his life; both his lives, the life of this, and the life of the next world too.

Yet a drop would redeeme a shoure, and a Sigh now a Storme then: Yet a teare from the eye, would save the bleeding of the heart, and a word from the mouth now, a roaring, or (which may be worse) a silence of consternation, of stupefaction, of obduration at that last houre. Truly, if the death of the wicked ended in Death, yet to scape that manner of death were worthy a Religious life. To see the house fall, and yet be afraid to goe out of it; To leave an injur'd world, and meet an incensed God; To see oppression and wrong in all thy professions, and to foresee ruine and wastefulnesse in all thy Posterity; and Lands gotten by one sin in the Father, molder away by another in the Sonne; To see true figures of horror, and ly, and fancy worse; To begin to see thy sins but then, and finde every sin (at first sight) in the proportion of a Gyant, able to crush thee into despair; To see the Blood of Christ, imputed, not to thee but to thy Sinnes; To see Christ crucified, and not crucified for thee, but crucified by thee; To heare this blood speake, not better things, then the blood of *Abel,* but lowder for vengeance then the blood of *Abel* did; This is his picture that hath been Nothing, that hath done nothing, that hath proposed no *Stephen,* No Law to regulate, No example to certifie his Conscience: But to him that hath done this, Death is but a Sleepe.

Many have wondred at that note of Saint *Chrysostom's,* That till Christ's time death was called death, plainly, literally death, but after Christ, death was called but sleepe; for, indeede, in the old-Testament before Christ, I thinke there is no one metaphor so often used, as Sleepe for Death, and that the Dead are said to Sleepe: Therefore wee wonder sometimes, that Saint *Chrysostome* should say so: But this may be that which that holy Father intended in that Note, that they in the old-Testament, who are said to have slept in Death, are such as then, by Faith, did apprehend, and were fixed upon Christ; such as were all the good

men of the old-Testament, and so there will not bee
many instances against Saint *Chrysostome's* note, That
to those that die in Christ, Death is but a Sleepe; to
all others, Death is Death, literally Death. Now of this
dying Man, that dies in Christ, that dies the Death of
the Righteous, that embraces Death as a Sleepe, must
wee give you a Picture too.

There is not a minute left to do it; not a minutes
sand; Is there a minutes patience? Bee pleased to remember that those Pictures which are deliver'd in a
minute, from a print upon a paper, had many dayes,
weeks, Moneths time for the graving of those Pictures
in the Copper; So this Picture of that dying Man,
that dies in Christ, that dies the death of the Righteous, that embraces Death as a Sleepe, was graving all
his life; All his publique actions were the lights, and
all his private the shadowes of this Picture. And when
this Picture comes to the Presse, this Man to the
streights and agonies of Death, thus he lies, thus he
looks, this he is. His understanding and his will is all
one faculty; He understands Gods purpose upon him,
and he would not have God's purpose turned any
other way; hee sees God will dissolve him, and he
would faine be dissolved, to be with Christ; His understanding and his will is all one faculty; His memory
and his fore-sight are fixt, and concentred upon one
object, upon goodnesse; Hee remembers that hee hath
proceeded in the sinceritie of a good Conscience in all
the wayes of his calling, and he foresees that his good
name shall have the Testimony, and his Posterity the
support of the good men of this world; His sicknesse
shall be but a fomentation to supple and open his
Body for the issuing of his Soule; and his Soule shall
goe forth, not as one that gave over his house, but as
one that travelled to see and learne better Architec-
ture, and meant to returne and re-edifie that house,
according to those better Rules: And as those thoughts
which possesse us most awake, meete us againe when

we are asleepe; So his holy thoughts, having been alwaies conversant upon the directing of his family,
the education of his Children, the discharge of his
place, the safety of the State, the happinesse of the
King all his life; when he is faln a sleepe in Death, all
his Dreames in that blessed Sleepe, all his devotions
in heaven shall be upon the same Subjects, and he
shal solicite him that sits upon the Throne, and the
Lamb, God for Christ Jesus sake, to blesse all these
with his particular blessings: for, so God giveth his
beloved sleep, so as that they enjoy the next world
and assist this.

So then, the Death of the Righteous is a sleepe;
first, as it delivers them to a present rest. Now men
sleepe not well fasting; Nor does a fasting Conscience,
a Conscience that is not nourish'd with a Testimony of
having done well, come to this Sleepe; but *dulcis
somnus operanti,* The sleepe of a labouring man is
sweete. To him that laboureth in his calling, even this
sleepe of Death is welcome. *When thou lyest downe
thou shalt not be afraid,* saith *Salomon;* when thy
Physician sayes, Sir, you must keepe your bed, thou
shalt not be afraid of that sick-bed; And then it followes, *And thy sleepe shall be sweet unto thee;* Thy
sicknesse welcome, and thy death too; for, in those
two *David* seems to involve all, *I will both lay me
downe in Peace, and sleep;* imbrace patiently my
death-bed and Death it selfe.

So then this death is a sleepe, as it delivers us to
a present Rest; And then, lastly, it is so also as it
promises a future waking in a glorious Resurrection.
To the wicked it is far from both: Of them God sayes,
*I will make them drunke, and they shall sleepe a per-
petuall sleepe and not awake;* They shall have no
part in the *Second Resurrection.* But for them that
have slept in Christ, as Christ sayd of *Lazarus,* Lazarus
Sleepeth, but I goe that I may wake him out of sleep,
he shall say to his father; Let me goe that I may wake

them who have slept so long in expectation of my coming: And *those that sleep in Jesus Christ* (saith the Apostle) *will God bring with him;* not only fetch them out of the dust when he comes, but bring them with him, that is, declare that they have beene in his hands ever since they departed out of this world. They shall awake as *Jacob* did, and say as *Jacob* said, *Surely the Lord is in this place,* and *this is no other but the house of God, and the gate of heaven,* And into that gate they shall enter, and in that house they shall dwell, where there shall be no Cloud nor Sun, no darkenesse nor dazling, but one equall light, no noyse nor silence, but one equall musick, no fears nor hopes, but one equal possession, no foes nor friends, but one equall communion and Identity, no ends nor beginnings, but one equall eternity. Keepe us Lord so awake in the duties of our Callings, that we may thus sleepe in thy Peace, and wake in thy glory, and change that infallibility which thou affordest us here, to an Actuall and undeterminable possession of that Kingdome which thy Sonne our Saviour Christ Jesus hath purchased for us, with the inestimable price of his incorruptible Blood. *Amen.*

DEATH'S DUELL: SERMON PREACHED AT WHITEHALL

February 25, 1630
(Psalms 68:20)

IX

EDITOR'S PREFACE

And then there is the last sermon John Donne
preached, the one called "Death's Duell." It is unlike
any other of his sermons. There is no sermon like it
in the whole literature of the Christian pulpit. There
can hardly be another such utterance in any literature.
It has been found morbid, shocking and terrifying. It
has also been identified as the great writing of Donne
"in the fulness of his powers." Whether either or both,
there is no understanding the extraordinary sermon
except in the even more extraordinary circumstances
of its delivery.

In 1629 Donne's failing health kept him out of his
pulpit more and more often. For the first time since
he went to St. Paul's as Dean, there is no Christmas
sermon from him. He preached again on the feast day
of the conversion of his beloved St. Paul, January 25,
1630. The Easter sermon of 1630 may have been
Donne's last appearance in the cathedral pulpit. In
August he went to visit his recently widowed and re-
married daughter, now Constance Alleyn, at her Essex estate, Aldborough Hatch. There the fever which
developed into his last illness (quinsy, malaria, or
both) overwhelmed him, and there he stayed, unable
to travel, until late in January, 1631, when he returned
to the London deanery.

Izaak Walton tells best how the last sermon was delivered.

He was appointed to preach upon his old constant day, the first Friday in Lent; he had notice of it, and had in his sickness so prepared for that employment, that as he had long thirsted for it, so he resolved his weakness should not hinder his journey; he came therefore to London some few days before his appointed day of preaching. At his coming thither, many of his friends—who with sorrow saw his sickness had left him but so much flesh as did only cover his bones—doubted his strength to perform that task, and did therefore dissuade him from undertaking it, assuring him, however, it was like to shorten his life; but he passionately denied their requests, saying he would not doubt that that God, who in so many weaknesses had assisted him with an unexpected strength, would now withdraw it in his last employment; professing an holy ambition to perform that sacred work. And when, to the amazement of some beholders, he appeared in the pulpit, many of them thought he presented himself not to preach mortification by a living voice, but mortality by a decayed body and a dying face. And doubtless many did secretly ask that question in Ezekiel: 'Do these bones live? or, can that soul organize that tongue, to speak so long as the sand in that glass will move towards its center, and measure out an hour of this dying man's unspent life? Doubtless it cannot.' And yet, after some faint pauses in his zealous prayer, his strong desires enabled his weak body to discharge his memory of his preconceived meditations, which were of dying; the text being, 'To God the Lord belong the issues from death.' Many that then saw his tears, and heard his faint and hollow voice, professing they thought the text prophetically chosen, and that Dr. Donne had preached his own funeral sermon.

"Being full of joy that God had enabled him to perform this desired duty, he hastened to his house; out of which he never moved, till, like St. Stephen, 'he was carried by devout men to his grave.'

Once back at home, Donne celebrated all the strange rites of his dying. He designed seals and rings for his closest friends, small "Heliotropian stones" engraved with the figure of Christ "extended upon an anchor" instead of a cross, the anchor being the emblem of hope. At least one of these gifts, the one sent to George Herbert, was accompanied by new poems in Latin and in English.

Early in March comes that bizarre incident memorialized still in marble in St. Paul's. Dean Donne was easily persuaded by friend Simeon Fox that a monument be readied for the dying Dean in the cathedral. But Donne insisted that he alone plan it and pay for it. Once that was agreed, he hurried the procedure. First a large wooden urn was made for him according to his exact requirements. It was delivered to his study along with a board just the height of Donne's own body, and with a portrait painter. Then,

Several charcoal fires being first made in his large study, he brought with him into that place his winding-sheet in his hand, and having put off all his clothes, had this sheet put on him, and so tied with knots at his head and feet, and his hands so placed as dead bodies are usually fitted, to be shrouded and put into their coffin or grave. Upon this urn he thus stood, with his eyes shut, and with so much of the sheet turned aside as might show his lean, pale, and death-like face, which was purposely turned towards the east, from whence he expected the second coming of his and our Saviour Jesus. In this posture he was drawn at his just height; and when the picture was fully finished, he caused it to be set by his bedside, where it continued and became his hourly object till his death, and was then given to his dearest friend and executor, Dr. Henry King, then chief Residentiary of St. Paul's, who caused him to be thus carved in one entire piece of white marble, as it now stands in that church . . . (Walton).

During the week of March 13-20, Donne called in his best friends one by one, bidding each goodbye with scriptural exhortations and a benediction. On March 20 he asked his servants to have all their accounts cleared with him by March 26, since "after that day he would not mix his thoughts with anything that concerned this world; nor ever did . . ."

A last poem, the splendid, seven-stanza "Hymn to God, My God, in My Sickness" was composed on March 23.

> Since I am comming to that holy roome,
>   Where, with thy Quire of Saints for evermore,
> I shall be made thy Musique; As I come
>   I tune the Instrument here at the dore,
> And what I must doe then, thinke here before . . .

The last days were a wasting patience. Toward midnight of March 31 he said, "I were miserable if I might not die," and then, "Thy kingdom come, Thy will be done." He closed his own eyes, stretched out his body and folded his hands to match the shrouded sketch by his bed, and died.

The whole elaborate death was, as Gosse suggests, "a piece of public tragedy, performed in solemn earnest, with an intention half chivalrous, half hortatory, by a religious humanist whose temper was of the sixteenth century . . . This was the Renaissance relation to human life, which was, after all, only a stage, on the boards of which a man of originality and principle must nerve himself to play *le beau rôle* to the last moment, in a final bout with a veritable Death, armed with scythe and hour-glass, a skeleton only just unseen, but accepted as something more than a mere convention." The last sermon certainly fits that picture. But it is not contained by that picture. More than a sixteenth-century grotesque in the seventeenth century, it is a sometimes brutal reminder of the blunt fact of death to anyone in any century who would look the other way.

DEATH'S DUELL OR, A CONSOLATION TO THE SOULE, AGAINST THE DYING LIFE, AND LIVING DEATH OF THE BODY.

Delivered in a Sermon at White-Hall, before the Kings Majesty, in the beginning of Lent (Feb. 25), 1630. Being his last Sermon, and called by his Majesties household THE DOCTORS OWNE FUNERALL SERMON.

Psalme 68. Vers. 20. In Finè. And Unto God the (Lord) Belong the Issues Of Death. i.e. From Death.

Buildings stand by the benefit of their *foundations* that susteine and *support* them, and of their *butteresses* that comprehend and *embrace* them, and of their *contignations* that knit and *unite* them: The *foundations* suffer them not to *sinke,* the *butteresses* suffer them not to *swerve,* and the *contignation* and knitting suffers them not to *cleave;* The body of our building is in the former part of this verse: It is this; hee that *is our God* is the *God of salvation; ad salutes,* of salvations in the plurall, so it is in the originall; the *God* that gives us spirituall and temporall salvation too. But of this *building,* the *foundation,* the *butteresses,* the *contignations* are in this part of the *verse,* which constitutes *our text,* and in the three divers *acceptations* of the words amongst our expositors. *Unto God the Lord belong the issues from death.* For *first* the *foundation* of this *building,* (that our *God* is the *God of all salvations*) is laid in this; That *unto* this *God the Lord belong the issues of death,* that is, it is in his power to give us an *issue* and deliverance, even then when wee are brought to the jawes and teeth of death, and to the lippes of that whirlepoole, the grave. And so in this acceptation of these words, and that upon which our *translation* laies hold, *The issues from death.* And then *secondly* the butteresses that comprehend and settle this building, That hee that is *our God,* is the *God of* all *salvations,* are thus raised; *Unto God the Lord belong the issues of death,* that is, the disposition and *manner of our death:* what kinde of *issue* and *transmigration* wee shall have out of this world, whether prepared or sudden, whether violent or naturall, whether in our perfect senses or shaken and disordered by sicknes, there is no condemnation to bee argued out of that, no Judgement to bee made upon that, for howsoever they dye, *precious in his sight is the death of his saints,* and with him are *the issues of death,* the *wayes* of our *departing* out of this *life* are in his *hands.* And so in this *sense* of the *words,* this *exitus mortis,* the *issue of death,* is *liberatio in morte, A deliverance in death;* Not that *God* will *deliver* us *from dying,* but that hee will *have a care* of us in the *houre of death,* of what kinde soever our passage be. And in this *sense* and acceptation of the *words,* the naturall frame and contexture doth well and pregnantly administer unto us; And then *lastly* the *contignation* and knitting of this building, that hee that is *our God* is the *God of all salvations,* consists in this, *Unto this God the Lord belong the issues of death,* that is, that this *God* the *Lord* having *united* and knit *both natures in one,* and being *God,* having also *come* into this *world,* in our *flesh,* he could have no other meanes to save us, he could have no other *issue* out of this world, nor *returne* to his former *glory,* but by *death;* And so in this sense, this *exitus mortis,* this *issue of death,* is *liberatio per mortem,* a *deliverance by death,* by the death of this *God* our *Lord Christ Jesus*. And this is Saint *Augustines* acceptation of the words, and those many and great persons that have adhered to him. In all these three lines then, we shall looke upon these words; *First,* as the *God* of *power,* the *Almighty Father* rescues his servants from the jawes of death: *And then* as the *God* of *mercy,* the glorious *Sonne* rescued us, by taking upon himselfe this *issue of death: And then* betweene these two, as the *God* of *comfort,* the *holy Ghost* rescues us from all discomfort by his blessed impressions before hand, that what manner of death soever be ordeined for us, yet this *exitus mortis* shall be *introitus in vitam,* our *issue in death* shall be an *entrance into everlasting life.* And these three considerations, our deliverance *à morte, in morte, per mortem, from death, in death, and by death,* will abundantly doe all the offices of the *foundations,* of the *butteresses,* of the *contignation* of this our *building;* That he that is our *God,* is the *God of all salvations,* because *unto* this *God the Lord belong the issues of death.*

First, then, we consider this *exitus mortis,* to bee *liberatio à morte,* that with *God* the *Lord* are the *issues of death,* and therefore in all our deaths, and deadly calamities of this life, wee may justly *hope* of a good *issue* from him. And all our *periods* and *transitions* in this life, are so many passages *from death* to *death;* our very *birth* and entrance into this life, is *exitus à morte,* and *issue from death,* for in our mothers *wombe* wee are *dead so,* as that wee doe *not know* wee *live,* not so much as wee doe in our *sleepe,* neither is there any *grave* so close, or so *putrid* a *prison,* as the *wombe* would be unto us, if we stayed in it *beyond* our time, or dyed there *before* our time. In the *grave* the *wormes* doe not kill us, wee *breed* and *feed,* and then *kill* those wormes which wee our selves produc'd. In the wombe the dead *child* kills the *Mother* that conceived it, and is a murtherer, nay a *parricide,* even after it is dead. And if wee bee **not** dead so in the *wombe,* so as that being dead wee kill her that gave us our first life, our life of *vegetation,* yet wee are dead so, as *Davids Idols* are dead. In the *wombe* wee have *eyes and see not, eares and heare not;* There in the wombe wee are fitted for *workes of darkness,* all the while deprived of light: And there in the *wombe* wee are taught *cruelty,* by being *fed with blood,* and may be *damned,* though we be *never borne.* Of our very making in the *wombe, David* sayes, *I am wonderfully and fearefully made,* and, *Such knowledge is too excellent for me,* for even that *is the Lords doing,* and it *is wonderfull in our eyes; Ipse fecit nos,* it is *hee that hath made us, and not wee our selves* nor our parents neither; *Thy hands have made me and fashioned me round about,* saith *Job,* and (as the *originall word is*) *thou hast taken paines about me,* and *yet,* sayes he, *thou doest destroy me.* Though I bee the *Master-peece* of the greatest *Master* (*man* is so), yet if thou doe no more for me, if thou leave me where thou madest mee, destruction will follow, The *wombe* which should be the *house of life,* becomes *death* it selfe, if *God* leave us there. That which God threatens so often, the *shutting of the womb,* is not so *heavy,* nor so discomfortable a *curse* in the *first,* as in the *latter* shutting, nor in the shutting of *barrennes,* as in the shutting of *weakenes,* when *children are come to the birth,* and there is not *strength to bring forth.*

It is the *exaltation of misery,* to *fall* from a *neare hope* of *happiness.* And in that vehement imprecation, the *Prophet* expresses the highest of *Gods* anger, *give them ô Lord, what wilt thou give them?* give them a *miscarying wombe.* Therefore as soone as wee are men, (that is, *inanimated,* quickned in the *womb*) thogh we cannot our selves, our parents have reason to say in our behalf, *wretched man that he is, who shall deliver* him *from this body of death?* for even the *wombe* is a *body of death,* if there bee no deliverer. It must be he that said to *Jeremy,* Before *I formed thee I knew thee,* and *before thou camest out of the wombe I sanc-tified thee.* Wee are not sure that there was no kinde of shippe nor boate to fish in, nor to passe by, till *God* prescribed *Noah* that absolute *form of the Arke.* That word which the *holy Ghost* by *Moses* useth for the *Arke,* is common to all kinde of *boates, Thebah,* and is the same word that *Moses* useth for the *boate* that he was *exposed in,* That *his mother layed him in an arke of bulrushes.* But we are sure that *Eve* had no *Midwife* when she was *delivered* of *Cain,* therefore shee might well say, *possedi virum à Domino, I have gotten a man from the Lord, wholly,* entirely from the Lord; It is the *Lord* that *enabled* me to *conceive,* The *Lord* that *infus'd a quickening soule* into that conception, the *Lord* that *brought into the world* that which himself *had quickened,* without all this might *Eve* say, My *body had bene* but the *house of death,* and *Domini, Domini sunt exitus mortis,* to *God the Lord* belong the issues of death.

But then this *exitus a morte,* is but *introitus in mortem,* this *issue,* this deliverance *from* that *death,* the death of the *wombe,* is an *entrance,* a delivering over to *another death,* the manifold deathes of this *world.* We have a winding sheete in our Mothers wombe, which growes with us from our conception, and wee come into the world, wound up in that *winding sheet,* for wee come to *seeke a grave;* And as prisoners discharg'd of actions may lie for fees, so when the *wombe* hath discharg'd us, yet we are bound to it by *cordes* of flesh by such a *string,* as that wee cannot goe thence, nor stay there; wee celebrate our owne funeralls with cries, even at our birth; as though our *threescore and ten years life* were spent in our mothers labour, and our circle made up in the first point thereof, we begge our *Baptisme,* with another *Sacrament,* with *teares;* And we come into a world that lasts many ages, but wee last not; *in domo Patris,* says our *Saviour,* speaking of *heaven, multæ man-*

siones, there *are many mansions,* divers and durable, so that if a man cannot possesse a *martyrs* house, (he hath shed no blood for *Christ*) yet hee may have a *Confessors,* he hath bene ready to glorifie *God* in the *shedding of his blood.* And if a woman cannot possesse a *virgins* house (she hath embrac'd the *holy state of mariage*) yet she may have a *matrons* house, she hath brought forth and brought up *children in the feare of God. In domo patris, in my fathers house,* in heaven there *are many mansions;* but here upon earth the *sonne of man hath not where to lay his head,* sayes he himselfe. *Nonne terram dedit filiis hominum?* how then hath *God given this earth* to the *sonnes of men?* hee hath *given* them *earth* for their *materialls* to bee made of earth, and hee hath given them *earth* for their *grave* and sepulture, to *returne* and resolve to *earth,* but not for their *possession: Here wee have no continuing citty,* nay no *cottage* that continues, nay no persons, no bodies that continue. Whatsoever moved Saint *Jerome* to call the journies of the *Israelites,* in the *wildernes,* mansions; The *word* (the word is *Nasang*) signifies but a *journey,* but a peregrination. Even the *Israel of God* hath no mansions; but journies, pilgrimages in this life. By that measure did *Jacob* measure his life to *Pharaoh; the dayes* of the years *of my pilgrimage.* And though the *Apostle* would not say *morimur,* that, whilest wee *are in the body* wee *are dead,* yet hee sayes, *Peregrinamur,* whilest wee are *in the body,* wee are but in a *pilgrimage,* and wee are *absent from the Lord;* hee might have said *dead,* for this whole *world* is but an *universall churchyard,* but one *common grave,* and the life and motion that the greatest persons have in it, is but as the shaking of buried bodies in the grave, by an *earth-quake.* That which we call life, is but *Hebdomada mortium,* a *weeke of deaths,* seven dayes, seven periods of our life spent in dying, *a dying seaven times over;* and there is an end. *Our birth dies* in *infancy,* and our

infancy dies in *youth,* and *youth* and the rest die in
age, and *age* also dies, and *determines all.* Nor doe all
these, youth out of infancy, or age out of youth arise
so, as a *Phœnix* out of the *ashes* of another *Phœnix*
formerly *dead,* but as a *waspe* or a *serpent* out of a
caryon, or as a *Snake* out of *dung.* Our *youth* is *worse*
than our *infancy,* and our *age worse* than our *youth.*
Our *youth* is *hungry* and *thirsty,* after those *sinnes,*
which our *infancy knew not;* And our *age* is *sory* and
angry, that it *cannot pursue* those *sinnes* which our
youth did; and besides, al the way, so many deaths,
that is, so many deadly calamities accompany every
condition, and every period of this life, as that death
it selfe would bee an ease to them that suffer them:
Upon this sense doth *Job* wish that *God had not given
him* an *issue* from the *first death,* from the *wombe,
Wherefore hast thou brought me* forth *out of the
wombe? O that I had given up the Ghost, and no eye
seene me! I should have beene as though I had not
beene.* And not only the impatiend *Israelites* in their
murmuring (*would to God wee had died by the hand
of the Lord in the land of Egypt*) but *Eliah* himselfe,
when he *fled* from *Jesabell,* and went for his life, as
that text sayes, under the *Juniper tree,* requested that
hee might die, and said, *it is enough now, O Lord,
take away my life.* So *Jonah* justifies his impatience,
nay his anger towards *God* himselfe. *Now ô Lord take,
I beseech thee, my life from mee, for it is better to die
than to live.* And when *God* asked him, *doest thou
well to be angry for this,* he replies, *I doe well to be
angry, even unto death.* How much worse a death than
death, is this life, which so good men would so often
change for death! But if my case bee as Saint *Paules*
case, *quotidiè morior,* that *I die dayly,* that something
heavier than death falls upon me every day; If my
case be *Davids* case, *tota die mortificamur; all the day
long wee are killed,* that not onely every day, but every
houre of the day some thing heavier than death falls

upon me, though that bee true of me, *Conceptus in peccatis, I was shapen* in *iniquity, and in sinne did my mother conceive me,* (there I dyed one death), though that be true of me *(Natus filius iræ) I was borne* not onely of the child of sinne, but *the child of wrath,* of the wrath of *God* for sinne, which is a heavier death; Yet *Domini Domini sunt exitus mortis,* with *God the Lord are the issues of death,* and after a *Job,* and a *Joseph,* and a *Jeremie,* and a *Daniel,* I cannot doubt of a deliverance. And if no other deliverance conduce more to his glory and my good, yet he hath the *keys of death,* and hee can let me out at that dore, that is, deliver me from the manifold deaths of this world, the *omni die* and the *tota die,* the *every days death* and *every houres death,* by that *one death,* the *finall dissolution* of body and sould, the end of all. But then is that the end of all? Is that dissolution of body and soule, the last death that the body shall suffer? (for of spirituall death wee speake not now) It is not. Though this be *exitus à morte,* It is *introitus in mortem;* though it bee an *issue from* the manifold *deaths* of this *world,* yet it is an *entrance* into the *death of corruption* and *putrefaction* and *vermiculation* and *incineration,* and dispersion in and from the *grave,* in which every dead man dies over againe. It was a *prerogative* peculiar to *Christ,* not to die this death, *not to see corruption:* what gave him this priviledge? Not *Josephs* great proportion of *gummes and spices,* that might have preserved his body from corruption and *incineration* longer than he needed it, longer than *three dayes,* but would not have done it for ever: what preserved him then? did his exemption and *freedome from originall sinne* preserve him from this corruption and *incineration?* 'tis true that original sinne hath induced this corruption and *incineration* upon us; If wee had not sinned in *Adam, mortality had not put on immortality,* (as the *Apostle* speakes) nor, *corruption had not put on incorruption,* but we had had our *transmigration* from this to the other world, without any *mortality,* and *corruption at all.* But yet since Christ tooke *sinne* upon him, so farre as made him *mortall,* he had it so farre too, as might have made him see this corruption and *incineration,* though he had no *originall sinne* in himself; what preserv'd him then? Did the *hypostaticall union* of both *natures, God* and *Man, preserve* him from this corruption and incineration? 'tis true that this was a most powerfull *embalming,* to be embalmd with the *divine nature* itselfe, to bee embalmd with *eternity,* was able to preserve him from corruption and *incineration* for ever. And he was embalmd so, embalmd with the *divine nature* it selfe, even in his *body* as well as in his *soule;* for the *Godhead,* the *divine nature* did not depart, but remained still *united* to his *dead body* in the *grave;* But yet for al this powerful *embalming,* this *hypostaticall union* of both natures, we see *Christ* did *die;* and for all this *union* which made him *God* and *Man,* hee became no man (for the *union* of the *body* and *soule* makes the man, and hee whose soule and body are separated by *death* as long as that state lasts is properly no man.) And therefore as in him the dissolution of *body* and *soule* was no *dissolution* of the *hypostaticall union;* so is there nothing that constraines us to say, that though the *flesh* of *Christ* had *seene corruption* and *incineration* in the grave, this had bene any *dissolution* of the *hypostaticall union,* for the divine *nature,* the Godhead might have remained with all the *Elements* and *principles* of *Christs* body, as well as it did with the two *constitutive* parts of his *person,* his *body* and his *soul.* This *incorruption* then was not in *Josephs gummes* and *spices,* nor was it in *Christs* innocency, and *exemption* from *originall sin,* nor was it (that is, it is not necessary to say it was) in the *hypostaticall union.* But this *incorruptiblenes* of his *flesh* is most conveniently plac'd in that, *Non dabis, thou wilt not suffer thy*

holy one to see corruption. Wee looke no further for
causes or *reasons* in the *mysteries of religion,* but to
the *will* and pleasure of *God: Christ* himselfe limited
his *inquisition* in that *ita est, even so Father, for so it
seemeth good in thy sight. Christs* body did *not see
corruption,* therefore, because *God* had *decreed* it
shold not. The humble soule (and onely the humble
soule is the religious soule) rests himselfe upon *Gods*
purposes and the decrees of *God,* which he hath declared and manifested not such as are *conceived* and
imagined in our selves, though upon some probability,
some *veresimilitude.* So in our present case *Peter* proceeds in his *Sermon* at *Jerusalem,* and so *Paul* in *his*
at *Antioch.* They preached *Christ* to have *bene risen*
without seeing *corruption* not onely because *God* had
decreed it, but because he had *manifested* that *decree*
in his *Prophet.* Therefore doth Saint *Paul* cite by
speciall number the *second Psalme* for that *decree;*
And therefore both Saint *Peter* and S. *Paul* cite for
it that place in the 16. *Psalme,* for when *God* declares
his *decree* and purpose in the expresse words of his
Prophet, or when he declares it in the reall execution
of the decree, then he makes it ours, then he manifests
it to us. And therfore as the *Mysteries* of our *Religion,*
are *not* the *objects* of *our reason,* but *by faith we rest*
on *Gods decree* and purpose, (It is so ô *God,* because
it is *thy will,* it should be so) so *Gods decrees* are ever
to be considered in the *manifestation* thereof. All
manifestation is is either in the *word* of *God,* or in the
execution of the *decree;* And when these two concur
and meete, it is the strongest *demonstration* that can
be: when therefore I finde those *markes* of *adoption*
and *spiritual filiation,* which are delivered in the *word*
of *God* to be upon me, when I finde that reall *execution* of his *good purpose* upon me, as that *actually*
I doe *live* under the *obedience,* and under the *conditions* which are *evidences* of *adoption* and *spiritual
filiation;* Then so long as I see these *markes* and live

so; I may safely comfort my selfe in a *holy certitude*
and a *modest infallibility* of my *adoption*. *Christ* determines himself in that, the purpose of *God* was manifest to him: S. *Peter* and S. *Paul* determine themselves
in those two wayes of knowing the *purpose* of *God*,
the *word* of *God* before, the *execution* of the *decree*
in the *fulnes of time*. It was *prophecyed before*, say
they, and it is *performed now, Christ is risen* without
seeing corruption. Now this which is so singularly
peculiar to him, that *his flesh should not see corruption*, at his *second coming*, his coming to *Judgement*,
shall extend to all that are then alive, their flesh
shall not *see corruption*, because as th' *Apostle* sayes,
and sayes as *a secret*, as *a mystery; Behold I shew you
a mistery, we shall not all sleepe,* (that is, not continue
in the state of the dead in the grave,) *but wee shall
all be changed in an instant,* we shall have a *dissolution,* and in the *same instant* a *redintegration,* a *recompacting* of *body* and *soule,* and that shall be
truely a death and truely a resurrection, but no sleeping in corruption; But for us that die now and sleepe
in the state of the dead, we must al passe this *posthume* death, this *death* after *death,* nay this death
after *buriall,* this *dissolution* after *dissolution,* this
death of *corruption* and *putrifaction,* of *vermiculation*
and *incineration,* of *dissolution* and *dispersion* in and
from the *grave,* when these bodies that have beene the
children of *royall parents,* and the *parents* of *royall
children,* must say with *Job, Corruption thou art my
father,* and *to the Worme thou art my mother and my
sister. Miserable riddle,* when the *same worme* must
bee *my mother,* and *my sister,* and *my selfe. Miserable
incest,* when I must bee *maried* to my *mother* and my
sister, and bee both *father* and *mother* to my *owne
mother* and *sister, beget* and *beare* that *worme* which
is all that *miserable penury;* when my *mouth* shall be
filled with *dust,* and the *worme* shall *feed,* and *feed
sweetely* upon me, when the *ambitious* man shall have

no satisfaction, if the *poorest alive* tread upon him, nor the *poorest* receive any *contentment* in being made *equal* to *Princes,* for they *shall bee equall* but *in dust.* One dyeth at his full strength, being wholly at ease and in quiet, and another dies in the *bitternes of his soul,* and never *eates* with *pleasure,* but they lye downe *alike* in *the dust,* and the *worme covers them;* In *Job* and in *Esay,* it *covers them and is spred under them,* the worme is spred *under thee,* and the *worme covers thee,* There's the *Mats* and the *Carpets* that *lie under,* and there's the *State* and the *Canapye,* that *hangs over* the greatest of the sons of men; Even those bodies that were *the temples of the holy Ghost,* come to this *dilapidation,* to ruine, to rubbidge, to dust, even the *Israel of the Lord,* and *Jacob* himselfe hath no other specification, no other denomination, but that *vermis Jacob,* thou *worme of Jacob.* Truely the consideration of this *posthume death,* this death after buriall, that after *God,* (with whom are the *issues of death*) hath delivered me from the *death* of the *wombe,* by bringing mee into the *world,* and from the manifold *deaths* of the *world,* by laying me in the *grave,* I must die againe in an *Incineration* of this *flesh,* and in a dispersion of that dust. That that *Monarch,* who spred over many nations alive, must in his dust lie in a corner of that *sheete of lead,* and there, but so long as that lead will laste, and that privat and *retir'd man,* that thought himselfe his owne for ever, and never came forth, must in his dust of the grave bee published, and (such are the *revolutions* of the *graves*) bee mingled with the dust of every high way, and of every dunghill, and swallowed in every puddle and pond: This is the most inglorious and contemptible *vilification,* the most deadly and peremptory *nullification* of man, that wee can consider; *God* seemes to have caried the declaration of his *power* to a great height, when hee sets the *Prophet Ezechiel* in the *valley of drye bones,* and says, *Sonne of man can these bones live?* as though it had bene impossible, and yet they did; The *Lord* layed *Sinewes upon them, and flesh, and breathed into them,* and *they did live:* But in that case there were *bones* to bee *seene,* something visible, of which it might be said, can this thing live? But in this death of *incineration,* and dispersion of dust, wee see *nothing* that wee call *that mans;* If we say, can this dust live? perchance it *cannot,* it may bee the meere *dust* of the *earth,* which never did live, never shall. It may be the dust of that mans *worme,* which did live, but shall no more. It may bee the dust of *another* man, that concernes not him of whom it is askt. This death of *incineration* and dispersion, is, to naturall *reason,* the most *irrecoverable death* of all, and yet *Domini Domini sunt exitus mortis, unto God the Lord belong the issues of death,* and by *recompacting* this *dust* into the *same body,* and *reinanimating* the *same body* with the *same soule,* hee shall in a blessed and glorious *resurrection* give mee such an *issue from* this *death,* as shal never passe into any other *death,* but establish me into a life that shall last as long as the *Lord of life* himself.

And so have you that that belongs to the *first acceptation* of these words, (*unto God the Lord belong the issues of death*) That though from the *wombe* to the *grave* and in the grave it selfe wee passe from *death* to *death,* yet, as *Daniel* speakes, the *Lord our God is able to deliver us, and hee will deliver us.*

And so wee passe unto our *second accommodation* of *these words* (*unto God the Lord belong the issues of death*) That it *belongs* to *God,* and *not* to *man* to *passe a judgement* upon us at our death, or to conclude a dereliction on *Gods* part upon the manner thereof.

Those *indications* which the *Physitians* receive, and those *presagitions* which they give for *death* or *recovery* in the *patient,* they receive and they give out of the grounds and the *rules of their art:* But we have no such rule or art to give a *presagition* of *spirituall death* and damnation upon any such *indication* as wee see in any *dying man;* wee see often enough to be sory, but not to despaire; wee may bee deceived both ways; wee use to comfort our selfe in the death of a *friend,* if it be testified that he went away like a *Lambe,* that is, without any *reluctation.* But, *God* knowes, that (he) may bee accompanied with a *dangerous damp* and *stupefaction,* and *insensibility* of his *present state.* Our blessed *Saviour* suffered *coluctations* with *death,* and a *sadnes even in his soule to death,* and an *agony* even to a *bloody sweate* in his *body,* and *expostulations* with *God,* and *exclamations* upon the crosse. He was a *devout man,* who said upon his death bed, or dead turfe (for hee was an *Heremit*) *septuaginta annis Domino servivisti, et mori times? hast thou served a good Master threescore and ten yeares,* and *now art thou loath to goe into his presence?* yet *Hilarion* was loath; *Barlaam* was a *devout* man (an *Heremit* too) that said that day hee died. *Cogita te hodie cœpisse servire Domino, et hodie finiturum. Consider this to be the first days service that ever thou didst thy Master,* to glorifie him in a Christianly and a constant death, *and if thy first day* be *thy last day too, how soone dost thou come* to *receive thy wages?* yet *Barlaam* could have beene content to have staid longer for it: Make no *ill conclusions* upon any mans *loathnes to die,* for the *mercies* of *God* worke *momentarily* in minutes, and many times *insensibly* to *bystanders* or any other than the party departing. And then upon *violent deaths* inflicted, as upon malefactors, *Christ* himselfe hath forbidden us by his owne death to make any *ill conclusion;* for his owne *death* had those impressions in it; He was *reputed,* he was *executed* as a *malefactor,* and no doubt many of them who concurred to his death, did beleeve him to bee so; Of *sudden death* there are scarce examples to be found in the *scriptures* upon *good men,* for *death* in *battaile* cannot be called *sudden death;* But *God* governes not by *examples,* but by *rules,* and therefore make no *ill conclusion* upon *sudden death* nor upon *distempers* neither, though perchance accompanied with some *words of diffidence* and distrust in the *mercies of God:* The *tree lies as it falles* its true, but it is *not* the *last stroake* that *fells* the *tree,* nor the *last word* nor *gaspe* that *qualifies* the *soule.* Stil *pray* wee for a *peaceable life* against *violent death,* and for *time* of *repentance* against *sudden death,* and for *sober* and *modest assurance* against *distemperd* and *diffident death,* but never make *ill conclusions* upon persons overtaken with such deaths; *Domini Domini sunt exitus mortis, to God the Lord belong the issues of death.* And *he* received *Sampson,* who went out of this world in *such* a *manner* (consider it *actively,* consider it *passively* in his *owne death,* and in those whom he *slew* with himselfe) as was subject to interpretation hard enough. Yet the *holy Ghost* hath moved S. *Paul* to celebrate *Sampson* in his *great Catalogue,* and so doth all the *Church: Our criticall* day is *not* the *very day* of our *death:* but the whole course of our life. I thanke him that *prayes* for me when the *Bell tolles,* but I thank him much more that *Catechises* mee, or *preaches* to mee, or *instructs mee how to live. Fac hoc et vives, there's* my securitie, the mouth of the *Lord hath said it, doe this and thou shalt live:* But *though I doe it,* yet I *shall die too,* die a bodily, a naturall death. But *God* never mentions, never seems to consider that death, the bodily, the naturall death. *God* doth not say, live well and thou shalt die well, that is, an easie, a quiet death; But *live well here,* and thou shalt *live well for ever.* As the first part of a sentence peeces wel with the last, and never respects, never hearkens after the *parenthesis* that comes betweene, so doth a *good life* here flowe into an *eternall life,* without any consideration, what *manner* of *death* wee dye: But whether the *gate* of *my prison* be *opened* with an *oyld key* (by a gentle and *preparing sicknes*), *or* the gate bee *hewen downe* by a *violent death,* or the gate bee *burnt downe* by a *raging* and *frantique feaver,* a *gate into heaven* I *shall have,* for *from* the *Lord is the cause* of *my life,* and *with God the Lord* are the *issues of death.* And further wee cary not this *second acceptation* of the *words,* as this *issue of death* is *liberatio in morte, Gods care* that the *soule* be *safe,* what *agonies* soever the *body suffers* in the *houre* of *death.*

But passe to our *third part* and last part; as this *issue of death* is *liberatio per mortem,* a *deliverance by the death* of another, by the death of Christ. *Sufferentiam Job audiisti, et vidisti finem Domini,* sayes Saint *James* 5. 11. *You have heard of the patience of Job,* says he, All this while you have done that, for in every man, calamitous, miserable man, a *Job* speakes; Now *see the end of the Lord,* saith that *Apostle,* which is not that end that the *Lord* propos'd to himselfe (*salvation to us*) nor the end which he proposes to us (*conformitie to him*) but *see the end of the Lord,* sayes he, The end, *that the Lord* himselfe *came to, Death* and a painefull and a shamefull death. But why did he die? and why die so? *Quia Domini Domini sunt exitus mortis* (as Saint *Augustine* interpreting this *text* answeres that question) because *to* this *God our Lord belong'd the issues of death. Quid apertius diceretur?* sayes hee there, what can bee more obvious, more manifest than this sense of these words. In the former part of this verse, it is said; *He that is our God, is the God of salvation, Deus salvos faciendi,* so hee reads it, the *God* that must save us. Who can that be, sayes he, but *Jesus?* for *therefore* that *name* was *given him,* because he was to *save us.* And to this *Jesus,* sayes he, this *Saviour, belong the issues of death; Nec oportuit eum de hac vita alios exitus habere quam mortis.* Being come into this life in our mortal nature, *He could not goe out of it* any other way *but by death. Ideo dictum,* says he, *therefore it is said,* To *God the Lord belong the issues of death; ut ostenderetur moriendo nos salvos facturum,* to *shew that his way to save us was to die.* And from this *text* doth Saint *Isodore* prove, that *Christ* was *truely Man,* (which as many *sects* of *heretiques denied,* as that he was *truely God*) because to him, though he were *Dominus Dominus* (as the *text* doubles it) *God* the *Lord,* yet to *him,* to *God the Lord belong'd the issues of death, oportuit eum pati* more can not be said, than *Christ* himselfe sayes of himselfe; *These things Christ ought to suffer,* hee had no other way but by death: So then *this part of* our *Sermon* must needes be a *passion Sermon;* since all his *life* was a *continuall passion,* all *our Lent* may well bee a *continuall good Friday. Christs* painefull life tooke off none of the paines of his death, hee felt not the lesse then for having felt so much before. Nor will any thing that shall be said before, lessen, but rather inlarge the devotion, to that which shall be said of his passion at the time of due *solemnization* thereof. *Christ* bled not a droppe the lesse at the last, for having bled at his *Circumcision* before, nor wil you shed a teare the lesse then, if you shed some now. And therefore bee now content to consider with mee how to *this God the Lord belong'd the issues of death.* That *God,* this *Lord,* the *Lord of life could die,* is a strange contemplation; That the *red Sea* could bee *drie,* That the *Sun* could *stand still,* That an *Oven* could be *seaven times heat* and *not burne,* That *Lions* could be *hungry* and *not bite,* is strange, *miraculously strange,* but *supermiraculous* that *God could die;* but that *God would die* is an *exaltation* of that. But even of that also it is a *superexaltation,* that *God shold die, must die,* and *non exitus* (said S.*Augustin, God* the *Lord had no issue but by death,* and *oportuit pati* (says *Christ* himself, all this *Christ ought to suffer,* was bound to suffer; *Deus ultionum Deus* says *David,*

God is the *God of revenges,* he wold *not passe* over
the *sinne of man* unrevenged, unpunished. But then
Deus ultionum liberè egit (sayes *that place*) The *God
of revenges workes freely,* he *punishes,* he *spares
whome he will.* And wold he *not spare himselfe?* he
would not: *Dilectio fortis ut mors, love is strong as
death,* stronger, it drew in death that naturally is not
welcom. *Si possible,* says *Christ, If it be possible, let
this Cup passe,* when his *love expressed in a former
decree* with his *Father,* had *made it impossible.* Many
waters quench not love, Christ tried many; He was
Baptized out of his *love,* and his love determined not
there. He *mingled blood* with *water* in his *agony* and
that determined not his love; hee *wept pure blood,* all
his blood at all his eyes, at all his pores, in his *flagella-
tion* and *thornes* (*to the Lord our God belong'd the
issues of blood*) and these *expressed,* but these did *not
quench his love.* Hee *would not* spare, nay he *could
not spare himselfe.* There was nothing more free,
more voluntary, more spontaneous than the death of
Christ. 'Tis true, *libere egit,* he *died voluntarily,* but
yet when we consider the *contract* that had passed
betweene his *Father* and *him,* there was an *oportuit,*
a kind of *necessity* upon him. All this *Christ ought to
suffer.* And when shall we *date* this *obligation,* this
oportuit, this *necessity?* when shall wee say *that begun?* Certainly this *decree* by which *Christ was to
suffer* all this, was an *eternall decree,* and was there
any thing before that, that was eternall? *Infinite love,
eternall love;* be pleased to follow this home, and to
consider it seriously, that what liberty soever wee can
conceive in *Christ,* to die or not to die; this *necessity
of dying,* this *decree* is as *eternall* as that *liberty;* and
yet how small a matter made hee of this *necessity* and
this *dying?* His *Father* cals it but a *bruise,* and but a
bruising of his heele (*the serpent shall bruise his
heele*) and yet that was that, the *serpent* should *practise* and *compasse* his *death.* Himselfe calls it but a

Baptisme, as though he were to bee the better for it.
I have a Baptisme to be Baptized with, and he was
in apine till it was accomplished, and yet this *Baptisme* was *his death.* The *holy Ghost* calls it *Joy* (for
*the Joy which was set before him hee indured the
Crosse*) which was not a *joy* of his reward after his
passion, but a joy that filled him even in the middest
of those torments, and arose from him; when *Christ*
calls his *Calicem, a Cuppe,* and no worse (*can ye
drink of my Cuppe*) he speakes not odiously, not with
detestation of it: Indeed it was a *Cup, salus mundo,
a health to all the world.* And *quid retribuam,* says
David, what shall I render to the Lord? answere you
with *David, accipiam Calicem, I will take the Cup of
salvation,* take it, that *Cup* is *salvation,* his *passion,* if
not into your *present imitation,* yet into your *present
contemplation.* And behold how that *Lord* that was
God, yet *could die, would die, must die,* for your *salvation.* That *Moses* and *Elias talkt with Christ* in the
transfiguration, both Saint *Mathew* and Saint *Marke*
tell us, but what they talkt of onely S. *Luke, Dicebant
excessum ejus,* says he, *they talkt of his decease,* of
his death which *was to be accomplished* at *Jerusalem,*
The *word* is of his *Exodus,* the very word of our *text,
exitus, his issue by death. Moses* who in his *Exodus*
had *prefigured* this *issue of our Lord,* and in passing
Israel out of *Egypt* through the *red Sea,* had foretold
in that actuall *prophesie, Christ passing of mankind
through* the *sea* of his *blood.* And *Elias,* whose *Exodus
and issue out of* this *world* was a *figure of Christs
ascension* had no doubt a great satisfaction in *talking*
with our *blessed Lord de excessu ejus,* of the *full
consummation of all this in his death,* which was to
bee *accomplished* at *Jerusalem.* Our *meditation* of his
death should be more *viscerall* and affect us more because it is of a thing already done. The ancient *Ro-
mans* had a certain tendernesse and detestation of the
name of death, they could not name death, no, not in

their wills. There they could not say *Si mori con-
tigerit,* but *si quid humanitus contingat,* not if, or
when I die, but when the course of nature is accomplished upon me. To us that speake daily of the *death*
of *Christ,* (he was *crucified, dead* and *buried*) can the
memory or the mention of our owne *death* bee irke-
some or bitter? There are in these latter times amongst
us, that name death freely enough, and the death of
God, but in *blasphemous oathes* and *execrations.*
Miserable men, who shall therefore bee said never to
have named Jesus, because they have named him *too
often.* And therefore heare *Jesus* say, *Nescivi vos, I
never knew you,* because they made themselves *too
familiar* with him. *Moses* and *Elias* talkt with *Christ*
of his *death,* only, in *a holy* and *joyfull sense* of the
benefit which *they* and *all* the world were to *receive
by that. Discourses of Religion* should not be *out* of
curiosity, but to *edification.* And then they talkt with
Christ of his *death* at that time, when he was in the
greatest *height of glory* that ever he admitted in this
world, that is, his *transfiguration.* And wee are afraid
to speake to the *great men* of this world of their *death,*
but nourish in them a *vaine imagination* of *immortality,* and *immutability.* But *bonum est nobis esse hic*
(as Saint *Peter* said there) It *is good to dwell here,* in
this *consideration* of his *death,* and therefore *trans-
ferre* wee our *tabernacle* (our *devotions*) through some
of those *steps* which *God* the *Lord* made to his *issue
of death* that *day.* Take in the *whole day* from the
houre that *Christ received* the *passeover* upon *Thurs-
day, unto* the *houre* in which hee *died* the *next day.*
Make *this* present *day* that *day* in thy *devotion,* and
consider what *hee did,* and remember what *you have
done.* Before hee *instituted* and *celebrated* the *Sacrament,* (which was *after* the *eating of the passeover*)
hee proceeded to that *act* of *humility,* to *wash his
disciples feete,* even *Peters, who* for a while *resisted*
him; In thy *preparation* to the holy and blessed

Sacrament, hast thou with a sincere *humility* sought a *reconciliation* with all the *world,* even with those that have beene *averse* from it, and *refused* that *reconciliation* from thee? If so, and not else thou hast spent that *first part* of his *last day,* in a *conformity* with him. After the *Sacrament* hee spent the time till night in *prayer,* in *preaching,* in *Psalmes;* Hast thou considered that a *worthy receaving* of the *Sacrament* consists in a *continuation* of *holinesse after,* as wel as in a *preparation* before? If so, thou hast therein also *conformed* thy selfe to him, so *Christ* spent his time till night; *At night* hee *went into the garden* to *pray,* and he prayed *prolixius* he spent *much time* in *prayer.* How much? Because it is literally expressed, that *he prayed there three severall times,* and that *returning to his Disciples* after his *first prayer,* and *finding them asleepe* said, *could ye not watch with me one houre,* it is collected that he *spent three houres* in *prayer.* I dare scarce aske thee *whither* thou *wentest,* or *how* thou *disposedst* of *thy self,* when it *grew darke* and after *last night:* If that time were spent in a *holy recommendation* of thy selfe to *God,* and a *submission* of *thy will* to *his,* It was spent in a *conformity* to him. In that *time* and in those *prayers* was *his agony* and *bloody sweat.* I will *hope* that thou didst *pray,* but not *every ordinary* and *customary prayer,* but *prayer actually* accompanied *with shedding of teares,* and *dispositively* in a readiness to *shed blood* for *his glory* in *necessary cases,* puts thee into a *conformity* with him; About midnight he was *taken and bound with a kisse.* Art thou not *too conformable* to him in that? Is not that *too literally,* too exactly *thy case?* at *midnight* to have *bene taken and bound with a kisse?* from thence he was *caried back to Jerusalem,* first to *Annas,* then to *Caiphas,* and (as late as it was) then hee was *examined* and *buffeted,* and *delivered over* to the custody of those *officers,* from whome he received all those *irrisions,* and *violences,* the *covering*

of his face, the *spitting upon his face,* the *blasphemies
of words,* and the *smartnes of blowes* which that *Gospell* mentions. In which compasse fell that *Gallicinium,* that *crowing of the Cock* which *called up Peter*
to his *repentance.* How thou passedst all that time
last night thou knowest. If thou didst any thing that
needed *Peters teares,* and hast *not shed them,* let me
be thy *Cock,* doe it now, Now thy *Master* (in the
unworthiest of his servants) *lookes back upon thee,*
doe it now; *Betimes,* in the morning, so soone as it
was day, the *Jewes held a counsell* in the *high Priests
hall,* and *agreed upon their evidence* against him, and
then caried him to *Pilate,* who was to be his *Judge;*
diddest thou *accuse* thy selfe when thou *wakedst this
morning,* and wast thou content even with *false accusations* (that is) rather to *suspect actions* to have
beene sin, which were not, than to *smother* and
justify such as were *truly sins?* then thou spentst that
houre in *conformity* to him: *Pilate* found *no evidence
against him,* and therefore to ease himselfe, and to
passe a *complement* upon *Herod, Tetrarch of Galilee,*
who was at that time at *Jerusalem* (because *Christ*
being a *Galilean* was of *Herods jurisdiction) Pilat sent
him* to *Herod,* and rather as a *madman* than a *malefactor, Herod* remaunded him *(with scornes)* to *Pilat*
to proceed against him; And this was about *eight* of
the *clock.* Hast thou been content to come to this
Inquisition, this examination, this agitation, this
cribration, this pursuit of thy *conscience,* to *sift* it, to
follow it from the *sinnes* of thy *youth* to thy *present
sinnes,* from the *sinnes* of thy *bed,* to the *sinnes* of
thy *boorde,* and from the *substance* to the *circumstance* of thy *sinnes?* That's *time spent* like thy
Saviours. Pilat wold have *saved Christ,* by using the
priviledge of the day in his behalfe, because that *day*
one *prisoner was to be delivered,* but they *choose
Barrabas.* Hee would have *saved* him *from death,* by
satisfying their fury, with *inflicting* other *torments*

upon him, *scourging* and *crowning with thornes*, and *loading* him with many *scornefull* and *ignominous contumelies;* But they regarded him not, they pressed a *crucifying*. Hast thou gone about to *redeeme thy sinne*, by *fasting*, by *Almes*, by *disciplines* and *mortifications*, in way of *satisfaction* to the *Justice* of *God*? that wil not serve, that's not the right way, *wee presse* an utter *Crucifying* of that *sinne* that governes thee; and that *conformes* thee to *Christ*. Towards *noone Pilat* gave *judgement*, and they made such *hast* to execution, as that *by noone* hee was *upon the Crosse*. There now hangs that *sacred Body* upon the *Crosse*, *rebaptized* in his *owne teares* and *sweat*, and *embalmed* in his *owne blood alive*. There are those *bowells of compassion*, which are so conspicuous, so manifested, as that you may *see them through his wounds*. There those *glorious eyes* grew faint in their light: so as the *Sun ashamed* to survive them, *departed with his light too*. And then that *Sonne of God*, who was *never from us*, and yet had now come a *new way unto* us in *assuming our nature*, delivers that *soule* (which was *never out* of his *Fathers hands*) by a *new way*, a *voluntary emission* of it into his Fathers hands; For though to this *God our Lord*, *belong'd these issues of death*, so that considered in his owne contract, he *must* necessarily *die*, yet at *no breach* or *battery*, which they had made upon his *sacred Body*, issued his soule, but *emisit*, hee *gave up the Ghost*, and as *God breathed a soule into* the *first Adam*, so this *second Adam breathed his soule into God, into the hands of God*. There wee leave you in that *blessed dependancy*, to *hang* upon *him* that *hangs* upon the *Crosse*, there *bath* in his *teares*, there *suck* at his *woundes*, and *lie downe in peace* in his *grave*, till hee vouchsafe you a *resurrection*, and an *ascension* into that *Kingdome*, which hee *hath purchas'd for you*, with the *inestimable price* of his *incorruptible blood*. Amen.

BIBLIOGRAPHY

THE SERMONS

SIMPSON, EVELYN M. and POTTER, GEORGE R. (editors). *The Sermons of John Donne*. Berkeley: University of California Press, 1953.

John Donne's sermons waited a long time for reliable presentation but when they finally received it, in these ten volumes, what they got was an irreproachably introduced, arranged, and annotated edition. Mrs. Simpson has long been an unchallengeable authority on Donne's prose work, and George Potter, who did not live to see the end of this enormous project, was a scholar of similar magnitude in the same galaxy. The rich big volumes in this set are indispensable not only for their definitive versions of the sermons but for their careful reconstruction of the facts of Donne's life. It is hard to imagine another edition of these sermons ever being necessary.

ALFORD, HENRY (editor). *The Works of John Donne*, D.D. (in six volumes). London: John W. Parker, 1839.

Between the original publication of Donne's sermons and the extraordinary Simpson-Potter edition, only the Alford volumes attempted a full representation. And Alford was none too full. His editing can be called only an expurgating edition. For nineteenth century Christians, Donne had to be expurgated! Modernizing the spelling, "improving" the punctuation did nothing to enhance the scholarly usefulness of the edition. But then, Alford was not concerned as much for scholarship as for distribution of sermons important to him as "a genuine body of orthodox divinity." Alford's Donne from now on is more interesting for what it tells about Alford than for what it tells about Donne. When the Simpson-Potter edition shortly is complete, Alford can be pushed far back on all shelves.

SMITH, LOGAN PEARSALL (editor). *Donne's Sermons* (Selected Passages). Oxford: Clarendon Press, 1920.

A rich treasury of nuggets from the vast mine of the sermons. Selections run from a few lines to a few pages long. The principle of selection seems to be mainly literary, the excerpts abounding more in general wisdom than in theological insight. In a way, therefore, Donne is made to look better than he is—and curiously thinner. The long introduction to the book is a graceful and ingratiating introduction to Donne.

BIOGRAPHY

WALTON, IZAAK. *Lives*. New York: Hurd and Houghton, 1865.

It is too much to ask factual precision from this biography. Walton was a friend and companion of the Dean of St. Paul's, and an unabashed hero-worshipper. The writing is all molten subjectivity. Yet the *Life of Dr. Donne*, readied for inclusion in the 1640 edition of *LXXX Sermons*, remains basic to subsequent biographies. Its principle attraction now, though, is as a genuine literary masterwork in its own right.

GOSSE, EDMUND. *The Life and Letters of John Donne* (2 volumes). New York: Dodd, Mead and Co., 1899.

This is still the fullest biography of John Donne, with most of his letters worked into the life story in their chronological order. Gosse's principle biographical facts have not been radically revised by subsequent scholarship, his literary appreciation of the sermons is just as hearty, and his reticence before the ultimate mystery of Donne's personality is commendatory. Later biographers may probe more fruitfully those personal depths with which we now think ourselves more familiar, but none will be more aware of those depths than was Gosse, to whom Donne was always "the most undulating, the most diverse of human beings."

HARDY, EVELYN. *Donne, A Spirit in Conflict*. London: Constable and Co., 1942.

Building on previous biographical studies, but full of subtle intuitions and private apprehensions, this is one of the latest and one of the most discerning studies of the ultimately inscrutable Dean.

DARK, SIDNEY. *Five Deans*. New York: Harcourt, Brace and Co., 1928.

Listed only for those who would balance Walton's starry-eyes and Gosse's inclined spirit with a largely negative reaction to Donne. The chapter given to him here is unsympathetic, bad spirited, choleric. The jibing pettiness does Dark far more discredit than Donne.

CRITICISM

GRIERSON, H. J. C. "John Donne." *The Cambridge History of English Literature*. Vol. IV, Chapter XI. Edited by A. W. Ward and A. R. Waller. Cambridge: University Press, 1909.

Criticism and Creation. London: Chatlo and Windus, 1949.

Grierson is the eminently sensible yet imaginatively discerning source back to which all contemporary Donne criticism ultimately traces.

SIMPSON, EVELYN M. *A Study of the Prose Works of John Donne*. Oxford: Clarendon Press, 1924.

Though the chapter given to the sermons in this book has been superseded by the full introductions and notes in the Simpson-Potter edition of the sermons, the book as a whole is still of interest and importance. In all the elaborate theorizing and rarified interpreting that has been perpetrated on Donne, it is good to begin with and to return to the sober, true analyses and explications of Evelyn Simpson. The most impressionistic flights of the poet-critics could hardly get high enough or go far enough to explore Donne's full mystery, and meanwhile Mrs. Simpson has all the facts we really have to go on.

DONNE, JOHN. *Essays in Divinity*. Edited by Evelyn M. Simpson. Oxford: Clarendon Press, 1952.

The interest here is not in the *Essays* themselves, which are very uneven with only occasional flashes of thought or style to suggest that this author had earlier written the poems or might later write the sermons. But Mrs. Simpson's careful introduction is important to the student of Donne's prose—as is everything which Mrs. Simpson writes on the subject.

SPENCER, THEODORE (editor). *A Garland for Donne*. Cambridge: Harvard University Press, 1931.

Issued to mark the 300th anniversary of Donne's death, this collection of essays is a tight little knot of Donne studies. Mark especially T. S. Eliot's "Donne in Our Times," Evelyn Simpson's "Donne's Paradoxes and Problems," John Hayward's "A Note on Donne the Preacher," Mary Paton Ramsay's "Donne's Relation to Philosophy," and Theodore Spencer's "Donne and His Age."

ELIOT, T. S. "Lancelot Andrewes" in *Selected Essays*. New York: Harcourt, Brace and Co., 1950.

Eliot has been very wise about Donne the poet on many occasions (see the essay "Metaphysical Poets" in this same volume), but Eliot does not have it in him to respond much to Donne the preacher. Or Eliot does very much have it in him to resist, reject, repress what he senses in Donne the man. There is a kind of well-bred alarm in Eliot over "a certain wantonness of spirit" he detects in the Dean and in those who respond to him. This may be, but it hardly follows of necessity, as it seems to for Eliot, that Bishop Andrewes must then be exalted for his chilly, distant purity.

WHITE, HELEN C. *The Metaphysical Poets, A Study in Religious Experience*. New York: Macmillan, 1956. Also, "John Donne and the Psychology of Spiritual Effort," in *The Seventeenth Century*, by Richard Foster Jones and others. Stanford: Stanford University Press, 1951.

The significant chapters in Miss White's recently reissued *The Metaphysical Poets* are I "The Intellectual

Climate," II "The Religious Climate," IV "The Conversions of John Donne," and V "The Divine Poetry of John Donne." Her insight is as felicitous as her expression.

BACKGROUNDS

WILLY, BASIL. *The Seventeenth Century Background*. London: Chatto and Windus, 1934.

The time and the temper.

RAMSAY, MARY PATON. *Les dectrines médiévales chez Donne le poète métaphysicien de l'Angleterre 1573-1631*. London: Oxford University Press, 1924. (2nd Edition.)

This rich, full study locates and labels every attachment between John Donne and medieval theology. It misses nothing. But in proceeding from the inevitable attachments to identification of Donne as a kind of late scholastic, it misses John Donne.

COFFIN, CHARLES MONROE. *John Donne and the New Philosophy*. New York: Columbia University Press, 1937.

As the Ramsay study presses Donne too firmly into his own background, this study projects him too explosively into the sequel. The book gives an engrossing account of the Copernican revolution that tore Donne's time. Accepting that, however, it is not necessary to proceed to the assumption that Donne was so grievously torn by the same revolution.

MOLONEY, MICHAEL FRANCIS. *John Donne, His Flight From Medievalism*. Urbana: The University of Illinois Press, 1944.

Moloney's book is a balanced account of the poet-preacher teetering in creative inbalance between times past and times to come.